Bed & Breakfast California

FIFTH EDITION

❧

Completely Revised and Expanded

Linda Kay Bristow

Printed in the United States of America.

Fifth Edition.

Library of Congress Cataloging-in-Publication Data:
Bristow, Linda Kay.
   Bed & Breakfast, California: completely revised and expanded / by
   Linda Kay Bristow.
       p. cm.
   Includes bibliographical references and index.
   ISBN 0-8118-0428-3
   1. Bed and Breakfast accommodations—California—Guidebooks.
2. California—Guidebooks. I.Title. II.Title: Bed and Breakfast, California.
TX907.3.C2B75 1994   93-40327
647.9479403—dc20   CIP

Book and cover design: Rob Hugel and Mary Leigh Henneberry,
XXX Design
Maps: Eureka Cartography
Cover: Hope-Merrill House
Cover photograph: © 1993 John Swain

Distributed in Canada by
Raincoast Books
112 East Third Avenue
Vancouver, B.C. V5T IC8

10 9 8 7 6 5 4 3 2 1

Chronicle Books
275 Fifth Street
San Francisco, CA 94103

Table of Contents

Preface iv

San Francisco/Bay Area **1**

Marin County **36**

Sonoma County **52**

Napa County **76**

The Mendocino Coast **116**

Humboldt County **148**

Yosemite **160**

The Gold Country/Sierra **172**

The Central Coast **214**

Southern California **238**

Bed and Breakfast Reservation and Referral Services **282**

Bed and Breakfast Associations **287**

Bed and Breakfast Publications **291**

Publications on How to Open and Operate a Bed and Breakfast Inn **298**

Cookbooks from Bed and Breakfasts **300**

Index **302**

Preface

When I began researching inns for the first edition of *Bed and Breakfast California* in 1980, I was looking for places that fit my preconceived notion of what a bed and breakfast should be: an owner-occupied home with four to six guest rooms, reasonably priced, with breakfast included. It didn't take long to realize that looking for the definition-perfect bed and breakfast was like looking for a needle in a haystack. Inns come in all sizes, shapes, and price ranges. And they vary greatly in atmosphere due to factors such as architecture, locale, and style of the owner.

At that time there were 50 bed and breakfasts in California. Today there are close to 800, and I hear of new ones continually. As the industry has evolved, so have the lines of demarcation, and bed and breakfast is currently being offered to the public in three similar but distinct forms: the homestay—similar to the European tradition of an inexpensive night's lodging in the spare room of someone's home; the commercial bed and breakfast inn—three to eight guest rooms in a building either previously owned by the hosts or purchased specifically for transformation to an inn; and the small hotel—10 to 30 guest rooms, often in a historic building, offering breakfast as part of its package. From the traveler's point of view, the homestay affords the least amount of privacy; the small hotel, the most. The commercial bed and breakfast inn strikes a balance between the two: rooms are available with either shared or private baths; some rooms have private entrances; and breakfast can be enjoyed either in the room or at the dining table with other guests, depending on the policy of the inn.

In the following pages of this, the fifth edition, you'll find a review of what I consider to be some of the best bed and breakfast establishments in the state. Most are commercial bed and breakfasts in areas of scenic or historic interest: the Wine Country, the Mendocino Coast, the Gold Country—to name a few. They are housed in buildings ranging in style from turn-of-the-century Queen Anne Victorians to former hunting lodges to newly built structures of concrete and glass. They may contain as few as three guest rooms to as many as 25. I have personally stayed at or visited all of them and have endeavored to give them a fair appraisal.

There is a certain etiquette involved with the bed and breakfast experience, and since forewarned is forearmed, here are some pointers to make you feel at home:

1. The basic modus operandi is the same as if you were staying at the home of a friend. Express appreciation for the offerings, be considerate, and don't treat the owner-innkeeper like a servant (although service is certainly at the heart of any professionallyrun bed and breakfast inn).
2. Don't hesitate to ask for what you want or need.
3. Clean up after yourself in a shared-bath situation.
4. Say goodbye when you check out, and return the key personally.
5. Follow house rules concerning checkout time, parking locations, payment arrangements, etc.

Some other points to remember. Rates are subject to change. The rate structure I've used throughout the book can be interpreted as follows: inexpensive—less than $75; moderate—$75 to $125; expensive—$125 to $175; very expensive—$175 plus. Reservations are a must. Though many inns book well in advance, last-minute cancellations do occur. Don't hesitate to phone or ask to have your name put on a waiting list. A private bath, which used to be hard to come by, has now become the norm. Don't, however, expect a telephone or television in your room or room service. Smoking is almost always discouraged, pets are unwelcome, and children are subject to house policy. Some inns require a two-night minimum stay, especially through weekend or holiday periods.

I enjoyed the inns, as I know you will, and I'd like to take this opportunity to extend my appreciation to the innkeepers throughout the state for putting me up as well as for putting up with me. A special note of thanks to the staff of Chronicle Books for their enduring support. Immeasurable gratitude to my dear friend Hany Farag for his computer expertise and to Gary Hanauer for his assistance in researching and writing this book.

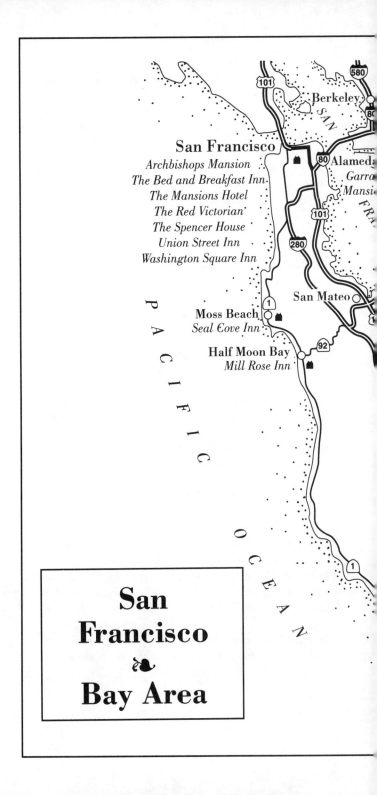

San Francisco

Archbishops Mansion
The Bed and Breakfast Inn
The Mansions Hotel
The Red Victorian
The Spencer House
Union Street Inn
Washington Square Inn

Berkeley

Alamed

Garra
Mansi

San Mateo

Moss Beach
Seal Cove Inn

Half Moon Bay
Mill Rose Inn

PACIFIC OCEAN

San
Francisco
&
Bay Area

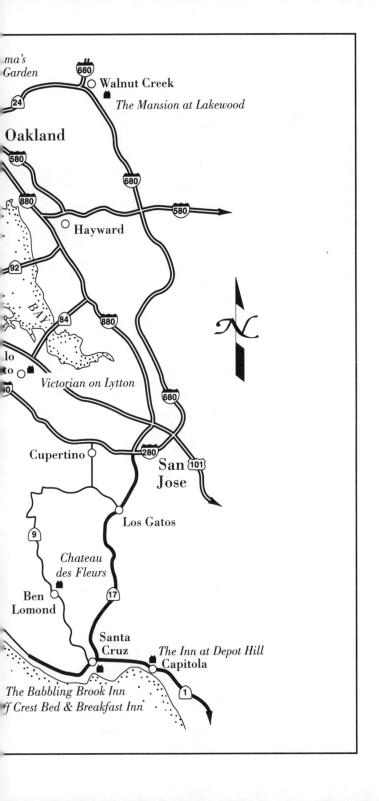

Garratt Mansion

900 Union Street
Alameda, California 94501; (510) 521-4779

INNKEEPERS: *Royce and Betty Gladden.*

ACCOMMODATIONS: *Six rooms, three with private bath; twin, double, and queen-size beds.*

RESERVATIONS: *Three weeks recommended.*

MINIMUM STAY: *None.*

DEPOSIT: *First night's lodging.*

CREDIT CARDS: *AE, MC, Visa.*

RATES: *Moderate.*

RESTRICTIONS: *No pets.*

The impressive Colonial Revival residence now known as the Garratt Mansion was built in 1893 for W. T. Garratt, an industrialist who had inherited a brass factory. Existing records show that the house originally cost over $14,000 to build, at a time when a $5,000 dwelling was considered an expensive home. The building eventually passed through the hands of several owners until its fate was sealed for over 50 years as a boarding house. But that's where Royce and Betty Gladden stepped in.

"We purchased the property as a boarding house with 23 single men living in it, and continued to run it like that for nearly four years," explains Betty. "Then we began remodeling the kitchen. Well, that made the cook mad, so she quit. Slowly, as fate would have it, our 'renovation' evolved into a bed and breakfast inn."

Over fifteen years have passed, but transformations still occur here. Weddings are frequently celebrated in the inn's spacious double parlor. Anniversaries, birthdays, and other special occasions are also honored with parties in these rooms. Betty has even been known to indulge her bed and breakfast guests with leftover wedding cake.

Downstairs, too, is a formal dining room where breakfast is served to hordes of hungry inn guests. Starting as early as 7:30 a.m. (or as late as 9:30, if that's the way you want it), a parade of fresh fruit (like sliced nectarines, blackberries, or just-picked strawberries) begins its regal march out of the kitchen followed by the likes of Grand Marnier French toast or pecan waffles. Freshly squeezed orange juice and a strong pot of coffee accompanies herbal tea cozied in silver service. Betty says her philosophy on food can be summed up as "fresh, healthy, and wholesome." Accordingly, she avoids overdoses of sugar in her morning menus.

Overnight quarters are located on the second and third stories of this 27-room mansion. A second-floor guest living room is supplied with a cabinet full of teacups and instant coffee. Books and magazines are scattered about the room as are snacks: a bowl of pistachio nuts and a plateful of chocolate chip cookies the day I breezed through. There's also a refrigerator stocked with cold drinks—a considerate touch, I thought. The orchestra balcony off the living room, which overlooks the home's ornately carved spiral staircase and grand foyer with stained-glass bay windows, is furnished with a comfortable settee and a supply of games and jigsaw puzzles.

A touch of whimsy in the second-floor accommodation known as Kelly's Room is the speakerphone hidden in a teddy bear. The room also has a queen-size bed, a ceiling fan, and an old Singer sewing machine. Bedside tables sport reading lamps. Feather pillows and white lace curtains adorning windows lend the room its homey touch. Diana's Room, also on the second floor, is popular for its gas fireplace and queen-size, bamboo four-poster bed. This room also has its own private bath with tub and shower and is amply stocked with such niceties (and necessities) as bath salts, toothpaste, talcum powder, shampoo, bandages, and a sewing kit.

The four rooms located on the third floor are the Attic Room, Martha's Room, Grandma's Room, and Angela's Room, which overlooks the treetops. (The antique oak bed here has been in the Gladden family through three generations.)

Clock radios provide soothing background music to each room and alert guests to all the time they have (or don't have) to fritter away. If the alarm goes off and you really do want to get up, there are bicycle paths, public tennis courts, a golf course, and a five-mile jogging trail on hand. Berkeley and San Francisco are, respectively, a 15- and 20-minute drive from the inn. But there's also a historic architectural walking tour still awaiting your presence in downtown Alameda, that is, if the Garratt Mansion hasn't already overwhelmed you with a sense of the past.

Gramma's Rose Garden Inn

2740 Telegraph Avenue
Berkeley, California 94705; (510) 549-2145

INNKEEPERS: *Kathy Kuhner and Barry Cleveland.*

ACCOMMODATIONS: *40 rooms, all with private bath; twin, double, queen-, and king-size beds.*

RESERVATIONS: *One month recommended for weekends.*

MINIMUM STAY: *None.*

DEPOSIT: *First night's lodging.*

CREDIT CARDS: *AE, MC, Visa.*

RATES: *Moderate to expensive.*

RESTRICTIONS: *No pets.*

Gramma's is the perfect example of a bed and breakfast inn that has outgrown itself. Since it opened, the inn has become so popular that it is now housed in not one, not two, but five separate buildings. But success has not dimmed Gramma's main appeal as a place for relaxation in an urban environment.

The establishment's story goes back to 1976 when Kathy Kuhner, fresh from B & B-hopping her way across Europe, decided she wanted to open an inn of her own. It wasn't until 1979 that she found what she thought was the perfect property: a grand old estate named the Fay House, which had been built around 1903. But its owner, a wealthy therapist, refused to sell.

Undaunted, Kathy felt certain that he would eventually come around, so in the meantime, she bought the house next door. By 1980, she'd renovated and made it into the 11-guest-room Main House of what is now the inn complex. She also restored the property's garden house. Finally, Kathy's waiting paid off. The Fay House, with its nine bedrooms and stained-glass windows across the top, was purchased along with its carriage house, which was converted into a four-guest-room annex. The Cottage House (eight guest rooms) was then built on the property and opened in 1991.

Washed in sun and surrounded by a fragrant garden of roses and wisteria, the inn is close to the famed University of California campus but still far enough away for the surrounding neighborhood to be quiet and residential. Elsewhere in Berkeley, street vendors ply their wares on Telegraph Avenue, nature lovers explore the Berkeley Rose Garden and Tilden Regional Park, and museum hounds tour the University of California Art Museum and Lawrence Hall of Science.

But a stay at Gramma's includes other bonuses, too. First and foremost are the rooms, most of which have queen- or king-size brass or Murphy beds and various combinations of such amenities as armoires, fireplaces, decks, chaise longues, wicker rocking chairs, love seats, and antique furnishings. If you really want to indulge yourself, check into Jewel's Retreat, the third-floor penthouse of Mrs. Jewel Fay's former home, which even comes with its own living room.

Although Berkeley is well known for its breakfast haunts, don't even think about going out to eat if you stay here. Served from 7:00 to 9:00 a.m. on weekdays and 7:30 to 9:30 on weekends, the scrumptious down-home repast includes croissants and muffins, yogurt, buckets of fresh fruit, an egg-based entrée, and three different kinds of cereal (Gramma's homemade granola is one). Wine and cheese are offered in the evening; coffee and cookies are on hand all day.

Who might turn up while you're staying here? Almost anyone, including such patrons as John Astin (he played the father on television's "Addams Family"), actress Amy Irving, and poet Yevgeny Yevtushenko. Although I didn't see any of these personages myself, I did come away with a wonderful T-shirt emblazoned with Gramma's logo and a photo I shot of Sterling, the inn's sleek gray house cat.

The Mansion at Lakewood

1056 Hacienda Drive
Walnut Creek, California 94598; (510) 945-3600 or (800) 477-7898

INNKEEPERS: *Michael and Sharyn McCoy.*

ACCOMMODATIONS: *Seven rooms, all with private bath; queen- and king-size beds.*

RESERVATIONS: *Three weeks recommended.*

MINIMUM STAY: *None.*

DEPOSIT: *First night's lodging.*

CREDIT CARDS: *AE, DC, MC, Visa.*

RATES: *Expensive to very expensive.*

RESTRICTIONS: *No pets.*

A quick turn off Ygnacio Valley Road onto tree-lined Homestead Avenue and then Hacienda Drive reveals beautiful, well-maintained private homes. How could a commercial bed and breakfast inn obtain a zoning permit here? you begin to think. But then you spy The Mansion at Lakewood's larger-than-life-size white iron gates and your car starts up the inn's circular drive. A step across the well-manicured lawn is like a step back in time.

"It took us one year and six public hearings to get zoning for a bed and breakfast inn—which we were only finally able to obtain under a historical building code," remembers owner Mike McCoy. "We wanted an urban inn, but a country setting. And we knew we could do a better job of innkeeping in an area we had already lived in."

The eight-thousand-square-foot 1860s home is graced with two majestic parlors, a library and drawing room, a formal dining room, seven private-bath guest rooms (two are suites), hardwood floors, and four wood-burning fireplaces. "This house was considered a white elephant by some, but we saw it as an unpolished gem," recalls Sharyn.

There are lots of heritage trees on the property: magnolia, shagbark hickory, cypress, tecalpa, and persimmon. One part of the lawn is even planted in ancient Mojave Desert cactus. The scent of the gardens' fragrant flowers and the sight of grazing deer and squirrels jumping from tree to tree can be enjoyed from the home's wide veranda.

Rabbits are common, too, but not real ones—only depictions in room wallpaper borders, ceramic vases, prints, and small figurines. In the drawing room, for example, an antique Oriental display case with inlaid brass and a glass front holds some of the mansion's cute bunnies. An 1861 burgundy velvet upholstered Victorian settee is flanked by matching Mr. and Mrs. chairs. These and a floral print wingback chair with Chippendale-style legs sit atop a burgundy area rug. French doors lead off to the redwood-paneled library with its collection of over 2,000 books, a multitude of parlor games, and an antique piano.

Also off the drawing room is the Terrace Suite with antique twin beds coupled as a king. A walnut armoire that matches the bed headboards is housed here, as is a cast-iron stove and a sitting area with table and chairs. The downstairs Estate Suite is nearly everyone's favorite guest room. It features a private deck and a private bath with a whirlpool Jacuzzi tub for two. Its sitting area has French doors that lead to the bedroom, decorated in a rose and cream tone. The highlight of the bedroom is surely the 1850s brass canopy bed sided by marble-top tables with brass lantern-style lamps. There's also a mirrored armoire and a lovely writing desk. An upstairs favorite is the Country Garden room, which is more moderately priced, with an English four-poster pine bed and pine armoire. Features that all the rooms share are goose down comforters and pillows, terry robes, private telephones, and AM/FM radios and tape players.

A delightful breakfast of freshly squeezed orange juice, mixed fresh fruit, almond croissants, and pancakes or Dutch babies is served in the dining room (or to the suites) on fine china with silver and crystal. The coffee is ready at 6:30 a.m., breakfast by 8:00 or as late as 10:00.

Mike and Sharyn exude a personal style of hospitality that has nearly all but vanished. They provide pink lemonade or iced tea with homemade cookies and cheese and crackers at check-in time. Dinner, entertainment, and shopping suggestions are also freely offered. Does a catered candlelight dinner at the inn with violin music, or perhaps, limousine service around town interest you? They'll arrange it. "Our hearts are open to you," they say. Well *I* say, welcome to Camelot.

Archbishops Mansion

1000 Fulton Street
San Francisco, California 94117; (415) 563-7872

INNKEEPERS: *Jonathan Shannon and Jeffrey Ross.*

ACCOMMODATIONS: *15 rooms, all with private bath; queen-size beds.*

RESERVATIONS: *Three to four weeks recommended.*

MINIMUM STAY: *Two nights on weekends.*

DEPOSIT: *First night's lodging.*

CREDIT CARDS: *AE, MC, Visa.*

RATES: *Expensive to very expensive.*

RESTRICTIONS: *No pets.*

They've outdone themselves, this irrepressible pair. And everyone is talking about it. Why, I could hardly complete my own interview with the innkeepers with all the calls coming in from reporters and radio talk-show hosts. It's the Archbishops Mansion, San Francisco's premier bed and breakfast inn. It renders European elegance in a style only Jonathan Shannon (with his impeccable taste and touch of flamboyance) and Jeffrey Ross (possessing an exhaustive knowledge of architectural history and restoration) could achieve.

Built in 1904 to house the offices and residences of the archbishops of San Francisco, this Second Empire French building with its 15 bedrooms and 18 working fireplaces is one of the city's three largest homes—30,000 square feet in all.

The interior follows the classical style of the French Renaissance (beaux arts), with receiving rooms located on the first floor and bedrooms occupying the second and third floors. The parlor, a buffer between the outside world and the one within, is handsomely appointed with Oriental carpets; fine oil paintings; a mix of European, Victorian, and Oriental antiques; a floor-to-ceiling gold-leaf mirror; and vases of tiger lilies in bloom. Take special note of the triple-vaulted ceiling, crystal chandelier, and massive carved redwood fireplace. A magnificent oval glass dome hovers above the stairwell leading to the guest rooms, which are named after romantic operas: La Boheme, Manon, Tosca, Carmen, Don Giovanni, Turandot, and Madame Butterfly.

Same-day laundry and dry-cleaning service, room service (for snacks), and complimentary soft drinks are among the amenities here—seldom heard of at other inns. Champagne and wine are available for purchase; afternoon wine tastings are a tradition. For breakfast, the inn serves an assortment of freshly baked pastries, along with orange juice and coffee.

The Archbishops Mansion overlooks Alamo Square, one of San Francisco's registered historic districts, which encompasses more Victorian architecture than any other neighborhood in the city. (You may recognize the row of Victorians along Steiner Street from a well-known picture postcard.) Davies Symphony Hall, the Opera House, the Museum of Modern Art, and the Civic Center are just eight blocks away.

The Bed and Breakfast Inn

4 Charlton Court
San Francisco, California 94123; (415) 921-9784

INNKEEPERS: *Robert and Marily Kavanaugh.*

ACCOMMODATIONS: *10 rooms, six with private bath; twin, double, queen-, and king-size beds.*

RESERVATIONS: *Two to three months recommended.*

MINIMUM STAY: *None.*

DEPOSIT: *First night's lodging.*

CREDIT CARDS: *Not accepted.*

RATES: *Moderate to expensive.*

RESTRICTIONS: *No children under 12. No pets.*

The Bed and Breakfast Inn, opened in 1976, was the first B & B in San Francisco. Many have opened since, but this is still one of the most popular in the city, evidenced by comments like this one in the inn's guest book: "In my fifteen years of coming to San Francisco this was my favorite visit because of you."

At the time of the inn's opening, the owners, Robert and Marily Kavanaugh, didn't realize they had hit on an idea whose time had come. Having traveled extensively, they were anxious to open an inn patterned after those they had stayed at in Wales and Scotland. Bob's background in real estate and building and Marily's industriousness and flair for decorating led them to purchase and restore this 100-year-old Victorian, which is located off fashionable Union Street in a quiet cul-de-sac that reminds one of a London mews.

Although today the Kavanaughs are assisted by a friendly staff of five, Marily explained that they did everything themselves for the first three years they were in business. I didn't find this hard to believe, as the afternoon I arrived I found her ironing table linens while Bob was busy with odd jobs in the garden.

It is apparent that the Kavanaughs take great pride in what they do—and they do it well. On arrival, guests are greeted on a first-name basis and escorted to their room, where personal touches such as fresh flowers and fruit are evident.

Many of the rooms, such as the Mayfair, Covent Garden, and Kensington Gardens, are named after areas of London. Each room is unique in decor; antiques and family heirlooms are judiciously scattered throughout.

My favorite room is Celebration, one of the six available with a private bath. And what a bath—complete with a sunken double tub, a hand-painted Sherle Wagner pedestal basin, plush towels, and scented soaps and bath oil. The bedroom, papered with a blue and white Laura Ashley print, features a love seat and a queen-size bed. Another popular guest room (and one of the two that open to the garden) is the Willows, decorated in a green and white print accented by white wicker furniture.

The Continental breakfast, served on Wedgwood china, includes fresh-squeezed orange juice, warm croissants, freshly ground coffee, and herbal tea. Evening sherry is complimentary; current magazines and good books are plentiful; and, unlike many other bed and breakfast inns, rooms with televisions and telephones are available.

The Bed and Breakfast Inn is located between Laguna and Buchanan in the heart of Union Street's nine blocks of boutiques, restaurants, and antique shops.

The Mansions Hotel

2220 Sacramento Street
San Francisco, California 94115; (415) 929-9444

INNKEEPER: *Robert Pritikin.*

ACCOMMODATIONS: *21 rooms, all with private bath; twin, double, and queen-size beds.*

RESERVATIONS: *Two to three weeks recommended.*

MINIMUM STAY: *None.*

DEPOSIT: *First night's lodging.*

CREDIT CARDS: *AE, DC, MC, Visa.*

RATES: *Expensive to very expensive.*

RESTRICTIONS: *None.*

Robert Pritikin's Mansions Hotel is one of those places I run into every once in a while that straddles the thin line separating an inn from a small hotel. But there are certain features that move me to include it here. First of all, it's housed in two historic properties that sit side by side: a grand, twin-turreted Queen Anne Victorian built by Utah State Senator Richard Chambers in 1887 and a 1903 four-story Greek Revival. Second, the innkeeper's colorful personality, wit, and varied background make for lively conversation. And finally, there is an opulent breakfast served in-room each morning.

The hotel is billed as "being in the middle of every-thing—yet a million miles away." "Everything" includes the not-too-distant downtown, Fisherman's Wharf, and North Beach areas as well as nearby Fillmore and Union streets. The "million miles away" is actually just a step away from the main entrance to the grand foyer, with its gigantic crystal chandelier and murals depicting the ro-mantic characters who inhabited The Mansions nearly a century ago.

To the right of the foyer is the Music Room, the setting for nightly classical concerts and magic shows. The inn-keeper ("America's foremost classical saw player") is your master of ceremonies. The piano here is said to have be-longed to Claudia Chambers, The Mansion's legendary haunt whose invisible fingers play classical requests. (Claudia's bad manners are purported to be the cause of a host of the hotel's troubles and problems. The staff snickers at the story of the night she unhinged a door that fell on the head of a guest who was being difficult.)

Another room worth noting is the Billiard Room. Beside the antique billiard table you'll find a stained-glass nickelodeon player piano pumping out the tunes of John Philip Sousa and Scott Joplin. A collection of beaded Victorian purses is displayed on the wall above an outsized dollhouse that was the original set from Edward Albee's New York Broadway production of *Tiny Alice*. Glass-fronted armoires hold memorabilia.

Guest rooms occupy the upper floors of the buildings. In the Chambers mansion a brass plaque on the door of each room identifies a historic personage to whom the room is dedicated, and the walls of the room are alive with murals depicting the legend of that person's life. High-end luxury suites fill the house next door.

Breakfast anyone? How does a French croissant, a wine glass full of fresh orange juice rimmed with a strawberry, eggs and sausages, cereal, a fruit cup, and freshly ground coffee sound?

Tennis? Lafayette Park is just a block away. Sauna? There's one in-house. Afternoon sherry? It's complimentary. Dinner? The hotel has its own intimate dining room. And last but not least are the front and back gardens displaying a collection of Beniamino Bufano sculptures, the most prominent of which are two towering bronze figures of Saint Francis of Assisi, patron saint of San Francisco.

The Red Victorian

1665 Haight Street
San Francisco, California 94117; (415) 864-1978

INNKEEPER: *Sami Sunchild.*

ACCOMMODATIONS: *18 rooms, four with private bath; twin, double, queen-, and king-size beds.*

RESERVATIONS: *Two weeks recommended.*

MINIMUM STAY: *Two nights on weekends and over holiday periods.*

DEPOSIT: *In full.*

CREDIT CARDS: *AE, MC, Visa.*

RATES: *Moderate.*

RESTRICTIONS: *Children by arrangement. No pets.*

Sami Sunchild is the artist-in-residence innkeeper; the Red Victorian is the grandest of all her works. This colorful upstairs bed and breakfast, located in the heart of San Francisco's ever-evolving Haight-Ashbury district, is a favorite of creative types and New Age thinkers. Psychologists and architects, futurists and poets come here from as near as a block away, as far as New Zealand and the Orient.

The turn-of-the-century building was originally constructed as a resort hotel to host the many people who came by cable car to take the fresh country air of Golden Gate Park. The hotel faded into a home for alcoholics and in the 1960s was invaded by hippies.

Sami purchased the property in 1977 and began single-handedly restoring the place to its original splendor. Today Sami believes that part of what makes the Red Victorian what it is, is what it's not. It's not downtown. It's not in a frequented tourist area. And it's not for those who want to get away from it all or to just be alone. It is, however, conveniently located near Golden Gate Park and is on major bus lines to all parts of the city.

The inn's street-level Global Village Networking Center is the setting for breakfast as well as lively discussions and occasional seminars where locals and guests meet and exchange ideas. Conversations continue here for hours, friendships for years.

Sami's calligraphic paintings decorate not only the downstairs Gallery of Meditative Art, but the building's second- and third-floor corridors as well. Guest rooms (located off long, narrow hallways) are moderately priced. The least expensive are the Butterfly and Peace rooms. Best of the house is the Peacock Suite with its stained-glass windows and king-size canopied bed. The rooms are all simply furnished; some are accented by Haight Street memorabilia and old photographs of the hotel.

A Continental breakfast of croissants, muffins, fresh fruit, and tea is served from 8:30 to 10:30 a.m. each morning.

The Spencer House

1080 Haight Street
San Francisco, California 94117; (415) 626-9205

INNKEEPERS: *Barbara and Jack Chambers.*

ACCOMMODATIONS: *Six rooms, all with private bath; double, queen-, and king-size beds.*

RESERVATIONS: *Three to four weeks recommended.*

MINIMUM STAY: *Two nights on weekends.*

DEPOSIT: *Full amount.*

CREDIT CARDS: *Not accepted.*

RATES: *Moderate to expensive.*

RESTRICTIONS: *Children discouraged. No pets.*

Barbara Chambers has an admitted fetish for beautiful linens. But you won't see them until you get inside her inn. And you won't get inside unless you read about it here or in one of very few other select publications, because Barbara, hostess at Spencer House, likes to maintain a low profile. Most of her guests currently come to her by word of mouth. There's no sign in the yard—or on the front door. The inn doesn't have a brochure. And most incredible of all, perhaps, is the fact that the phone number is unlisted. A San Francisco resident myself, I had driven by hundreds of times, assuming the great Queen Anne straddling the corner of Haight and Baker streets was a private home.

Built in 1887 by the Spencer family, the house was purchased in 1984 by the Chambers. "My first night here was spent in the dark," reflects Barbara. "The building had so deteriorated over the years that there was no electricity or working plumbing; previous occupants had even roller-skated on the parlor's hardwood floors."

Its original graciousness now restored, the home brims with European and Oriental antiques, and fabrics, draperies, and linens purchased in France. A priceless 285-year-old grandfather clock marks time in the Oriental-motif entryway. The oak hall seat and mirror here were original to the house. Oriental carpets partially cover the quarter-sawn, oak geometric-patterned floors. Just off the entry is the parlor filled with two forest green velvet love seats facing each other in front of a tiled fireplace. Ivy, a ficus tree, and built-in bookshelves offset a collection of original artwork. Two particularly interesting pieces are a floor-to-ceiling oil portrait of a Frenchman and a freestanding bust of Napoleon.

The formal dining room with its oak paneling and golden Lincresta Walton wainscoting impregnated with a seashell design is made cozy by a fireplace and 1906 brass lamp fixtures with their original filament bulbs. A long oak table, capable of seating twelve, is dressed for breakfast with silver candlesticks on a white lace table runner. Fine china and a silver tea service are also set out. The bountiful gourmet breakfast that Barbara serves starts out with a fresh watermelon sorbet topped by a lime wedge. Two fresh-ground blends of coffee are poured: a French and a dark Colombian roast. The tangy sweetness of the just-squeezed orange juice is further enhanced by Belgian waffles drowning in orange butter syrup topped with ripe berries.

Guests descend the staircase for breakfast at around 8:00 a.m. Of all the second-floor bedrooms, the French Room is the most highly prized. A brass, gas-burning lamp fixture once owned by Sally Stanford is a focal point of this room decorated in cool shades of aqua. French Provincial furnishings consist of an armoire carved with a cupid motif and matching bed with a fabric half-canopy. The cupid theme is also expressed in curios, pictures, and lamp shades.

The Small Queen Anne is the inn's least expensive accommodation. Its high-backed bed has a feather mattress. Walls are covered with padded forest green fabric and co-ordinating Victorian reproduction Bradbury wallpapers; the floor is draped with an Oriental carpet. This room has a small private bath with shower and an antique sink set in a cast-iron pedestal. The Large Queen Anne has fabric walls in shades of pink, rose, and green floral fabric. There's a queen-size, burlwood bed with matching armoire, and a breakfast table in the room's bay window tower. Prints of Victorian ladies reclining on chaise longues decorate the walls. All of the rooms are supplied with his-and-hers plush terry robes.

"If you're good to people, they'll go home and tell someone else," Barbara says. "I guess that's why we've been able to build up such an outstanding clientele." With no sign, no brochure, and not even a listed phone number, it must be that Barbara and Jack have been very, very good.

Union Street Inn

2229 Union Street
San Francisco, California 94123; (415) 346-0424

INNKEEPER: *Helen Stewart.*

ACCOMMODATIONS: *Five rooms, all with private bath; twin, queen-, and king-size beds. Carriage House with Jacuzzi.*

RESERVATIONS: *Four to six weeks recommended.*

MINIMUM STAY: *Two nights on weekends and some holiday periods.*

DEPOSIT: *First and last night's lodging.*

CREDIT CARDS: *AE, MC, Visa.*

RATES: *Expensive to very expensive.*

RESTRICTIONS: *No pets.*

For Helen Stewart, owning and operating a bed and break-fast inn is a third career. As a mother she raised five children, and she has also taught school. As an innkeeper she is a natural. Helen's appealing calmness is reflected in the decor and surroundings of her Union Street Inn.

This two-story house, an Edwardian built around the turn of the century, is slightly set back from the bustle of Union Street. A few steps lead to a small front porch that opens to the reception area and downstairs parlor. The parlor, where guests gather in the late morning and early evening, has a soft apricot velvet wall covering, a brick fireplace, bay windows, and glass doors that open out to a back deck and beautiful English garden. The furnishings, rich in tone and texture, are contemporary with a mix of antiques; the most unusual pieces are a pair of iron and brass chairs, with leather backs and seats, that were made in Australia. A bowl of potpourri made from the flowers in the garden sits on one of the end tables.

There are five bedrooms in the house, all with private bath. And although the rooms range in price from $125 to $225 per night, I found each one to be just as nice as the next. Wildrose (one of the larger rooms with a Jacuzzi) has a king-size bed with wicker headboard, a comfortable lounge chair and matching ottoman, an abundance of healthy-looking plants, and a garden view. The Golden

Gate room, with a queen-size canopy bed in contrasting shades of midnight blue and mocha cream, looks out to Union Street. The English Garden room is characterized by French doors that lead to a private deck, and the Carriage House, with its own patio, garden, and Jacuzzi, is a very romantic hideaway.

The morning I spent at the Union Street Inn I relaxed on the sun deck with a glass of orange juice, a steaming hot cup of coffee, and one of the most delicious croissants I've ever tasted. Helen told me that she and her staff taste-tested just about every croissant made in San Francisco until they finally settled on one made at a French bakery a few blocks away. Between the breakfast, the morning sun, and the gentle breeze that filled my senses with the fragrance of the many varieties of flowers in the garden, I found it difficult to leave.

Those who can manage to tear themselves away from this peaceful and visually pleasant environment will find some of the city's finest shops and restaurants just a short distance from the door. Fisherman's Wharf, Pier 39, Davies Symphony Hall, the Opera House, and downtown San Francisco are minutes away.

Washington Square Inn

1660 Stockton Street
San Francisco, California 94133; (415) 981-4220 or (800)
388-0220

INNKEEPERS: *Nan and Norm Rosenblatt.*

ACCOMMODATIONS: *15 rooms, 10 with private bath; twin, double, queen-, and king-size beds.*

RESERVATIONS: *Six to eight weeks recommended.*

MINIMUM STAY: *None.*

DEPOSIT: *First night's lodging.*

CREDIT CARDS: *AE, MC, Visa.*

RATES: *Moderate to expensive.*

RESTRICTIONS: *No pets.*

San Francisco's Nan and Norm Rosenblatt "got the bug" for a bed and breakfast inn of their own while traveling through Europe and staying at little inns along the way. Nan is an interior designer, Norm a financial wizard. Together they turned two dilapidated buildings that sat back-to-back into one fantastic inn: the Washington Square Inn.

A stay at the inn is so pleasant that it's tempting to remain inside, especially if you have one of the two rooms that overlook the square. Although the rooms are individually decorated, a European country theme prevails. Furnishings are a well-blended mix of antique and contemporary. The beds are all modern, but some have fabric canopies that blend with the soft floral-patterned drapes and bedspreads. Most rooms have a private bath and all have a telephone. Televisions are available on request. As in most of the other inns in this book, there are fresh flowers in every room.

Complimentary breakfast in bed runs to flaky croissants, scones, cheese brioches, fresh fruit, freshly squeezed orange juice, Italian coffee (in keeping with the neighborhood), and herb tea. Or if you prefer to meet and mingle with the other guests, you can enjoy breakfast at the formal dining table in the reception lobby.

Though it may be tempting, don't linger over breakfast too long. Washington Square is in the heart of the city's colorful Italian district, which offers plenty to see and do. This area, called North Beach, is a favorite of locals and visitors alike for its specialty shops, bakeries, cafes, and night-clubs, all within a few blocks' radius.

And if that's not enough, the inn's concierge can arrange a car, theater tickets, a tour of the city, a picnic, or even a stenographer if you've come here to get down to business (heaven forbid). Because the inn is midway between Fisherman's Wharf and the financial district, it appeals to tourists and businesspeople alike.

Tea and cookies, wines, imported cheeses, and cucumber sandwiches each afternoon are complimentary.

Victorian on Lytton

555 Lytton Avenue
Palo Alto, California 94301; (415) 322-8555

INNKEEPERS: *Susan and Maxwell Hall.*

ACCOMMODATIONS: *10 rooms, all with private bath; twin, queen-, and king-size beds.*

RESERVATIONS: *Four to six weeks recommended.*

MINIMUM STAY: *None.*

DEPOSIT: *First night's lodging.*

CREDIT CARDS: *AE, MC, Visa.*

RATES: *Moderate to expensive.*

RESTRICTIONS: *Children discouraged. No pets.*

Guests of the Victorian on Lytton bed and breakfast in Palo Alto enter the blue, white, and rose painted Queen Anne through an archway of delicate white potato-bud flowers that drape the home's bay front porch. Classical music plays softly in the parlor amidst a mix of contemporary and antique furnishings: a wingback chair and matching sofa in a soft beige and brown print, and a Louis XV armoire.

With five guest rooms (and a five-guest-room carriage house), this two-story dwelling was originally built in 1895 as a retirement residence for Miss Hannah Kezia Clapp and her longtime companion, Elizabeth C. Babcock. Miss Clapp, descendant of Massachusetts Bay colonist Roger Clapp (1630) and daughter of a midwestern pioneer family, reputedly crossed the plains on horseback riding side-saddle from Michigan to California with a pistol held tightly in her belt. Once settled in the West, she accomplished considerable gains in the educational field, founding a highly regarded preparatory school called Sierra Academy in Carson City, Nevada.

Susan and Maxwell Hall discovered Miss Clapp's home in 1985. At the time, it had been operating for over 50 years as an eight-unit apartment complex. The pair was motivated to purchase and renovate it as an inn after discovering that the landmark was slated to be torn down to make way for condominiums.

The Halls' guest rooms are named after Queen Victoria and each of her nine children. Commonalities are the private baths, separate sitting areas, and telephones, and the fluffy down comforters, neck rolls, and embroidered lace pillows on all of the beds. A coffee or tea setup with fresh fruit and "thoz" cookies—Susan's own recipe of oatmeal-based cookie dough with white and dark chocolate chips—awaits each guest.

The Duke of Edinburgh sits across the upstairs hall from the Queen Victoria. The Duke's California-king four-poster bed has a pink and white fabric canopy overhead. Walnut bedside tables hold a clock radio and a telephone. The Queen herself is decked out with a four-poster, this one with a canopy of white lace. Her partially painted, partially papered walls are regal blue with English rose wallpaper. A triple-mirrored vanity, gateleg table, and English black-walnut corner wardrobe are among the room's curious antiques. (The portraits of Victoria and Albert that grace the wall by the bed were sent compliments of past inn guests.)

Of the five rooms in the carriage house, Princess Louise and Princess Royal were dressed quite prettily. Louise is decorated in shades of white and soft lavender. She holds a 120-year-old pine armoire shipped over from Germany and a king-size burlwood bed with a floral fabric swag draped above it. Princess Royal, on the other hand, is decorated in rich maroon colors. The maroon walls show off botanical prints. A pecan four-poster matches a double-mirrored pecan wood dresser, and a fireplace lights up one corner of the room. A Continental breakfast of fresh fruit, muffins or croissants, and coffee, tea, and juice is served to the rooms between 7:00 and 9:00 a.m.

A United States senator, an eminent Russian scientist, and a famous horticulturalist from Spain have all been recent guests of the Victorian on Lytton. CEOs, VPs, and VIPs of Silicon Valley's numerous high-tech industries are also frequent guests. The Halls and their staff are known to respond to requests with loving hearts and listening ears. "I remember the morning we washed and ironed one guest's shirt for an important business meeting," laughs Susan. It's all in a day's work.

Seal Cove Inn

221 Cypress Avenue
Moss Beach, California 94038; (415) 728-7325

INNKEEPERS: *Rick and Karen Herbert.*
ACCOMMODATIONS: *10 rooms, all with private bath; twin, queen-, and king-size beds.*
RESERVATIONS: *Six weeks recommended.*
MINIMUM STAY: *Two nights over holiday periods.*
DEPOSIT: *First night's lodging.*
CREDIT CARDS: *AE, DC, MC, Visa.*
RATES: *Expensive to very expensive.*
RESTRICTIONS: *No pets.*

Karen (Brown) Herbert has come up with the recipe for a perfect inn: place one English-style manor in a meadow of wildflowers overlooking the ocean. Mix in some antiques. Add an attractive young couple with impeccable taste, boundless enthusiasm, and a love for travel. There you have it—Seal Cove Inn. And who better to envision and create the ideal hostelry than the author and publisher of the successful *Karen Brown's Country Inns* book series. (Current editions cover country inns and bed and breakfasts in England, France, Germany, Italy, Ireland, Austria, Portugal, Spain, and Switzerland.)

Each of Seal Cove's 10 guest rooms offers the amenities of a hotel—television with VCR, telephone, towel warmer, a well-stocked refrigerator—but then Karen and husband Rick believe in catering to *all* their guests' needs. A case in point: one room has been designed specifically for the disabled. This wheelchair-accessible room is awash in colorful flowers. Its iron bed is covered in a pink and green flowered bedspread. Matching curtains draw back to reveal French doors that open to a patio and garden. Comfortable chocolate brown wicker chairs with down cushions face the bedroom's intimate fireplace, and the television and VCR are hidden out of sight in a handsome walnut armoire.

In the vaulted-ceiling Fitzgerald Room, yards of cream and beige fabric drape a canopied king-size bed. The inviting sofa—upholstered to match both bedding and draperies—is positioned in front of an oak-framed fireplace.

Active guests will appreciate a relaxing soak in the bathroom's private Jacuzzi. Juliette balconies offer a spectacular sweeping ocean view.

Karen has one surefire way of pampering her guests— with delectable home cooking. One morning you'll be served fresh-squeezed orange juice, a baked apple with granola, and Grand Marnier French toast with steamy French roast coffee. The next day may bring a bowl of ripe strawberries sprinkled with brown sugar and sour cream and a spicy egg-filled tortilla topped with salsa and guacamole. Guests have the choice of having breakfast served to their room or in the inn's spacious dining room. An afternoon buffet consisting of California wine, cheese and crackers, a crudité platter, meatballs, and fresh fruit is also available in the dining room. Late-night snackers will appreciate the homemade chocolates thoughtfully placed on the pillows when their beds are turned down.

Seal Cove is conveniently located just 30 minutes south of San Francisco. At nearby Fitzgerald Marine Reserve seals sun themselves on the ocean rocks while you explore marine life in the tide pools. Your hosts can help make arrangements for an afternoon of horseback riding along the beach, a whale watching cruise, or dinner at the popular Moss Beach Distillery, which is within walking distance of the inn.

Mill Rose Inn

615 Mill Street
Half Moon Bay, California 94019; (415) 726-9794

INNKEEPERS: *Eve and Terry Baldwin.*

ACCOMMODATIONS: *Six rooms, all with private bath; queen- and king-size beds.*

RESERVATIONS: *Four to six weeks recommended.*

MINIMUM STAY: *Two nights on weekends and holidays.*

DEPOSIT: *In full.*

CREDIT CARDS: *AE, MC, Visa.*

RATES: *Very expensive.*

RESTRICTIONS: *No children. No pets.*

Just at the end of four-block-long Mill Street is perhaps one of the most spectacular floral displays to be found in all of San Mateo County, but most certainly in the area of Half Moon Bay, which is itself a flower-producing center. This intense profusion of color with an English country garden accent is the work of ornamental horticulturist Terry Baldwin, who, with his interior decorator wife, Eve, turned what was once a nondescript, two-bedroom cottage into an inn that transforms bed and breakfast lodging into a luxurious living experience.

The Baldwins' garden sports lilies, sweet peas, daisies, poppies, irises, delphiniums, lobelia, and English lavender. In addition to the hundreds of carefully groomed annuals and perennials, there are over 200 different varieties of roses in bloom.

Guest rooms at Mill Rose could conceivably grace the pages of *Architectural Digest*. All are equipped with full-size private baths, hand-painted tile fireplaces, cable televisions with VCRs, and even private-line telephones. Not that this resembles a small hotel either—no, indeed. Rooms are also furnished with both fresh and silk flower arrangements, fancy soaps and plush towels, his-and-hers Japanese dressing gowns, stereo cassette players, and well-stocked refrigerators. A copy of the morning newspaper is delivered to each room's door.

Favorite hideaways include the Renaissance Rose (where I've stayed two or three times), Bordeaux Rose

Suite, Botticelli Rose, and the Burgundy Rose Room with its clawfoot tub for two. All rooms have canopy or brass beds and European antiques. A hydrotherapy spa with high-powered jets sits inside a garden gazebo surrounded by tropical blooms and a charming brick courtyard with fragrant vines and a cascading fountain.

The evening wine and cheese hour affords the opportunity to mingle with other guests you might not have met previously, due to the fact that most of the accommodations at Mill Rose feature their own private entrances. The innkeepers are on hand to expound the joys of sightseeing in the area and to place calls for dinner reservations, as most bed and breakfast hosts do.

Half Moon Bay is a town that flows with the seasons: The annual Pumpkin Festival in late October attracts visitors from near and far; in December the area's Christmas tree farms allow you to select or cut down your own at prices that are remarkably affordable; the elephant seals at Año Nuevo are a big draw October through March; there's an annual Fourth of July parade with fireworks; whale-watching tours are popular in winter; and farm-fresh produce is available all year round.

Needless to say, Eve incorporates these locally grown fruits and vegetables into her morning meal. Quiche Lorraine, an herb omelette, or fresh fruit crepes usually comprise the entrée. Champagne is a standard accompaniment as is a choice of coffee, tea, or Mexican hot chocolate. The Baldwins even offer an afternoon dessert bar.

Mill Rose's location, just 35 miles south of San Francisco, makes it a prime candidate for a midweek break for some relaxation or rest. It's also a good stopping point for a late Friday evening escape heading south to Carmel or the Central Coast. Mill Rose is good to keep in mind, too, if you're making your way up the coast on Highway 1 from Los Angeles or San Diego.

Chateau des Fleurs

7995 Highway 9
Ben Lomond, California 95005; (408) 336-8943

INNKEEPERS: *Lee and Laura Jonas.*

ACCOMMODATIONS: *Three rooms, all with private bath; queen-size beds.*

RESERVATIONS: *Two to three weeks recommended.*

MINIMUM STAY: *None.*

DEPOSIT: *First night's lodging.*

CREDIT CARDS: *AE, MC, Visa.*

RATES: *Moderate.*

RESTRICTIONS: *No children. No pets.*

Snug in the Santa Cruz foothills of the Coastal Range is one of the homiest additions to Santa Cruz County's roster of bed and breakfast inns. Chateau des Fleurs, a late-1870s Victorian, once belonged to William Bartlett, who brought the Bartlett pear from Europe to northern California. He and his wife Flora derived their livelihood selling pears from their orchard to the canneries of nearby Santa Cruz. After Will died and the canneries closed down, Flora was frequently seen in her green Ford peddling pears along Highway 9, perhaps making a living the only way she knew how.

Needless to say, four Bartlett pear trees sit proudly on the property that surrounds the home today—now under the tender care of Lee and Laura Jonas. These, along with stately redwoods and large apple trees, can be viewed from a long wall of picture windows in the family room, hub of the inn's activities.

This family room is packed with all sorts of games, including darts and horseshoes, plus a 46-inch color television, an extensive library, and a piano used for frequent sing-alongs. An adjoining parlor holds blue velvet recliners, a comfortable floral print sofa, a fireplace, and a century-old pump organ.

Lee and Laura's home features three guest rooms with queen-size beds and private baths. The Orchid Room, with its white wicker chairs, looks out onto a sunny deck. The interior is friendly: an oak dresser, a desk, a big white iron bed with down comforter, a bouquet of silk orchids, and a ceiling fan.

While lying in the Violet Room's brass-trimmed bed, you can gaze out at the tall trees through the beige Bishop Sleeve-style lace curtains. Silk wallpaper that swirls with clusters of tiny violets and a white table with a burgundy and violet flower arrangement lend the room its name. This room also contains an oak dresser and two wood and cane captain's chairs.

Rose is the color (and name) of the largest and most luxurious of the guest rooms. With rose-painted walls, rose bouquets on the dresser, and several flower-filled oil paintings, a stay here is akin to an afternoon in a garden. Even so, one of its main draws is the antique clawfoot tub enclosed by lace curtains on a raised wooden platform.

A piping hot breakfast is served at 9:00 a.m. sharp in the formal dining room downstairs. Sitting around an oblong dark oak table that seats six, with an inviting fireplace off to the side, guests are served juices, coffee, fresh fruit or baked apples, banana nut muffins with honey butter, or, if Laura feels like making an old family recipe, an almond-filled pastry called Swedish kringler that's highly addictive. Cheese blintzes smothered with strawberries, quiche Lorraine, cheese souffle, waffles, and French custard toast are other favorites your hostess occasionally whips up.

Think of your stay in this mountain retreat as a center for exploring such nearby attractions as Santa Cruz's sandy beaches, Henry Cowell State Park (lots of hiking trails), Roaring Camp (ride the full-scale steam train and eat barbecue or bring your own picnic), and the more than 20 antique shops scattered between Lee and Laura's home and the coast.

The Babbling Brook Inn

1025 Laurel Street
Santa Cruz, California 95060; (408) 427-2437

INNKEEPER: *Helen King.*

ACCOMMODATIONS: *12 rooms, all with private bath; queen- and king-size beds.*

RESERVATIONS: *Three to four weeks recommended.*

MINIMUM STAY: *Two nights on weekends.*

DEPOSIT: *Half of full amount.*

CREDIT CARDS: *AE, DC, MC, Visa.*

RATES: *Moderate to expensive.*

RESTRICTIONS: *Children discouraged. No pets.*

A gazebo by a cascading waterfall, a meandering creek and a footbridge, flower gardens exploding with color, and pine trees and redwoods collectively set the stage for a romantic evening or weekend at The Babbling Brook Inn.

The first bed and breakfast to open in Santa Cruz, and still the largest, Babbling Brook features 12 cozy guest rooms that exude a French country air. Most have fireplaces, private decks, and outside entrances; all have private baths, telephones, and even televisions.

A great place to get away, hide away, or merely slow down the pace is the inn's secluded Cezanne room. Larger than some of the other guest quarters, its peach and ivory tones in wallpaper, prints, and bed covering elicit a soothing effect. The room has a queen-size bed and a wood-burning corner fireplace along with a spacious bath.

Also favored is the FMRS Garden Room. Cream, forest green, and camel are the predominant colors in carpeting, bedding, and walls. A king-size bed is covered in a floral print comforter with four fluffy pillows. The bureau holds an antique coffee urn that has been transformed into a lamp. Two wooden rockers nestle up to the Franklin stove elevated on a tile platform, and a wall of glass looks out to a wishing well.

A lover's fantasy is the inn's Honeymoon Suite trimmed in Laura Ashley linens of ivory and blue. An embroidered comforter sits atop the four-poster, canopied bed. There's also a raised corner fireplace and private deck overlooking a 16-foot-tall historic waterwheel and a waterfall. The bath's antique, recessed tub is encased in wood.

With over 20 wineries surrounding Santa Cruz, it's not surprising that check-in is closely followed by a wine and cheese social hour in the inn's living room. Hostess Helen King pours wines that are locally produced as she chats with guests and offers snacks from the buffet. Also served buffet style is a tantalizing breakfast that runs from 8:00 to 10:00 a.m. The morning repast commences with a bowl of fresh fruit overflowing with pineapple, melon, strawberries, grapes, and peaches. Granola and a pitcher of milk sit next to fruit-flavored yogurt. A variety of croissants and muffins can be smothered with butter, cream cheese, or one of two types of jam. There's also homemade frittata (usually artichoke or turkey sausage and mushroom). The eye-opening beverages available are coffee, tea, and tangy fresh-squeezed orange juice.

Built in 1909 on the site of an 1870s-era tannery, a 1790s-era grist mill, and an Indian fishing village that dates back well over 2,000 years, the inn abounds with historical interest as well as romance. If space permitted, I'd tell you about the 1911 silent film classic that was made here or the tale of the Austrian countess who once owned the home. A Russian czar's vice consul also figures into Babbling Brook's history, as does Jesse Grant, son of Ulysses S. Grant, who wrote a book about his father while occupying the house. But I guess I'll have to leave those stories for Helen King to relate. After breakfast, perhaps?

Cliff Crest Bed & Breakfast Inn

407 Cliff Street
Santa Cruz, California 95060; (408) 427-2609

INNKEEPERS: *Bruce and Sharon Taylor.*

ACCOMMODATIONS: *Five rooms, all with private bath; queen- and king-size beds.*

RESERVATIONS: *One month for summer weekends.*

MINIMUM STAY: *Two nights on weekends and over holidays.*

DEPOSIT: *First night's lodging.*

CREDIT CARDS: *AE, MC, Visa.*

RATES: *Moderate.*

RESTRICTIONS: *No pets.*

Cliff Crest is a bed and breakfast inn that offers a quiet location from which to enjoy Santa Cruz's sandy beaches, fishing pier, and nostalgia-filled boardwalk. But Cliff Crest is a local historical landmark as well. It's the former residence of William Jeter, lieutenant governor of California (1890) and one-time mayor of Santa Cruz.

The home's five guest rooms are graced with antiques and fresh flowers. The Empire Room, a large room with fireplace on the main floor, features a four-poster bed, an armoire, hardwood floors with plum carpeting, and a garden view. A cozy upstairs hideaway is the Apricot Room, with its antique iron and brass bed. The Grey Room (shades of soft blue and pale gray) offers a French queen-size bed and a tiled shower for two. The Rose Room, a sunny upstairs room with views of Monterey Bay and the Santa Cruz Mountains, has an Eastlake Victorian canopied bed, a sitting area, and an across-the-hall bath with a Victorian clawfoot tub and shower. The Pineapple Room, named for its four-poster bed with pineapples carved on the posts, harbors an 1887 stained-glass window.

Innkeepers Bruce and Sharon Taylor describe themselves as friendly and easygoing. And it's evident they have gone out of their way to provide guests with the comforts of a home away from home: an umbrella table and chairs on the terrace, stimulating games (Trivial Pursuit, Scrabble), and subscriptions to three daily newspapers (the *San Fran-*

cisco Chronicle, the *Santa Cruz Sentinel,* and the *Wall Street Journal*).

Sharon serves an inviting breakfast to the room—juices, fresh fruits in season, French toast, phyllo dough specialties, muffins, and coffeecakes, along with coffee, tea, and hot chocolate. If preferred, breakfast can be enjoyed on the terrace or in the solarium, with its picture windows looking out to the beautifully landscaped gardens designed by Mr. Jeter's friend, John McLaren, the landscape architect of San Francisco's Golden Gate Park.

The Inn at Depot Hill

250 Monterey Avenue
Capitola-By-The-Sea, California 95010; (408) 462-3376

INNKEEPERS: *Suzie Lankes and Dan Floyd.*

ACCOMMODATIONS: *Eight rooms, all with private bath; queen- and king-size beds.*

RESERVATIONS: *Two weeks for weekdays, two months for weekends.*

MINIMUM STAY: *Two nights if stay includes a Saturday.*

DEPOSIT: *Full amount.*

CREDIT CARDS: *AE, MC, Visa.*

RATES: *Expensive to very expensive.*

RESTRICTIONS: *Children discouraged. No pets.*

All aboard for an evening in Paris, a sun-drenched afternoon on the French Riviera in Cote d'Azur, or a leisurely weekend in the timeless beauty of Italy's Portofino or England's Stratford-on-Avon. You travel first class in the luxurious Pullman-car-style Railroad Baron's Suite. Can dreams like this come true at Capitola-By-The-Sea? They certainly can. Or you can stroll through an English gardenlike atmosphere in Sissinghurst, or enjoy a taste of Holland in The Inn at Depot Hill's Delft room.

Adventure, glamour, and romance are all a part of a grand tradition resurrected in contemporary form at this turn-of-the-century seaside railroad depot. Originally built in 1901 to serve the Southern Pacific Railroad, today's spiffed-up version of the depot sits proudly by the now rarely used railroad tracks.

The dining room (which was once Southern Pacific's ticket office) and living room are original to the railway station. The remainder of the inn, including the guest rooms, is all-new construction. Credit for this loving and painstakingly detailed transformation goes to owner Dan Floyd and his innkeeper partner Suzie Lankes. Open just three months on the occasion of my springtime visit, the inn already had a two- to three-month reservation waiting list for summer weekends. "Our guests are rebooking as they check out," explained Dan.

Custom-made furnishings, featherbeds, fireplaces, stereos, out-of-sight televisions, VCRs, and telephones are all common features of the rooms. Downstairs bedrooms open to private gardens or patios with Jacuzzi tubs. And all guest rooms have fully private marble baths stocked with bathrobes and hair dryers—some with Japanese soaking tubs and two-headed showers. But this is where the similarities end. Each room is cleverly (and uniquely) decorated to evoke a singular time, place, and frame of mind.

Breakfast-time extends mutual conviviality to guests seated around a glass-topped table in the dining room or privacy for two at a dining-car-style side table against a painted countryside, ocean-view backdrop with a wire luggage rack and vintage suitcases overhead. A wine and hors d'oeuvre hour also commences at this spot around 5:00 p.m., and homemade desserts and a glass of port await returning dinner guests.

Overfed, you can stretch your legs in the back garden landscaped in the classical mode. A herringbone brick patio, pergola, and reflecting pond are clothed in roses, azaleas, ferns, lobelia, and colorful trumpet vines.

The jewel-box village of Capitola is a mini-resort with its cluster of main-street shops, restaurants, and art galleries, to say nothing of its popular beach. Shopping, beachcombing, golfing, boating, or wine tasting are all daytime possibilities. But I think you'll find that The Inn at Depot Hill is a destination in and of itself.

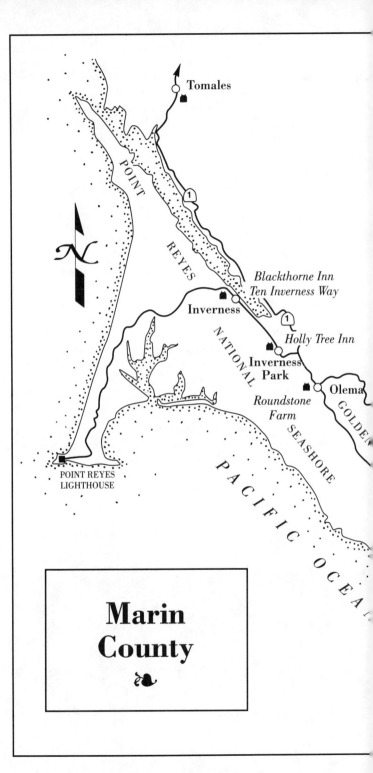

Tomales

POINT REYES

Blackthorne Inn
Ten Inverness Way

Inverness

Holly Tree Inn

Inverness
Park

*Roundstone
Farm*

Olema

NATIONAL

SEASHORE

GOLDEN

POINT REYES
LIGHTHOUSE

PACIFIC OCEAN

**Marin
County**

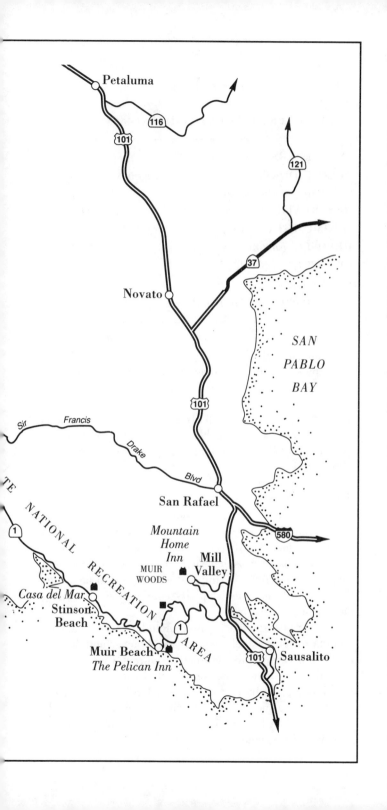

Mountain Home Inn

810 Panoramic Highway
Mill Valley, California 94941; (415) 381-9000

INNKEEPERS: *Ed and Susan Cunningham.*
ACCOMMODATIONS: *10 rooms, all with private bath; queen- and king-size beds.*
RESERVATIONS: *Four to six weeks recommended.*
MINIMUM STAY: *None.*
DEPOSIT: *First night's lodging.*
CREDIT CARDS: *MC, Visa.*
RATES: *Expensive.*
RESTRICTIONS: *Children discouraged. No pets.*

After searching out over 100 sites for a bed and breakfast inn in California, Ed Cunningham found Mount Tamalpais's Mountain Home Inn right in his own backyard. The inn, the last remaining commercial establishment on the mountain, is located on a scenic ridge just above Muir Woods. Originally built in 1912 by a Swiss couple homesick for their beloved Alps, it is bordered by over 340,000 acres of parklands and hundreds of miles of hiking trails.

The grand national park hotels of the thirties, such as the Ahwahnee at Yosemite, the Timberline Lodge at Mount Hood, and the Glacier Park Lodge, served as inspiration for the building's three-tiered redwood, cedar, and glass reconstruction. All 10 guest rooms have gorgeous views and private baths. Most have terraces; some, fireplaces and Jacuzzis. Each room is supplied with trailhead maps, although guests here feel equally comfortable in evening clothes or hiking attire.

Room rates, quoted for two, include a full breakfast. Mountain Home's chef also prepares lunches and dinners for the inn's on-premise gourmet restaurant. Cuisines from around the world are represented with fresh, local ingredients forming the base of each meal. Recharged travelers can request a picnic lunch to go. The offerings include grilled chicken breasts or sandwiches, fresh fruit, cake, and even champagne.

Mount Tamalpais has always been an international meeting place: Transplanted Europeans, tourists, and Bay Area residents alike revel in the splendor of the wilderness and the sweeping panoramas. Until 1884, the only access to Mount Tam was by cow trail. Later, a wagon road was followed by a scenic railway dubbed "the crookedest railroad in the world" because of its 22 trestles and 281 curves. Today's smoothly paved, two-lane road makes going up the mountainside much more pleasant.

Located at the junction of many popular hiking trails, Mountain Home Inn is also just a mile and a half from the outdoor Mountain Play Theatre, site of summertime theater productions. Scenic Muir Woods is two miles from the inn. Audubon Canyon Ranch, a sanctuary for great blue herons, and the Point Reyes Bird Observatory are no more than a 20-minute drive. There are also nearby stables for horseback rides.

Stinson Beach, with the largest beach in southwestern Marin County, is the nearest coastal town to the inn. Stinson Beach's many arts and crafts shops, surf equipment rental facilities, bookstore, and library are of interest. The delis in town can also provide the fixings for an impromptu beach picnic.

The Pelican Inn

10 Pacific Way
Muir Beach, California 94965; (415) 383-6000

INNKEEPER: *Barry Stock.*

ACCOMMODATIONS: *Seven rooms, all with private bath; queen-size beds.*

RESERVATIONS: *Six months recommended for weekends.*

MINIMUM STAY: *None.*

DEPOSIT: *In full.*

CREDIT CARDS: *MC, Visa.*

RATES: *Expensive.*

RESTRICTIONS: *No pets.*

For bed and breakfast in the spirit of sixteenth-century England's west country, plan to stay at The Pelican Inn. The Pelican is located at Muir Beach, scarcely 20 minutes north of the Golden Gate Bridge.

It was here on the Marin Coast that Sir Francis Drake beached his Pelican (the ship was renamed the Golden Hinde in mid-voyage) some 400 years ago to claim California for Queen Elizabeth I and her descendants.

The inn is a weathered-looking English Tudor-style farmhouse that sits nestled between the ocean and the redwoods of the Golden Gate National Recreation Area. The main floor of the building houses a traditional English pub and a public dining room. Pub grub includes both fish 'n' chips and bangers and mash; prime rib and beef Wellington are listed among the dinner entrees. The bar, with its low beams, dart board, and good fellowship, is well stocked with imported brew (Bass, Watney, and Irish Harp on tap), wine, port, and sherry.

Overnight accommodations are located on the second floor. The rooms, with their low doorjambs and leaded windows, are graced with English antiques, heavily draped half-tester (canopy) beds, and Oriental rugs that cover the hardwood floors. Each room has a private bath.

Renaissance music, burning candles, and a roaring fire in the great inglenook set the tone for the proper English breakfast of bangers, bacon and eggs (any style), broiled tomatoes, toast with Scotch marmalade, orange juice, coffee, and tea. A stay of any length is like an ongoing tea party. And speaking of tea, Darjeeling tea with biscuits and "all things nice" can be had throughout the day by the fire or while curled up in bed with a good book.

Casa del Mar

37 Belvedere Avenue
P.O. Box 238
Stinson Beach, California 94970; (415) 868-2124

INNKEEPER: *Rick Klein.*

ACCOMMODATIONS: *Five rooms, all with private bath; queen-size beds.*

RESERVATIONS: *Three to four weeks for weekends.*

MINIMUM STAY: *Two nights on weekends, three over holiday periods.*

DEPOSIT: *Full amount.*

CREDIT CARDS: *AE, MC, Visa.*

RATES: *Expensive.*

RESTRICTIONS: *Children discouraged. No pets.*

Pull your chair up to Casa del Mar's sturdy dining table for what may be one of the most memorable breakfasts you'll ever be privileged to experience at any of California's finer bed and breakfast inns.

Prepared by chef-turned-innkeeper Rick Klein, the morning menu begins, say, with a homemade blueberry and poppyseed coffeecake. A steaming hot cup of coffee probably already sits alongside your glass of freshly squeezed orange juice. Then out comes a whopping plateful of huevos rancheros atop whole wheat tortillas, all simply smothered in fresh salsa. But there's more. Black bean, scallion, and fresh gingerroot pancakes are accompanied by side plates overflowing with fresh fruit.

The next morning you ask yourself: "What could Rick possibly do to top yesterday's meal?" when out of the kitchen's frying pan pops a three-egg omelette filled with fresh-from-the-garden sugar snaps and piled high with grated Romano cheese. Then there's that delicious lemon walnut bread. And once again, fresh fruit, this time a mix of strawberries, cantaloupe, and kiwi. Will this food extravaganza ever end? you think. No, Rick still has fresh apple and ricotta cheese pancakes flavored with cinnamon up his sleeve.

Rising above its hillside terraces, Rick's stately peach and white Mediterranean-style home was built as an attempt to lure nature indoors. Walls of picture windows surround both the living and dining rooms. French doors open out to balconies and decks. Some rooms have skylights; others, ocean views.

The spacious, open living room is filled with rattan chairs and facing rattan sofas in front of a fireplace. Original artwork by local artists like Stinson Beach's Gary Stephens and Inverness's Billy Rose bears a colorful Southwestern influence. Upstairs, five guest rooms show similarities in furnishings, size, and decoration with queen-size platform beds the focal point of each room. Beds are covered with down comforters and massed with plump pillows. Baths offer fluffy towels, modern tiled showers, and pedestal basins.

Guests are welcome, even encouraged, to work in the inn's exotic gardens that feature plants from around the world. There's a microgarden, a vegetable plot, succulents, an herb garden, fruit-bearing trees, and a water-resourceful xeriscape.

One note of caution though: While puttering around the garden there are lessons to be learned. Take, for example, the subtle art of pruning. In gardening, as in life, the cutting away of old growth actually stimulates growth in a new direction. And like the plants of a garden, a person's soul, too, must be nurtured.

"That's what I'm attempting to accomplish here at Casa del Mar," expounds Rick. "To create a mood people can come home to, where they feel nourished and cared for." Oh, to tarry longer in this kind of garden . . .

Roundstone Farm

9940 Sir Francis Drake Boulevard
P.O. Box 217
Olema, California 94950; (415) 663-1020

INNKEEPER: *Inger Fisher.*

ACCOMMODATIONS: *Five rooms, all with private bath; queen- and dual king-size beds.*

RESERVATIONS: *Two weeks recommended.*

MINIMUM STAY: *Two nights on weekends.*

DEPOSIT: *First night's lodging.*

CREDIT CARDS: *AE, MC, Visa.*

RATES: *Moderate.*

RESTRICTIONS: *No children. No pets.*

Gently rolling hills and picturesque views of Tomales Bay and the Point Reyes National Seashore distinguish a 10-acre horse ranch known as Roundstone Farm. Home to Inger Fisher, breeder of fine Arabians and Irish Connemaras, Roundstone is actually a new construction, built just seven years ago, of cedar batten and board, with a passive solar design. So deserving of adjectives like serene, remote, and soul-satisfying in nature is its reflective isolation that most visitors experience a desire for a stay of indeterminable length, rather than just a night or two.

"This house doesn't seem to demand anything of people," says its hostess, Inger. "The rooms are comfortable and pretty, yet simple."

Designed to blend into the surrounding hillside, the house sits on five different levels. The living room with its 16-foot ceilings, slanted wood beams, skylights, eclectic furnishings, and wood-burning stove is on the ground floor. Sliding glass doors lead from the living room out to a deck that overlooks the constant activity of birds and ducks on a pond. A few steps up from the living room is the dining room decorated with prints of stallions from the Danish kings' stables, and furnished with an oval table and chairs and a buffet from a Sussex farmhouse. Guest quarters, located on the third, fourth, and fifth levels of the spacious house, embrace armoires purchased in England and Denmark. All of the rooms' stable-gate-design bed headboards were custom made to Inger's specifications by a local craftsperson. Floral print bedspreads, white goose down comforters, and other linens were imported from Switzerland. Reading lamps sit comfortably on tables beside the beds. Fireplaces are also common to the rooms, as are private baths with tubs and showers.

A 9:15 a.m. seating around the dining room table yields cuisine that might include a baked egg casserole with cottage cheese and mushrooms or apple-puffed pancakes and fresh-ground sausage patties. Juice and fresh fruit are often accompanied by home-baked scones or muffins. An assortment of teas and French roast coffee are also served.

Located less than an hour's drive north of San Francisco is this pristine porthole into another, perhaps more ordered, world. Besides its location within the bounds of the Golden Gate National Recreation Area, the inn enjoys views of Mount Wittenburg, Point Reyes National Seashore, Inverness Ridge, Olema Valley, and the rolling hills of neighboring ranches. The easily accessed mountains, forests, meadows, and beaches emanate an island-in-time appeal to a wide variety of folks: sightseers, hikers, cyclists, bird-watchers, nature lovers, *and* equestrians.

Holly Tree Inn

3 Silverhills Road
Inverness Park, California
Mailing address: P.O. Box 642
Point Reyes Station, California 94956; (415) 663-1554

INNKEEPERS: *Diane and Tom Balogh.*

ACCOMMODATIONS: *Four rooms, all with private bath; queen- and king-size beds. Two guest cottages.*

RESERVATIONS: *Four weeks recommended.*

MINIMUM STAY: *Two nights on weekends.*

DEPOSIT: *In full.*

CREDIT CARDS: *MC, Visa.*

RATES: *Expensive.*

RESTRICTIONS: *No pets.*

Diane Balogh relates a story about the afternoon a young couple rode up on horses to inquire about a room for the night. But this was nothing unusual as the Baloghs' B & B—the Holly Tree Inn—is located just a mile or so from the Point Reyes National Seashore, which offers a variety of outdoor activities, among them hiking, fishing, boating, bird-watching, beachcombing, whale watching, and, of course, horseback riding.

This comfortable and spacious two-story home reminiscent of a hunting lodge was built by a Swede in the late 1930s. The Baloghs, who had set their hearts on an inn of their own after staying at one in Maine, found the 19-acre estate on their first trip out with a realtor. They concluded the deal within a matter of days, moved in, and rented the downstairs as an apartment while the second-story conversion was taking shape.

Central to the inn is the light, airy living room with its huge brick fireplace and overstuffed sofas upholstered in provincial prints. This is a wonderful place for conversation, a cup of tea in the afternoon, or a daydream or two.

The living room opens up to the dining area, which also features a fireplace and a cozy setting for the country-style breakfast. One morning it might include Johnnycakes and braised apples served with coffee, tea, and orange juice.

The next you might get a sampling of Diane's quiche or an omelette with homemade poppyseed bread.

There are four guest rooms—the Laurel Room, the Holly Room, the Ivy Room, and Mary's Garden. The Laurel Room is the most private as well as the largest. Decorated in shades of pale blue and white, it has a comfortable sitting area and a king-size bed. The lace-edged sheets and ruffled curtains set the mood in the pink and white Ivy Room, with its view of the flowery hillside and ivied lattice-work just outside one of the cottage windows. The Holly Room overlooks the front lawn with its flower-covered wishing well. Country antiques and peace and quiet are shared features among the rooms.

The Baloghs also let out two cottages short distances away from their home. Just up the valley is Cottage in the Woods, furnished with a king-size bed, pearwood antiques, and overstuffed chairs. It also features a Pullman kitchen and a small fireplace. Sea Star Cottage is a rustic accommodation built over the tidal waters of Tomales Bay with a dock leading up to the front door. It has a wood-burning fireplace in its cozy living room, a fully equipped kitchen, and a solarium with hot tub.

Unlike many other inns, the Holly Tree welcomes children.

Blackthorne Inn

266 Vallejo
P.O. Box 712
Inverness, California 94937; (415) 663-8621

INNKEEPERS: *Bill and Susan Wigert.*

ACCOMMODATIONS: *Five rooms, three with private bath; one double and four queen-size beds.*

RESERVATIONS: *Six to eight weeks for weekends; two weeks for weekdays.*

MINIMUM STAY: *Two nights on weekends.*

DEPOSIT: *In full.*

CREDIT CARDS: *MC, Visa.*

RATES: *Moderate to expensive.*

RESTRICTIONS: *No pets.*

Best described by *Sunset* magazine, Bill and Susan Wigert's Blackthorne Inn is "a carpenter's fantasy, with decks, hot tub, fireman's pole, and spiral staircase." But then Blackthorne Inn, which resembles a giant treehouse, has gotten so much press. Its Eagle's Nest, an octagonal, glassed-in tower was named "the most romantic, magical room on the coast" by Simon and Schuster's *West Coast Bed and Breakfast Guide*.

Blackthorne had its inception in the early seventies when the Wigerts purchased a one-acre parcel on the northern side of Fish Hatchery Creek Canyon. "We used to hike the area," remembers Susan, "and always wished for our own place here." When they purchased the property, only a two-room cabin occupied the land. Well-meaning friends suggested that Bill add on a deck, and that was just the beginning of what turned out to be a three-year project. As the dwelling grew, room by room, another pal suggested that the couple turn the ever-expanding home into a bed and breakfast operation.

Actually, five guest rooms span the structure's four stories. The Studio, the inn's most spacious guest room, occupies part of the first floor. It offers a private entrance, a queen-size bed, and a separate sitting room with forest view, as well as a private redwood deck. The Hideaway, the other first-floor room, is a must for night owls or late sleepers. It not only has a private entrance but is situated so that it filters out the early morning light and sounds. Overlook and the Lupine Room are third-floor accommodations that each have a private bath. Stained-glass windows in the Overlook Room depict three common local wildflowers: poppy, iris, and thistle. The room also holds a queen-size bed, a beveled mirror, and an antique dresser. The Lupine Room, with its queen-size bed, is connected by bridgeway to a hillside deck where the hot tub is located.

The second floor of the house is masculine, even robust, in decor with strong lines and features. It encompasses a giant stone fireplace, a stained-glass window, skylights, and is surrounded by a 3,500-square-foot deck. Oriental area rugs cover hardwood floors; contemporary furnishings, antiques and collectibles, books, a stereo system, and menus from local restaurants fill the living room. Breakfast is served buffet style in the adjacent dining room at 9:30 a.m. Two kinds of coffeecake (apricot and poppyseed are not unusual), a home-baked quiche, tangy orange juice, fresh fruits, yogurt, and granola follow the early morning coffee and tea. An afternoon dessert is also provided here, compliments of the inn.

Located just an hour north of San Francisco, near the Point Reyes seashore, the inn offers a spectacular setting: long stretches of beach dotted with tide pools, nearby lagoons and bird sanctuaries, rolling hillside pastures, and densely wooded forests. "The words that come to mind when I think of this peninsula are primordial," reflects Susan, "prehistoric."

Ten Inverness Way

10 Inverness Way
Inverness, California 94937; (415) 669-1648

INNKEEPER: *Mary Davies.*

ACCOMMODATIONS: *Four rooms and a suite, all with private bath; queen-size beds.*

RESERVATIONS: *Four to six weeks recommended.*

MINIMUM STAY: *Two nights on weekends.*

DEPOSIT: *In full.*

CREDIT CARDS: *MC, Visa.*

RATES: *Moderate to expensive.*

RESTRICTIONS: *No pets.*

Ten Inverness Way is a four-bedroom guest house that was built in 1904. The living room still has its original Douglas fir paneling and massive stone fireplace, and the guest rooms that were once family bedrooms retain that character. The entire house is furnished with what the proprietor calls "comfortable antiques," and the rooms are filled with fresh flowers (daisies, fuchsias, carnations, and poppies, to name just a few) from the garden that surrounds the house.

Mary Davies, a former Sacramento legislative director, has owned and operated Ten Inverness Way for the past 14 years. She brings to it what might best be described as "a woman's touch": a flair for decorating, a feel for comfort, and the warmth of a friendly smile.

The living room is a great place to curl up with your favorite book. If you didn't bring one along you can choose from the wide selection that fills the bookshelf. The books reflect the broad range of interests of the innkeeper, ranging in subject from religion to the arts, psychology to the classics. The player piano or the recently installed backyard hot tub provide the evening's entertainment; complimentary beverages can be enjoyed by the fire. The bedrooms, all on the second floor, feature antique furniture, handmade rugs, and patchwork quilts. One of the more popular rooms in the house is at the top of the stairs. It sports a view of Tomales Bay from its four multipaned windows.

There's a full American-style breakfast to start the day off right. Banana-laden buckwheat pancakes and cheese-

and-basil scrambled eggs are just two specialties. Egg-based dishes might be complemented by homemade bread one morning and freshly baked spice coffeecake the next. Fresh fruit, coffee, and tea come with every breakfast.

Ten Inverness Way is located just off Sir Francis Drake Boulevard (the main street that runs through town). From the inn you can reach the village shops, restaurants, and Point Reyes National Seashore on foot. Golden Gate Transit provides service between San Francisco and Inverness; the bus stop is a block from the inn's front door.

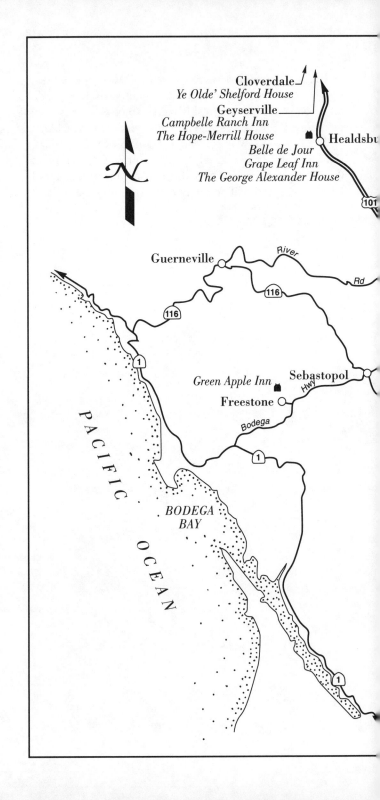

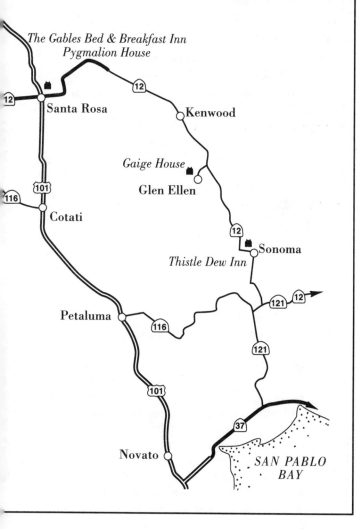

Sonoma
County

The Gables Bed & Breakfast Inn
Pygmalion House

Santa Rosa

12

Kenwood

Gaige House

Glen Ellen

Cotati

Sonoma

Thistle Dew Inn

Petaluma

Novato

SAN PABLO
BAY

Thistle Dew Inn

171 West Spain Street
Sonoma, California 95476; (707) 938-2909

INNKEEPERS: *Larry and Norma Barnett.*

ACCOMMODATIONS: *Six rooms, all with private bath; queen-size beds.*

RESERVATIONS: *Six to eight weeks recommended.*

MINIMUM STAY: *None.*

DEPOSIT: *Full amount.*

CREDIT CARDS: *AE, MC, Visa.*

RATES: *Moderate.*

RESTRICTIONS: *Children discouraged. No pets.*

When Larry Barnett asked himself if there was an occupation that combined his three favorite interests (cooking, gardening, and interacting with people), the answer "innkeeping" popped into his head.

Having frequented bed and breakfasts in both Europe and the United States while traveling as publisher of Sierra Club greeting cards, Larry was keenly aware of what distinguished an ordinary overnight stay from one that was memorable. "I found that personal touches counted for more than a room's decoration—a feeling of welcome, a sense of importance, these were the elements that lingered," he explains. Larry's wife, Norma, also has a first-hand understanding of the needs people have to feel special and cared for. She is a psychologist with a private practice in Oakland. Three days a week she goes off to work and leaves her easygoing, domesticated husband to run the show.

Perhaps one reason the Barnetts were attracted to Thistle Dew, an Arts-and-Crafts-style home, is that its structural design is conducive to conversation. When guests gather around the dining room table for breakfast, they've usually already met in the fire-lit parlor (central to the home's floor plan) or at the backyard picnic table the night before.

A showcase for the Arts-and-Crafts period (circa 1910), the home's common rooms brim with collector pieces of Mission-style furniture, most of them personally signed by

Gustav Stickley or Charles Limbert, two leading figures of the movement. (Arts and Crafts was a swing from the overly ornate Victorian style to one that gained its strength of character from quality of workmanship and materials rather than frivolous detail.)

Thistle Dew's six guest rooms are similarly dressed in Stickley furnishings with queen-size beds and ceiling fans. Fresh flowers, wine glasses, feather pillows, and scented soaps were some of the personal touches that I noted. Complimentary bicycles are also provided for guest use, as is a hot tub. And free passes to a local health club that offers aerobics, weight machines, an outdoor swimming pool, and sauna and steam room are available from the innkeepers.

After a workout, or the drive to the inn, guests greatly appreciate the afternoon refreshments provided by the Barnetts. Sonoma County wines are served along with exotic hors d'oeuvres and freshly cut vegetables and dip. Some of the recipes I pinched were for the Turkish eggplant caviar and hummus with pita bread. Other delicacies with an international flair that Larry whips up are deep-fried spiced pork wontons with sweet mustard sauce, potato-filled Indian samosas, Middle Eastern meatballs, and Indonesian sate with hot peanut sauce.

A decidedly substantial breakfast starts another day of touring off right with an Italian omelette stuffed with salami, roasted peppers, onion, fresh tomato, and three varieties of cheese. This menu, which varies each day, is accompanied by homemade cinnamon brioche, fresh cut fruit, and juice.

I've already rebooked another stay at Thistle Dew. The thing is, I can't decide whether my impending return was prompted by the Barnett's special brand of hospitality, the hot tub, or the food!

Gaige House

13540 Arnold Drive
Glen Ellen, California 95442; (707) 935-0237

INNKEEPER: *Ardath Rouas.*

ACCOMMODATIONS: *Eight rooms, all with private bath; queen- and king-size beds.*

RESERVATIONS: *Four weeks recommended.*

MINIMUM STAY: *Two nights on weekends and through holiday periods.*

DEPOSIT: *First night's lodging.*

CREDIT CARDS: *AE, DC, MC, Visa.*

RATES: *Moderate to expensive.*

RESTRICTIONS: *Children discouraged. No pets.*

Antique hounds will appreciate Gaige House for its central location to the numerous shops located in and around Santa Rosa, Sonoma, and Petaluma. Nature lovers are encouraged by the inn's proximity to Jack London State Historic Park and Sugar Loaf Ridge and Annadel state parks. Possibilities for horseback riding, golf, hiking, canoeing, and wine tasting are also nearby. But the home's spacious centrally air-conditioned rooms and the perfectly maintained backyard swimming pool are where guests frequently hang out.

Situated on an acre of property bounded by Calabezas Creek and the wooded hills of the California Coast Range, Gaige House is best described as Italianate in style with Queen Anne detail. Built in 1890 as a family home for A. E. Gaige, whose butcher shop and slaughterhouse were across what was then called Glen Ellen Avenue, the home has also offered up its services over the years as a boarding house, an elementary school, and, in the 1920s, a bordello (although this rumor is unconfirmed). Another highlight: Gaige himself was said to personally deliver meats in his horse and wagon to writer Jack London at the London family ranch. And, of course, it was London who popularized, or rather romanticized, this area of California when he penned *Valley of the Moon.*

Twenty-four rooms on three levels supply guest parlors, bedrooms, and innkeeper's quarters. Owner Ardath Rouas has filled the inn with her personal collection of modern art. The central living room and parlor are furnished with contemporary sofas and love seats that sit amidst Victorian chairs and settees. Leather bound, two-volume sets of Jack London's works are found in each of the eight guest rooms.

Breakfast is a communal affair served weekdays between 8:00 and 9:00 a.m.; weekends beginning at 8:30. French toast with applewood-smoked bacon, a cantaloupe wedge, orange juice, Peet's coffee, and tea comprised the menu I sampled.

The home's hospitality room is stocked with a refrigerator full of complimentary sodas and mineral water (none of that honor bar stuff you find in hotels). Tea and coffee are also made available, as are wine glasses and ice buckets. Ardath plays host to a formal wine and cheese hour in the parlor between 4:00 and 6:00 p.m. Featured wines such as Chateau St. Jean, Kenwood, Grand Cru, and, of course, Glen Ellen are locally produced.

Food writers (like Julia Child), television producers, and soap-opera stars (Robert and Loyita Wood) are numbered among past guests of Gaige House. People employed in or merely interested in the wine industry also stay here. A wine distributor attempting to describe his experience wrote this in the inn's guest book: "Great complexity, depth, and character. (A night at Gaige House is) . . . to be enjoyed for years."

The Gables Bed & Breakfast Inn

4257 Petaluma Hill Road
Santa Rosa, California 95404; (707) 585-7777

INNKEEPERS: *Michael and Judy Ogne.*

ACCOMMODATIONS: *Seven rooms, all with private bath; double, queen-, and king-size beds.*

RESERVATIONS: *Three weeks recommended.*

MINIMUM STAY: *Two nights on weekends and holiday periods.*

DEPOSIT: *First night's lodging.*

CREDIT CARDS: *AE, MC, Visa.*

RATES: *Moderate to expensive.*

RESTRICTIONS: *Children in cottage only; no children under 10 in main house. No pets.*

Horse ranches, hay farms, melon patches, brightly painted red and white barns, grazing sheep, and "Oreo cookie" striped cows are all familiar sights along Santa Rosa's Petaluma Hill Road. Also situated on this country road just three and a half miles out of town is Sonoma County Historical Landmark #128, a home completed in 1877 by William Roberts as part of his dairy farm—today fondly known as The Gables Bed & Breakfast Inn.

Heralded as a near-perfect example of the High Victorian Gothic Revival architectural style, the home is constructed of redwood with shiplap siding characterized by wide endboards. Fifteen gables, which supply the clue to the inn's historic name, crown the dwelling's unusual keyhole-shaped windows with their original wooden shutters.

The interior floor plan of the home is also classic Victorian, with a central hallway extending from the front veranda all the way through the house to the back porch. Brightened by newly-installed burgundy and rose floral-patterned carpeting, an ornately-carved spiral mahogany staircase, and a 120-year-old grandfather clock, the entry opens to a parlor in the main floor pentagon with a marble fireplace facing blue velvet upholstered Victorian settees comfortably arranged on an Oriental carpet. The Venezuelan harp that sits next to the fireplace was discovered by innkeepers Michael and Judy Ogne at a garage sale. An oak showcase along the room's north wall holds a stereo set, audio tapes, books, and a Regulator clock that

Michael made himself. Beige lace curtains with rose-colored valances cover the four windows of the room.

The centered-bay dining room's oak table, set in front of a marble fireplace, is decked out with white lace place mats and delicately patterned, gold-rimmed white china, a silver service, and fresh cut flowers. The morning I partook, breakfast began with a crystal goblet filled with freshly squeezed orange juice and a flavorful cup of coffee. Chocolate chip coffeecake with walnuts emerged from the inn's spacious kitchen and was followed shortly by a granola-stuffed baked apple bathed in a pool of fresh cream. Frosted butterhorns topped with sliced almonds preceded the cream cheese and plum marmalade-stuffed French toast in a buttermilk batter topped with fresh fruit and a Grand Marnier, orange marmalade, butter, and honey sauce. Link sausages framed the French toast, and coffee refills were endlessly poured.

An ascent up the staircase disclosed five of the inn's seven guest rooms. The Garden View, with its fresh sponge-painted walls with floral wallpaper borders in bright raspberry and mint green tones, turned out to be my favorite bedroom. It held a queen-size brass bed with a rose down comforter, an oak table with two antique oak chairs, and an antique sewing machine converted into a wash-stand. Ivy plants and gay floral wreaths decorated walls and ledges, and the room's tall windows were draped in white lace swags.

Popular among honeymooners or family members vacationing together is the separate backyard William and Mary Cottage with its hide-a-bed sofa living room, wood-burning Franklin stove, fully equipped kitchenette, and second-level sleeping loft.

The Ognes recommend that after breakfast their guests embark on a drive down Crane Canyon Road to Highway 12 through Glen Ellen for a winery tour and then on to Sonoma for a picnic in the park. Another favorite route is a seventy-mile loop from Highway 12 to Bodega Bay then north to Jenner and on to River Road for a tour of the Korbel Champagne Cellars. Along the way, suggested stops might include a seafood lunch, shopping at any number of unique gift and antique stores, a look at the sea lions that sun themselves on the sandbar where the Russian River meets the sea at Jenner, or browsing in the art gallery at Duncan Mills.

Pygmalion House

331 Orange Street
Santa Rosa, California 95401; (707) 526-3407

INNKEEPER: *Lola Wright.*

ACCOMMODATIONS: *Five rooms, all with private bath; twin, double, queen-, and king-size beds.*

RESERVATIONS: *Three weeks recommended.*

MINIMUM STAY: *None.*

DEPOSIT: *First night's lodging.*

CREDIT CARDS: *AE, MC, Visa.*

RATES: *Inexpensive.*

RESTRICTIONS: *Children by arrangement. No pets.*

Santa Rosa was never on my top 10 list of places to visit in California. But since I was searching out bed and breakfast inns and had heard of one that opened there, I thought I'd stop by. From the freeway I spotted a beautifully restored, freshly painted Victorian, and something (perhaps intuition, perhaps experience) told me that if there was a bed and breakfast in downtown Santa Rosa, this was it. I followed directions a friend had jotted down: Downtown exit from 101. Third to Railroad Street. Left turn. Two blocks to Laurel. Another left. A right onto Orange. Last house on the right. It came as no surprise that the last house on the right and the house I saw from the freeway were one and the same: Pygmalion House.

The house is a classic example of what one expects of a bed and breakfast. It exudes homeyness and history, and from a bed-and-breakfast enthusiast's point of view, it's just the right size. Each of the five bedrooms offers a private bath, and each is named for the predominant color of its decor. The Blue Room wins my vote of approval: blue and white flowered wallpaper, plush blue carpeting, French Provincial furnishings, lace curtains, and a king-size bed. The bathroom has an old-fashioned clawfoot tub with brass fixtures.

Guests enjoy a bountiful breakfast: corn flakes and granola, fresh fruit in season, yogurt, ham, bacon, or sausage and eggs, a hot bread basket, coffee, and freshly squeezed orange juice. Other amenities: the morning paper, fresh flowers in the room, and cheese and crackers with sparkling apple cider in the late afternoon.

Lola Wright brings to Pygmalion House 25 years of experience staying at bed and breakfasts throughout Europe and 10 years as manager of an inn in Hawaii. Accordingly she defines her innkeeping style as incorporating European comfort and attention with Southern hospitality and lots of aloha spirit.

Pygmalion House is adjacent to Railroad Square, the historical section of Santa Rosa that has rapidly gained popularity for its shops and fine restaurants. And, as I discovered, Santa Rosa is central to many areas of interest: the Napa and Sonoma wine country, the Russian River, San Francisco, Point Reyes National Seashore, and the Pacific Ocean.

Belle de Jour

16276 Healdsburg Avenue
Healdsburg, California 95448; (707) 431-9777

INNKEEPERS: *Tom and Brenda Hearn.*

ACCOMMODATIONS: *Four rooms, all with private bath; queen- and king-size beds.*

RESERVATIONS: *Two weeks recommended.*

MINIMUM STAY: *Two nights on weekends and some holidays.*

DEPOSIT: *First night's lodging.*

CREDIT CARDS: *MC, Visa.*

RATES: *Moderate to expensive.*

RESTRICTIONS: *No pets.*

In 1986 Tom and Brenda Hearn left the fast-paced life of Los Angeles for the serenity of Sonoma County and a business venture they could call their own. They purchased Belle de Jour, an 1875 Italianate Victorian that was formerly not only an inn but a working farm as well. Out went the sheep, rabbits, and goats. In marched four friendly felines.

Six acres of flower, herb, and vegetable gardens, fruit-bearing trees, and cozy little nooks set the stage for the guest accommodations: four separate cottages overlooking the home's back meadow. The cottages, freshly painted and nestled in the pines, have fireplaces and wood-burning stoves. All include ceiling fans, and some also come with whirlpool tubs for two. Overall, the mix of contemporary and antique pieces make up what the innkeepers call a California country decor.

Guests enter the main house through the kitchen, with its gleaming copper pots and pans, large commercial range, and glass-front refrigerator—all an indication that this couple takes breakfast seriously. "We emphasize three things," notes Brenda of the bountiful breakfast produced here each morning and served either on the deck or in the kitchen dining area at 9:00 a.m. sharp. "Freshness, variety, and abundance."

The house blend of java and a selection of fresh juices kick off the morning meal. Home-baked breads are accompanied by waffles or egg-and-cheese dishes with an abundance of fresh fruit.

Belle de Jour's location seldom leaves guests with nothing to do—that is, unless it's by choice. The countryside invites a crisp morning run or a bike ride. Golf, tennis, swimming, canoeing, and kayaking are all available nearby. Local wineries are among the finest, and the backroads offer quaint country charm. A real treat, though, is a backroads/wineries tour in the Hearns' 1923 Star touring car.

To reach Belle de Jour from Highway 101, take the Dry Creek Road offramp. Turn right on Dry Creek to the stoplight, then left on Healdsburg Avenue and continue for approximately one mile. The Simi Winery tasting room is on the left, Belle de Jour on the right.

The George Alexander House

423 Matheson Street
Healdsburg, California 95448; (707) 433-1358

INNKEEPERS: *Christian and Phyllis Baldenhofer.*

ACCOMMODATIONS: *Four rooms, all with private bath; double, queen and king-size beds.*

RESERVATIONS: *Two to three weeks recommended.*

MINIMUM STAY: *None.*

DEPOSIT: *First night's lodging.*

CREDIT CARDS: *MC, Visa.*

RATES: *Moderate.*

RESTRICTIONS: *Only one room available for children. No pets.*

Distinguished by its quatrefoil front windows and octagonal tower, The George Alexander House pays tribute to the late Queen Anne architectural style. Erected in 1905, it was built by George Alexander, the tenth and last child of Cyrus Alexander, whose surname is to this day synonymous with the region—the Alexander Valley—and its wine producing fame.

Wine tasting is an activity held in high regard in and around the small Sonoma County town of Healdsburg. From this bed and breakfast you can easily walk to five different tasting rooms or get in your car for a short drive through spectacular hills and valleys that lead to nearly 50 more such edifices. But Healdsburg also offers great antique stores, historic late 19th-century homes, and fine dining in restaurants like John Ash & Company and Madrona Manor.

"Innkeeping reinforces our faith in the goodness of people," reflects Christian and Phyllis Baldenhofer, expatriots of big city living who bought the Alexander home after 11 years of operating a coffee, tea, and spice shop on Haight Street in San Francisco. The Baldenhofers, also one-time art gallery owners, have stocked their house with Oriental rugs and African artifacts, as well as a large collection of books ranging from art and architecture to homeopathy and armchair travel.

Stained and leaded glass corner windows grace the home's front parlor as do Victorian love seats, an 1800s signed Wright and Mansfield English desk, and a recliner that once belonged to George Alexander. "We found it in the basement," notes Phyllis. A second, smaller parlor exudes the warmth of a fireplace, which makes it ideal for sitting around and mapping out the day's sightseeing plans. This room is furnished with a wicker settee and matching side chairs.

Guest accommodations include the stately Mr. and Mrs. George Alexander Room with its fireplace, Eastlake bed, and shower for two. A Victorian-era four-poster with burl head- and footboard dominates the cheery Lucille Alexander Room. The Butler's Room, just off the kitchen, is decorated with an antique spindle bed and Eastlake chairs, and contains a cozy bath with dual showerheads. The largest and most private accommodation offered here is called The Back Porch. It features a small deck and private entrance, a king-size bed, an environmentally correct wood-burning stove, and private bath with a Jacuzzi tub.

Breakfast is served in the inn's dining room at 9:00 a.m., but the Baldenhofers are most accommodating when it comes to obliging earlier breakfast requests. Freshly brewed Guatemalan coffee provides the wake-up call, after which Phyllis proceeds to serve, for example, baked pears in cinnamon sauce topped with yogurt sweetened with maple syrup and cornmeal pancakes stuffed with banana yogurt alongside mixed fruit compote. Other goodies that The George Alexander House's kitchen is known for include a breakfast bread pudding, lemon ricotta pancakes, oatmeal scones, and custard French toast. Rave about the offerings and you're apt to walk away with complimentary recipes.

Grape Leaf Inn

539 Johnson Street
Healdsburg, California 95448; (707) 433-8140

INNKEEPERS: *Karen and Terry Sweet.*

ACCOMMODATIONS: *Seven rooms, all with private bath; queen- and king-size beds.*

RESERVATIONS: *Two months recommended.*

MINIMUM STAY: *Two nights on weekends.*

DEPOSIT: *First night's lodging.*

CREDIT CARDS: *MC, Visa.*

RATES: *Moderate.*

RESTRICTIONS: *No children under eleven. No pets.*

Grape Leaf Inn, a seven-bedroom, seven-bath gem that is surely the envy of the competition, is located in the small town of Healdsburg, a short bike ride from one of California's premier grape-growing regions, the Alexander Valley.

In keeping with the natural surroundings, the proprietors have named the guest rooms after grape varietals: Merlot, Pinot Noir, Gamay Rose. Cabernet Sauvignon has skylight windows in both bedroom and bath. The Chardonnay Suite features stained-glass windows, an antique armoire, and a separate sitting room; there's an old-fashioned pull-chain toilet and a double-sink oak vanity in the bath. Sauvignon Blanc's brass and iron bed faces a bay window with a love seat. And the Zinfandel Room has a king-size bed, an antique oak dresser, and an Oriental rug that covers the hardwood floor. (The four upstairs rooms all have sloped roofs and two-person whirlpool tub/showers.)

Innkeepers Karen and Terry Sweet pour a sampling of Sonoma County wine to go along with the Sonoma County cheeses that are served in the front parlor late each afternoon. Books, magazines, and games are available, or one can just sit and relax on the sofa in front of the fireplace. A collection of local artists' paintings and photographs is on display throughout the inn.

A full country breakfast is served at 9:00 a.m. in the dining room. Featured dishes include Mexican eggs with guacamole, bacon and broccoli frittata, or quiche Lorraine; fresh blueberry or banana-almond coffeecake (the inn's most requested recipe); cereal and milk; fresh fruit in season (baked apples in winter); freshly ground coffee; and freshly squeezed orange juice.

Within walking distance of the inn are river beaches and night-lighted tennis courts. Bicycles can be rented just three blocks away for informal tours of the wine country. The innkeepers will make dinner reservations or arrangements for river canoe trips and other recreational activities.

Campbell Ranch Inn

1475 Canyon Road
Geyserville, California 95441; (707) 857-3476

INNKEEPERS: *Mary Jane and Jerry Campbell.*

ACCOMMODATIONS: *Five rooms, all with private bath; king-size beds.*

RESERVATIONS: *Two to three weeks recommended.*

MINIMUM STAY: *Two nights on weekends; three-night minimum over some holiday periods.*

DEPOSIT: *First night's lodging.*

CREDIT CARDS: *MC, Visa.*

RATES: *Moderate.*

RESTRICTIONS: *No children. No pets.*

A generous man will prosper; he who refreshes others will himself be refreshed.—Proverbs 11:25

I not only feel right at home at the Campbell Ranch, I feel as though I could return again and again. This is due in part to the serenity experienced here. Perhaps it is also due to the fact that since the Campbells' living quarters are not separate from their inn operation, one immediately feels like part of the family. Then again, it might just have something to do with that delicious homemade pie that is served at the kitchen table just before bedtime. But no one describes the Campbell Ranch experience better than Mary Jane when she says, "People come here to *stay!*"

There's plenty to stay for—picturesque hilltop views of lush rolling vineyards, a well-maintained swimming pool and hot tub spa, a tennis court, Ping-Pong, and horseshoes, not to mention bicycles and peaceful country roads.

The Campbell Ranch is a modern, split-level ranch-style home with traditional furnishings. The living room's two floral-patterned sofas sit face to face in front of a massive brick fireplace that divides the living room from the family room, where guests find chess, checkers, jigsaw puzzles, a stereo, and yes, even a television set.

The bedroom on the lower level (room 1) affords the most privacy, as it is the sole bedroom on this floor and is equipped with a private (though detached) bath. Here you will find wood-paneled walls, plants, a desk, and a comfortable reading chair, as well as a collection of *National Geographic* magazines dating from 1959—enough to keep an armchair traveler holed up here for years.

My favorite room was the one I stayed in overnight—preselected from the brochure for its Baldwin piano and balcony with a view of the countryside (room 2). There was a spacious closet, a desk, ivy plants, and shelves abounding with good reading material. Rooms 3 and 4 also share in the panoramic views. Room 5, the cottage, is a two-bedroom accommodation ideal for families vacationing together.

Mary Jane cites her job as a maid during college and her experience as a wife and mother (three boys) as the training ground for operating a bed and breakfast. "Jerry's the handyman around here," she says. "He does all the grass cutting and repairs, though he loves socializing and sharing his model railroad."

The kitchen provides the setting for breakfast, which is served until 10:00 a.m. Monday through Saturday and until 9:00 a.m. on Sundays. Selections include a choice of a grapefruit half, freshly squeezed orange juice, stewed prunes, or sliced bananas with sugar and cream. "Group B" selections consist of cold cereal, a cheese omelette, fried eggs and potatoes, or the Campbell Ranch egg puff (loaded with fresh sauteed mushrooms and Monterey Jack cheese). From "Group C" you can choose between white toast, zucchini bread, sour cream coffeecake, homemade honey-wheat loaf, or blueberry or bran muffins. And finally, the beverages: coffee, tea, milk, or hot chocolate.

There's plenty to do after breakfast for those who aren't content to just *stay*: winery tours, a nearby dam and fish hatchery, and canoeing or tubing on the Russian River just seven minutes away. Snoopyland, home of cartoonist Charles Shulz, is in nearby Santa Rosa. The inn also provides a central location for easy day trips to Mendocino, Napa, Sonoma, and even San Francisco.

The Hope-Merrill House

21253 Geyserville Avenue
P.O. Box 42
Geyserville, California 95441
 (707) 857-3356 or (800) 825-4BED

INNKEEPERS: *Bob and Rosalie Hope; Kim Hope-Taylor.*

ACCOMMODATIONS: *Seven rooms, all with private bath; double and queen-size beds.*

RESERVATIONS: *Three to four weeks recommended.*

MINIMUM STAY: *Two nights on weekends, May through October.*

DEPOSIT: *First night's lodging.*

CREDIT CARDS: *MC, Visa.*

RATES: *Moderate.*

RESTRICTIONS: *No pets.*

Victoriana buffs, arise—and head straight to Geyserville for one of the finest overnight experiences on the bed and breakfast circuit—The Hope-Merrill House, named after the present owners-innkeepers, Bob and Rosalie Hope, and the original builder-occupant, J. P. Merrill.

This circa 1875 Eastlake/Stick Victorian is a virtual museum of the trends and treasures of its time, from the carefully researched and reproduced wall coverings to the period furnishings and fixtures. Of special interest are the Lincrusta-Walton wainscoting in the entranceway and up-stairs hall and the tin ceiling in the kitchen. The Hopes' collection of glassware and bric-a-brac, as well as their books on Victorian gardens, furnishings, and house build-ing (and one on gas lighting in America), delight the eye and captivate the mind.

The reasonably priced guest accommodations include the Victorian Room with its chaise longue, antique per-fume bottles, and walnut carved headboard from the 1860s; the Peacock Room, the only downstairs bedroom with a fireplace, queen-size bed, and whirlpool bath; the Bachelor's Button, with antique bed, chestnut dresser, and Maxfield Parrish prints; and the Carpenter Gothic and Briar Rose rooms. Two recently completed guest accommo-dations (the Bradbury Room and Vinyard View) include showers for two in their baths. Also new are the outdoor gazebo, Victorian gardens, heated swimming pool and Pac-A-Picnic lunch basket offered at a slight additional charge.

Victoriana buffs, awake—to one of the most delicious gourmet breakfasts found on the bed and breakfast circuit. Rosalie and Kim, caterers whose creations are highly respected by the top names in the county, are known for their hot poached pears with ginger, fresh peaches with zabaglione, chili egg puff with salsa, French toast like no other, sour cream coffeecake, homemade apple butter, and homemade jams.

The slow-paced, rural atmosphere makes one inclined to linger, perhaps too long, while scenic views along Highway 128 and tours and tastings along the Russian River Wine Road await. Bob offers wine tasting advice and cites this, along with lovemaking, as the two activities his guests seem to be most interested in. "Canoeing runs a distant third," he adds.

"Our desire was to authentically recreate a living history of the Victorian era for people to enjoy," Bob explains. Victoriana buffs, acclaim—well done!

Ye Olde' Shelford House

29955 River Road
Cloverdale, California 95425; (707) 894-5956

INNKEEPERS: *Al and Ina Sauder.*

ACCOMMODATIONS: *Six rooms, all with private bath; queen- and king-size beds.*

RESERVATIONS: *Three to four weeks recommended for summer weekends.*

MINIMUM STAY: *Two nights on weekends.*

DEPOSIT: *First night's lodging.*

CREDIT CARDS: *DC, MC, Visa.*

RATES: *Moderate.*

RESTRICTIONS: *No pets.*

With a locale among the backroads of Cloverdale's Wine Country (where 10 wineries are clustered within 11 miles of each other), a fringe-topped horse-drawn surrey, and a bicycle built for two, Ye Olde' Shelford House brims with scenic adventure possibilities.

Run by Al and Ina Sauder, Shelford House is an authentically restored 1885 Victorian, comfortably furnished with antiques, some of which were made by Al's grandfather.

The home was originally built by Eurastus Shelford on property given to him by his father, who purchased the land in 1863 as part of the Rancho Musalacon. It stayed in the Shelford family over the next 110 years, and by the time the Sauders found the two-story house after Al retired from teaching in 1984, it had been turned into a rental unit.

Many new homeowners try to modernize their properties. But not Ina and Al. "The first thing we had to do was demodernize, starting with the downstairs bathroom," laughs Al. "Out came the new tub and toilet and in went a clawfoot tub and an antique, pull-chain water closet."

The result of this lovable couple's work is a delightful little country inn. Because the home faces acres of vineyards, the view is incredible. There are three bedrooms in the main house (and three in a newly built carriage house) with lots of windows for viewing the surrounding grapevines. Each room also has beautiful homemade quilts, plants, and fresh flowers from the surrounding gardens.

One of the personalized touches here is that bedrooms are named after Ina and Al's mothers. Some are even furnished with their parents' heirlooms.

Upstairs are the Laura May Colmery Room (named after Al's adopted mother), with Laura's queen-size bed and wedding set from the 1920s, and the Helen Gabriel Linton Room (named after Ina's mom), with its antique Belgian oak bed covered with a garden-patterned quilt. The upstairs bath has family antiques as well: Laura's old washstand and an old oak potty chair. The Mary Oakes Green Room (named after Al's real mother), which features a queen-size oak bed and a private bath with clawfoot tub, is downstairs.

If the upstairs skylight arboretum, a game of Ping-Pong in the recreation room, or a song on the player piano isn't enough to captivate you, you can take a romantic dip in the inn's across-the-lawn hot tub or a swim in the pool.

In the morning the aroma of fresh, oven-baked breakfast wafts through the house. Ina's feast starts off with a cool glass of fresh orange juice and leads on to such delights as quiche (Lorraine, seafood, or broccoli), just-made breads, jams, fresh fruit, and coffee, tea, or milk. Iced tea, lemonade, and homemade cookies are laid out in the afternoon.

After breakfast, you can arrange to take a ride down memory lane aboard the Sauders' turn-of-the-century carriage. The ride leaves the inn at 10:00 each Saturday and Sunday morning (May through October) for a leisurely jaunt down quiet country lanes that ends with an outdoor picnic. Another option is Al's 1929 Model A Ford tour of five local wineries with a picnic lunch stop at Lake Sonoma.

Cloverdale is the gateway to Lake Sonoma, which has great bass, catfish, and trout fishing, plus picnic and swim areas, and even a fish hatchery.

Green Apple Inn

520 Bohemian Highway
Freestone, California 95472; (707) 874-2526

INNKEEPERS: *Rogers and Rosemary Hoffman.*

ACCOMMODATIONS: *Four rooms, all with private bath; double and queen-size beds.*

RESERVATIONS: *Two weeks recommended.*

MINIMUM STAY: *Two nights on weekends and over holiday periods.*

DEPOSIT: *First night's lodging.*

CREDIT CARDS: *MC, Visa.*

RATES: *Moderate.*

RESTRICTIONS: *No children under seven.*

In the mid-19th century two brothers, joint owners of one of the original homes in the town of Freestone, had a serious falling-out. The burning issue has long since been forgotten, but the consequence remains. Showing more logic than good sense, one brother sawed off what he claimed to be his half of the house and took it elsewhere. Astonished, the other brother rolled in another house and tacked it on to the wounded building.

Although the general consensus within the village is that this story is true, there is a strong difference of opinion about which of the Freestone homes the story applies to.

Rogers and Rosemary Hoffman, proprietors of the Green Apple Inn, invite you to note the different structural styles within their home, and they make the case that, indeed, it is this house that resulted from the historic feud.

The Hoffmans' Green Apple Inn is located on five acres of meadowland and redwood groves. Its sitting room and four guest rooms provide an intimate atmosphere for socializing and spinning a few yarns of one's own. Heirlooms and family treasures fill the house; the most unusual of these are Rogers' great-grandfather's Civil War gun (a portrait of the late Thomas Rogers hangs above the fireplace mantel), the 100-year-old Seth Thomas mantel clock, a Japanese wood carving, a coal scuttle from the turn of the century, a French Revolution-era etching, and a 250-year-old brass coffee urn. Guest rooms hold iron and brass beds with fluffy patchwork and floral print comforters, marble-topped dressers, wicker pieces, and wildflowers.

As expected, apple-based dishes make up the breakfast menu at the Green Apple Inn. Typical fare includes French toast with walnuts and apples, a fresh fruit salad or baked apple in wintertime, freshly baked apple bread with home-made marmalade, and coffee.

After breakfast you can take a walking tour of Freestone's award-winning nursery; visit an antique store, a homespun clothing boutique, or a Japanese enzyme health spa; hike through the surrounding hills and valleys; or play Frisbee with Jeannie, the Hoffmans' pet Labrador.

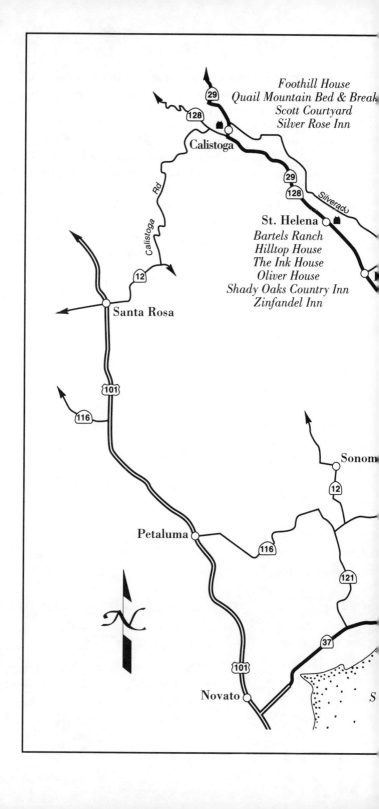

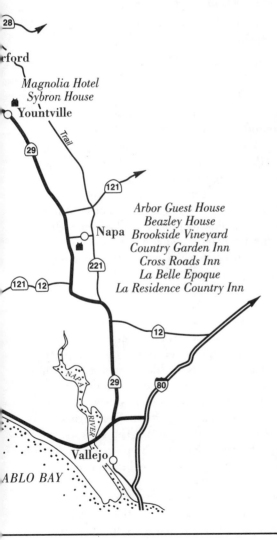

Napa County

28 →

rford

Magnolia Hotel
Sybron House
Yountville

29

Trail

121

Arbor Guest House
Beazley House
Napa   *Brookside Vineyard*
Country Garden Inn
Cross Roads Inn
La Belle Epoque
La Residence Country Inn

221

121 12

12

NAPA

29   80

RIVER

Vallejo

ABLO BAY

Arbor Guest House

1436 G Street
Napa, California 94559; (707) 252-8144

INNKEEPERS: *Rosemary and Bruce Logan.*

ACCOMMODATIONS: *Five rooms, all with private bath; queen-size beds.*

RESERVATIONS: *Five to six weeks recommended.*

MINIMUM STAY: *Two nights on weekends.*

DEPOSIT: *First night's lodging.*

CREDIT CARDS: *MC, Visa.*

RATES: *Moderate.*

RESTRICTIONS: *No children under 10. No pets.*

The Arbor Guest House, a colonial transition, was built in 1906 by the appropriately named Rumbles, who left San Francisco just after the historic rumbling of the 1906 earthquake. Mr. Rumble was a lather, and the exterior and interior of Arbor Guest House is a stunning example of his artful woodworking. The inn's proprietors, Bruce and Rosemary Logan, are the third owners of the house. Bruce (an architect and contractor by profession) has remodeled the main and carriage houses and restored them to their turn-of-the-century elegance with contemporary touches.

Many of the guests comment that the Arbor Guest House reminds them of their grandmother's home in the Midwest. The warmth is apparent in the graceful living and dining room combination. A clawfooted French couch and chair (covered in fabric the color of café au lait with hints of blue) have their colors reproduced in the tiled fireplace that boasts a pair of family heirloom andirons from Stratford-on-Avon. A mahogany Jacobean dining room table with side chairs and marble-topped sideboard complete the homey picture. You'll be particularly intrigued by the etched glass in the entryway doors: The fern pattern was created by a process called glue chipping. When glue spread on glass is heated by the sun, it shrinks and chips the glass away to create a design.

This bed and breakfast is like two inns in one. The carriage house has two guest rooms (Rose's Bower and Autumn Harvest) and the main house has three (Winter

Haven, Spring Fancy, and Summer Garland). Rose's Bower is a Victorian fantasy come to life with a wood-burning fireplace, rose-patterned wallpaper, ruby cut-glass lamps beside a queen-size mahogany bed, and an opaque glass window etched with a bouquet of roses. Rose's Bower occupies the entire second floor of the carriage house. Downstairs, Autumn Harvest is done in fall tones of peach, cream, and brown. A Federal queen-size bed in the lace-curtained alcove is covered with a satin, suede, and eyelet spread of champagne and peach. A double razor strap bed with a dark champagne spread makes the room ideal for two or more traveling companions. Autumn Harvest's private bath features a recently added shower and whirlpool spa tub.

These two rooms were the most requested until Winter Haven was completed in the main house. That room is a harmony of greens and dusty rose tones. And it also has a two-person whirlpool tub, only this one is actually in the bedroom facing a fireplace. Sheer bliss. If you choose, you can sit by the fire in one of the Victorian chairs. The queen bed has an Amish quilt with a dahlia pattern.

Linger over breakfast under the umbrella table on one of the three separate patio areas Bruce built in the orchardlike yard filled with cedar, cherry, orange, walnut, olive, peach, and lemon trees. Rosemary indulges her guests with Good Morning Muffins (moister than most, made with carrots, coconut, and raisins), or apple walnut coffeecake made from ingredients grown on the property. A full breakfast (most guests skip lunch) includes French toast with fresh peach syrup or a spicy ham and cheese quiche also filled with tomatoes, spinach, and peppers. Guests staying in the carriage house have the option of dining in their room.

During the spring the lavender trumpet vine flowers drape over the arbor that separates the main house from the carriage house. "That's not the only reason we named the inn Arbor Guest House," Rosemary and Bruce inform us. "An arbor is a secluded place, a refuge from the world." While their home certainly provides a relaxing retreat, it is also in a prime location to some of Napa's best known attractions. The Napa Valley Wine Train, for one, is just half a mile from the inn.

Beazley House

1910 First Street
Napa, California 94559; (707) 257-1649

INNKEEPERS: *Jim and Carol Beazley.*

ACCOMMODATIONS: *11 rooms, all with private bath; queen-size beds.*

RESERVATIONS: *Two to three weeks recommended.*

MINIMUM STAY: *Two nights on weekends.*

DEPOSIT: *First night's lodging.*

CREDIT CARDS: *MC, Visa.*

RATES: *Moderate to expensive.*

RESTRICTIONS: *Children under 12 discouraged. No pets.*

Fond memories of the Beazley House: friendly people (Jim and Carol Beazley), the smell of freshly baked muffins wafting from the kitchen, a warm and snuggly down comforter, and one of the finest old homes in Napa, an early California town with more than its share of distinguished literary and business personalities.

This two-story, Colonial Revival/Shingle-style house was built in 1902. Its hardwood floors, wainscoting, cove ceilings, and stained-glass windows bespeak its Edwardian origins. There's a large living room with a fireplace and a window flanked by bookshelves. (The Beazleys also keep plenty of games on hand: backgammon, chess, Yatzee, and dominoes are all available.) To the right of the music room is the formal dining room, where a breakfast of fresh fruits, yogurt, cheeses or quiche, home-baked muffins, coffee and tea, and fruit juice is served. Guest rooms are individually decorated and named according to theme. In addition to the six accommodations in the main house, the Carriage House provides five rooms with fireplaces and private baths (all with two-person spas).

The Beazleys are as comfortable and accommodating as their home. Both are unabashedly people oriented. Carol served as a full-time nurse for 14 years; Jim was a photojournalist with the *Reno Evening Gazette* and *Nevada State Journal*. A tour of bed and breakfasts in England and California left them with a confirmed belief in the owner operated philosophy of innkeeping.

Beazley House is three blocks from central Napa, a city that is experiencing a rebirth as a tourist destination. It offers historic-architecture walking tours within the immediate area. There is also hot air ballooning, cycling, gliding, horseback riding, and the Robert L. Stevenson Museum, all within a few miles.

Visitors will have no difficulty finding this attractive wine country inn with its bright blue and white awnings and gracefully hipped roof. But despite its impressive exterior, the memories most people take away are of the warm and familylike atmosphere inside.

Brookside Vineyard

3194 Redwood Road
Napa, California 94558; (707) 944-1661

INNKEEPERS: *Tom and Susan Ridley.*

ACCOMMODATIONS: *Three rooms, all with private bath; queen- and king-size beds.*

RESERVATIONS: *Two to three weeks recommended.*

MINIMUM STAY: *Two nights on weekends.*

DEPOSIT: *First night's lodging.*

CREDIT CARDS: *Not accepted.*

RATES: *Moderate.*

RESTRICTIONS: *No children. No pets.*

"We're probably the only bed and breakfast in Napa Valley that has its own Christmas tree farm," laughs Susan Ridley of Brookside Vineyard. Susan and husband Tom are the proprietors of an inn complex that features not only Christmas trees, but a free-form swimming pool, a romantic gazebo, a fruit orchard, and a working vineyard.

Tom Ridley has a wealth of information to share with his guests about grape growing and winemaking, as well as years of hands-on experience that you are unlikely to encounter on a one-to-one basis at any full-scale winery in the valley that you might choose to visit.

During the preharvest season (mid-August through the first weeks of September), guests who don't mind setting their alarm clocks for 5:00 a.m. are welcome to help Tom gather grapes that will be crushed and tested for sugar content. If harvesting sample grapes isn't your idea of a relaxing vacation, you might consider paying a visit during the fall pruning season when you can collect grapevines for homemade Christmas wreaths.

The Ridleys' adobe home with red tile roof has an idyllic setting on Napa's Redwood Creek. Douglas fir trees provide a lush green backdrop to the property throughout the year. Spring is a riot of flowering fruit trees, and in the autumn months the chardonnay vines turn a vivid amber. Built in the 1950s, the house is best described as early California mission. Its library and living room have a Mediterranean feel with cream-colored walls, arched doorways, and cathedral-beamed ceilings. Furnishings are a mix of old family favorites (like the tuxedo-style sofa in a cream and green print) and a collection of European and American antiques. A steamer trunk displays an antique Belgian terra-cotta horse; an early American silver pitcher is used as a vase.

Each of the guest rooms (Britannia, Americana, and France) is decorated in its own distinctive style with a decided international flair. Britannia, in muted shades of gray, brown, and brass, has both a fireplace and an enclosed patio. A sauna and private bath are added attractions to this oversized room. Americana is decorated with beige and blue Laura Ashley fabrics that drape walls, windows, tables, and the room's queen-size bed. American accent pieces consist of an antique Boston rocking chair and a steamer trunk that serves as a dresser. Sliding glass doors lead from the bedroom to a walkway that ends at the swimming pool.

An *al fresco* breakfast (available between 8:00 and 9:30 a.m.) is offered in the gazebo. Fresh-squeezed orange juice, a selection of seasonal fruits, creamy yogurt, and Susan's signature muffins are set out buffet style; the ever-changing daily entrée is served tableside. Waffles with chopped pecans and syrup, individual garden quiches with Jarlsberg cheese, and popovers brimming with fresh raspberries and blueberries are just a few of Susan Ridley's favorite recipes.

ॐ

Country Garden Inn
1815 Silverado Trail
Napa, California 94558; (707) 255-1197

INNKEEPERS: *Lisa and George Smith.*

ACCOMMODATIONS: *10 rooms, all with private bath; queen- and king-size beds.*

RESERVATIONS: *Three to four weeks recommended.*

MINIMUM STAY: *Two nights on weekends.*

DEPOSIT: *First night's lodging.*

CREDIT CARDS: *AE, MC, Visa.*

RATES: *Expensive.*

RESTRICTIONS: *No children. No pets.*

Nostalgic for that bed and breakfast where you spent your honeymoon while exploring the English countryside? No need to fly to Heathrow. Just book a room at the secluded Country Garden Inn and leave your passport behind. This inn has it all: a great location on the banks of the Napa River in the heart of the wine country, an elegant country decor with antique-filled guest rooms, including one in a private country cottage, and an English-born and -bred innkeeper.

Once you reach Country Garden Inn, just off the Silverado Trail, I'm sure you will be convinced that a little bit of heaven has planted itself squarely here. The inn is hidden among one and a half acres of wooded riverside property. The circular rose garden with a lily pond and fountain are shaded by a canopy of trees. In summer, the grounds offer a peaceful verdant retreat; autumn days are similarly spectacular when the red leaf maple reaches full color.

You may, however, have a difficult time deciding which guest room to choose; there are 10 in all. Six are in the main house, three in the newly completed Rose House, and one, the Willow, is that private cottage I mentioned. It comes complete with its own Jacuzzi, fireplace, and private deck.

The Rose Room (in the main house) is a long-standing favorite of honeymooners and anniversary couples with its rose satin and beige lace canopied king-size bed and expanse of beveled glass windows that bring the garden surroundings into the room. A sunken Jacuzzi tub is a key feature of the room's private bath. A wood beam ceiling in the Orchid Room sets an old-world tone for a canopied queen-size bed covered with an antique patchwork quilt.

A champagne breakfast is served from 9:00 until 10:00 a.m. in the Smiths' delightful Morning Room. While sipping your complimentary glass of bubbly you may select from an assortment of seven or eight fresh fruits followed by homemade coffeecake (cinnamon walnut is a favorite), scones or croissants, and (if you have any room) grilled sausages, scrambled eggs (or eggs Benedict or a soufflé), fried bread and potatoes, and the grilled tomatoes that round off this hearty English-style breakfast.

And what would an English inn be without a proper tea time? Or, you may prefer a cool glass of fresh mint-garnished lemonade or a piping hot cup of coffee. Sample one (or all!) of the homemade cookies: shortbread, chocolate chip, peanut butter, and oatmeal. An hour after tea you'll find a half carafe of white zinfandel in your room accompanied by a dish of spicy deviled almonds roasted with cayenne pepper. And don't forget the 5:30 happy hour hosted on the backyard patio. A choice of wines and sherry is offered with a cheese board, homemade chutneys, pickles, crackers, and fresh-baked French bread.

After dinner come back to the inn for dessert. An array of dessert wines complement hand-dipped truffles, chocolate mints, fudge, macaroons, and an Amaretto torte. The Smiths promise that calories don't count when their guests are on holiday.

Cross Roads Inn

6380 Silverado Trail
Napa, California 94558; (707) 944-0646

INNKEEPERS: *Sam and Nancy Scott.*
ACCOMMODATIONS: *Four rooms, all with private bath.*
RESERVATIONS: *Six to eight weeks recommended.*
MINIMUM STAY: *Two nights on weekends and holidays.*
DEPOSIT: *First night's lodging.*
CREDIT CARDS: *MC, Visa.*
RATES: *Very expensive.*
RESTRICTIONS: *No children under 16. No pets.*

One of the great joys of visiting Napa Valley is watching the popular hot air balloons ascend into the heavens. At the Cross Roads Inn you can not only see the balloons make their spectacular journey, you can hear them. Perched in the Mayacaymus mountain range, the inn has an eye-level view of the expanse of colorful sky, as well as a bird's-eye view of the entirety of Napa County. This fact alone would make it worth your while to vacation at this mountain-top bed and breakfast, but there's more to Cross Roads Inn than meets the ear, or the eye.

The inn's lounge area (in subtle tones of brown and beige) has four wingback chairs and an inviting sofa just made for sitting around the fireplace. And what a fireplace it is. Made from rocks found on the property, the circular fireplace, glassed in at the center, rises to the full 20-foot ceiling. A wall of windows allows for enjoyment of the view. After a day in the wine country, you may want to work out in the Scotts' game room: You can ride one of the stationary bikes or work up a sweat on the rowing machine. Or you can read that hot new novel in the library, just off the kitchen, snuggled in one of the red leather chairs.

High tea and sherry are served each afternoon in the dining area, a traditionally appointed room with mahogany Queen Anne table and chairs, a china cabinet and buffet, an Oriental rug, and a crystal chandelier.

The four guest rooms are named after Beatrix Potter characters: Mrs. Rabbit, Puddle Duck, Peter Rabbit, and Mrs. Ribby. Each has a charming music box appointed to carry out the fanciful theme. I particularly liked the fact that each bedroom is located in a separate wing of the house, providing the utmost in privacy and quiet, and each has its own private bathroom and deck. Jacuzzi tubs are also common to the rooms, as are antiques like the Victorian-style white iron beds, mahogany Italian secretary, and inlaid chess set that the Scotts have meticulously collected over the years.

Nancy pampers her guests with breakfast in bed, a mark of hospitality that has become all too rare. A culinary perfectionist, she makes her own preserves, grinds fresh Vienna coffee beans daily, and offers a selection of nearly two dozen different types of tea. Fresh fruit (melon, pineapple, kiwi, and bananas) is accompanied by homemade breads and muffins. Nancy's eggs Benedict are the best ever, and her French toast, made with melted Haagen-Daz rum raisin ice cream, is downright sinful.

Built on 23 acres of mountainous land covered with oak trees and wildflowers, this three-story country chalet is a nature lover's paradise. Much to the guests' amusement (and the Scotts' dismay) deer occasionally wander into the rose garden to sample Sam's horticultural efforts. Bird watchers may catch sight of a red-tail hawk or a scrub blue jay; quails are easy to spot—thousands live here. Coyotes and jackrabbits also claim this part of the Napa Valley as their home, and rumor has it cougars live here, too. I didn't see one, but maybe you will.

La Belle Epoque

1386 Calistoga Avenue
Napa, California 94558; (707) 257-2161

INNKEEPERS: *Merlin and Claudia Wedepohl.*
ACCOMMODATIONS: *Six rooms, all with private bath; queen- and king-size beds.*
RESERVATIONS: *Four to six weeks recommended.*
MINIMUM STAY: *Two nights on weekends.*
DEPOSIT: *First night's lodging.*
CREDIT CARDS: *AE, DC, MC, Visa.*
RATES: *Moderate.*
RESTRICTIONS: *Children discouraged. No pets.*

La Belle Epoque (The Beautiful Era) innkeepers Claudia and Merlin Wedepohl's turn-of-the-century Queen Anne Victorian, resplendent with its high-hipped roof, multi-gabled dormers, and semicircular windows, is the perfect setting to show off Claudia's obsession—collecting antiques. The first owner, Minnie Shwarz, (her father, Herman Shwarz, a local Napa merchant, had the house built for her) would undoubtedly approve of how the Wedepohls have restored the home and painted it in a gold-leaf highlighted, 10-color scheme.

You may want to linger a moment and study the stained-glass design on the double door entrance, but you are soon distracted by the imposing Bavarian carved oak entry piece with mirror, table, and umbrella stand. The adjoining living and dining rooms are painted a soft gray, an ideal background for the splash of colors emanating from stained-glass transoms and windows in both rooms. A square grand piano, made by Hallet Davis and Company in the 1850s, hails from Boston. But the most unusual item is a Victorian mahogany curio cabinet with brass rails that has detailed carvings of seemingly every conceivable style. The storage areas have glass doors and shelves where Claudia has displayed, among other things, an antique vase, a crystal paperweight, and a grouping of old-fashioned postcards.

Bedrooms (named Plumwood, Fleur de Lis, Petite Fleur, Wedgwood, Victorian Garden, and Rosebriar) are filled with more of Claudia's wonderful relics from the past. Her grandfather's walnut bedroom set is in Rosebriar. The vanity in Victorian Garden is an antique dining buffet. And other guest rooms have similar treasures: a tapestry tufted Victorian chair and a French oak armoire carved with a design of leaves, nuts, and berries. Many of the guest rooms have the home's original stained glass. In fact, one guest claims to have had a religious experience watching the sun rise through his bedroom window.

The cozy parlor on the upper floor, in restful colors of gray and mauve, is a perfect spot to curl up in your robe and read the latest bestseller. But don't get so engrossed that you fail to come down for breakfast. Claudia, a dedicated cook, makes all her own jams and breads (two of her specialities are orange date bread and banana chocolate chip). Typical of her breakfast's not-to-be-missed offerings are the cream cheese coffeecake with chocolate chips and baked sourdough French toast with walnuts and brown sugar (worth every extra calorie). An asparagus and egg casserole baked with English muffins and roasted chicken and artichokes topped with a poached egg are other dishes worth mentioning.

From 5:30 until 7:30 p.m., Claudia and Merlin offer a variety of Napa Valley wines free for the sampling in their newly remodeled home tasting room. Great believers in holding on to memories associated with the home from out of the past, they are carrying on a tradition left over from the Prohibition era, when Napa's Eagle Cycle Club reportedly held "high-spirited" meetings in their attic.

La Residence Country Inn

4066 St. Helena Highway North
Napa, California 94558; (707) 253-0337

INNKEEPERS: *Craig Claussen and David Jackson.*

ACCOMMODATIONS: *Nine rooms, seven with private bath; queen-size beds. 11-guest-room French barn.*

RESERVATIONS: *Two to four weeks recommended.*

MINIMUM STAY: *Two nights on weekends.*

DEPOSIT: *First night's lodging.*

CREDIT CARDS: *MC, Visa.*

RATES: *Moderate to expensive.*

RESTRICTIONS: *Children discouraged. No pets.*

Harry C. Parker was a New Orleans river pilot who caught gold fever and arrived in San Francisco in 1849. After a career as a merchant in Stockton and San Francisco, he moved to Napa County in 1865 and took up farming. In 1870 he built his dream house, a Gothic Revival with a distinctly Southern flavor. Today his home still projects this amalgamation of regional styles, and the clientele attracted by its modern-day owners reflects the adventurous spirit of its original creator and inhabitant.

There is elegance here, as befits a home built by a man from the land of magnolias. Rooms are filled with 19th-century antiques, chandeliers, and plantation shutters, and the majority of guest rooms also have fireplaces. The library is well stocked with mysteries, with a preponderance of the English drawing room genre. One room even boasts a small library containing the works of Robert Louis Stevenson, the 19th-century English literary light who lived nearby.

Bicycle enthusiasts will find a bike trail, beginning right across the road, that runs all the way to Yountville, then along the Silverado Trail to Calistoga. Runners are encouraged to enjoy the fresh Napa air and sunshine on the same trail. Balloonists frequently stay here because of the proximity of the ballooning facilities, and the proprietors are happy to recommend tours at the local wineries.

But if it's simply rest and relaxation you thirst after, you will not be disappointed. Each bedroom has its own sitting area, and the parklike setting gives the entire area a secluded and restful ambience. Its two acres boast magnolias (naturally); California live oaks; and orange, walnut, fig, apple, and pear trees. There's also a heated swimming pool, a Jacuzzi, a gazebo, and an abundance of patios and decks.

The morning breakfast consists of orange juice; eggs or French toast; fresh fruit in season; pastries, muffins, breads, or caramel nut rolls; and the house blend of coffee or tea. It is served from 8:30 to 10:00 a.m. in the light and airy dining room.

Magnolia Hotel

6529 Yount Street
Yountville, California 94599
(707) 944-2056 or (800) 788-0369

INNKEEPERS: *Bruce and Bonnie Locken; Craig Locken.*

ACCOMMODATIONS: *12 rooms, all with private bath; double, queen-, and king-size beds.*

RESERVATIONS: *One to two months for weekends.*

MINIMUM STAY: *Two nights on weekends.*

DEPOSIT: *In full.*

CREDIT CARDS: *Not accepted.*

RATES: *Moderate to expensive.*

RESTRICTIONS: *No pets.*

It was built as a hotel in 1873, of brick and native fieldstone—reputedly from the Silverado Trail. In the intervening years it has been a bordello, a hotel for laborers, a 4-H headquarters, and, during Prohibition, a speakeasy. It was rescued from oblivion and is now owned by Bonnie and Bruce Locken, who have turned the Magnolia Hotel into one of the most fashionable country inns in the vineyards of California.

Class tells right from the moment you enter and spy the antique rolltop desk in the lobby. There is a formal parlor; the second floor has a very large deck, perfect for sipping wine and looking out over the surrounding vineyards. (The wine cellar is stocked with over 200 California wines.)

Each room has its own handmade theme doll specially created by Bonnie. In the Magnolia Room I discovered a private balcony overlooking the heated pool. (I also found a welcome decanter of port.) There is a heated Jacuzzi with a redwood deck in the rear. My bedspread pattern was cleverly keyed to correspond to wall decor, and I liked the fireplace, the needlepoint chair design, and the pink lace curtains. Other rooms have iron and brass beds, handmade quilts, and lace coverlets; each room has a private bath and plush towels. And it is worth noting that the Magnolia is air-conditioned during the summer.

Bruce Locken has been in the hostelry trade for over 30 years serving at famous spots such as San Francisco's Clift Hotel. But he yearned for something different. "I wanted to get back to the small, intimate kind of operation—which is really how the business began," he says. He searched for eight years. In the late seventies he found the Magnolia already in operation. It was love at first sight.

Bonnie takes charge in the kitchen, as one would expect of a former dietician. For breakfast she serves up French toast baked in rounds; homemade hot port wine syrup; sausage or double-thick bacon; eggs baked or as an omelette; old-fashioned oatmeal with brown sugar, banana chips, and cream; and fresh orange juice. Breakfast is served family style in the dining room.

If you can break away from the Lockens' famous collection of cookbooks, nearby attractions include a petrified forest, over a hundred wineries, a geyser named Old Faithful after its prototype in Yellowstone, and a mud bath (yes, a mud bath). Bruce, Bonnie, or their son Craig, are happy to assist with information and reservations. This is an operation that marries the old with the very modern and makes it work.

Sybron House

7400 St. Helena Highway
Yountville, California
Mailing address: Napa, California 94558
(707) 944-2785

INNKEEPERS: *Cheryl and Sybil Maddox.*

ACCOMMODATIONS: *Four rooms, all with private bath; queen-size beds.*

RESERVATIONS: *Four to six weeks recommended.*

MINIMUM STAY: *Two nights on weekends, three over holiday periods.*

DEPOSIT: *Full amount.*

CREDIT CARDS: *AE, MC, Visa.*

RATES: *Moderate to expensive.*

RESTRICTIONS: *Not suitable for children. No pets.*

Sybron House bed and breakfast inn is one of those unexpected "finds" that takes your breath away. Perched on a hill a mile and a half north of Yountville overlooking the heart of the Napa Valley, the inn sits like a sentinel against green and golden vistas. Looking out at the rolling fields from the three-story neo-Victorian, you feel like you're smack-dab in a pastoral painting by one of the French Impressionists.

The surprising thing is what you may see from the Maddox' stately masterpiece. On summer mornings between 6:30 and 7:30 a.m., expect a panorama of colorful hot air balloons launching from the valley floor. "One day I counted 27," says Cheryl, whose in-laws, Sybil and Ronald, built the inn in 1978. "Another time, 18—one after the other—came sailing right over the house!"

But it's the inside of the house that's special. Care and thought has gone into each of the home's four rooms, three of which are on the second floor. The accommodations all have queen-size beds, high molded ceilings, and antiques.

Top of the line is the first-floor honeymoon suite, also known as the Cottage Room. It features a four-poster Battenburg lace canopy bed, down comforters and pillows, handmade quilt, porcelain pedestal sink, writing desk, two overstuffed chairs, and lace window curtains that blow in the breeze, which imbues the setting with the scent of honeysuckle from the two-acre garden. Even better: the room comes with its own fireplace and Jacuzzi tub.

Upstairs, expect more pleasures. Sybil's Room has a four-poster bed with antique lace coverlet, Jacuzzi tub, stained-glass window that creates the feeling of moonlight at night, vanity with two double sinks and polished brass fittings, and a sitting area with love seat overlooking the valley (perfect for balloon watching).

Next to Sybil's former quarters you'll find a hideaway surrounded by so much greenery it's called the Treetop Room. An antique enameled iron bed with brass trim, paintings by Swedish artist Carl Larson, antique chest, eight French artichoke plates, an antique white pedestal porcelain sink, glass chandelier, tub/shower, and a private wrought iron staircase to the yard are some of the treats.

Finally, down the hall, there's a room that's reminiscent of something you'd find in a New England inn. Highlights of the aptly named Rose Room include rose-covered wallpaper, portrait miniatures, and a lovely view of the property's beautiful rose garden, as well as nearby Mount St. Helena. It also has its own tub/shower and sink, plus tall shutter doors that cut the area off from the hall and give it the appearance of a small apartment. Also on the second floor: a huge living room with grand piano, library, writing desk, sunroom, balconies, and would you believe, a fireplace made of limestone strewn with fossils.

If you rise early, you can sample the living room's wet bar for coffee, tea, and chocolate. Otherwise, be prepared for sheer indulgence at 9:00 a.m. when Cheryl whips up a breakfast that always includes a seasonal fruit and something from the garden. The morning of our visit she served rhubarb sour cream coffeecake, made from rhubarb picked minutes before, nectarines and blueberries with an orange marmalade and Grand Marnier sauce, orange juice, Irish porridge, and, of course, freshly brewed coffee. Sybron, which is named after Sybil and her husband, Ron, puts out cheese, crackers, bread, and beverages in the afternoon. For dinner, all you have to do is walk across the street to Mustards Grill, which, like Berkeley's famous Chez Panisse, was one of the founders of California cuisine.

Bartels Ranch

1200 Conn Valley Road
St. Helena, California 94574; (707) 963-4001

INNKEEPER: *Jami Bartels.*

ACCOMMODATIONS: *Four rooms, all with private bath; queen- and king-size beds.*

RESERVATIONS: *Eight to ten weeks recommended.*

MINIMUM STAY: *Two nights on weekends, three over holiday periods.*

DEPOSIT: *Half of full amount.*

CREDIT CARDS: *AE, DC, MC, Visa.*

RATES: *Moderate to very expensive.*

RESTRICTIONS: *Children by special arrangement only. No pets.*

Not only is Bartels Ranch, also known as the Conn Valley Ranch, unusual because it was personally built by its female innkeeper, but it stands out from the crowd because of what it offers. Consisting of only four rooms, Jami Bartels' self-described "elegant country dream" combines bed and breakfast vacationing with the kind of options usually found only at luxury resorts.

From the very first things you see outside—a quarter-mile long driveway, 250-year-old oak grove, and towering, 24-foot-high overhang above the redwood and rock entrance—to the first sights inside—a sunken living room with baby grand piano, an 18-foot-long formal dining room—everything about the 7,000-square-foot inn exudes sumptuousness.

A special favorite among guests is the Napa Valley Game Room, just off the dining room. For starters, it has cathedral ceilings, walls of glass, and three separate views of the valley, oak grove, and the inn's very unusual swimming pool. Then there are all the "games": billiards, Ping-Pong, a television, VCR, an organ, jukebox, exercise bike, and, in the adjacent library, baskets containing "every game that's ever been invented": Scrabble, Trivial Pursuit, Monopoly. The game room also has a floor-to-roof brick fireplace.

The Brass Monarch Room features an Empire Period queen-size brass bed and English walnut dresser (both from the 1850s), a showcase of seashells, and bathroom with tub/shower and skylight. The dreamy-feeling Hillside Suite has appeared in *Brides* magazine and offers a California king, walk-in closet, Italian writing desk, white sofa, decorative fireplace, and large bathroom, including tub, shower, and skylight. Then there's the Blue Valley Room, with queen-size canopied bed with brass headboard, antique oak armoire, decorative fireplace, private deck, and Softub for two. And a real stunner, the Heart of the Valley Suite, boasts its own private wing and entrance to pool area and deck, not to mention a fireplace, 1870 English armoire, table, sofa, gigantic two-room bathroom (including a sunken, heart-shaped Jacuzzi tub for two and steam sauna/shower), and a custom-made adjustable bed that's actually bigger than a California king. All rooms have a television, VCR, and stereo.

Jami doesn't just build big. She also has big plans: tennis courts and a $1.5 million vineyard. For now, though, the inn's showstopper is its pool. "It's got a black bottom," Bartels explains, "because I wanted it to blend in with the surrounding environment and not look too garish." She also designed it to have an antique keyhole shape.

The service at the ranch is outstanding. Jami loves to help guests plan trip itineraries; upon arrival, each guest also gets a complimentary bottle of champagne. Moreover, the humongous breakfast (Iowa raisin bread pudding, almond croissants, quiche or frittata, and cinnamon rolls are typical offerings along with fresh fruit, English muffins, and a yogurt/granola/banana compote) is supplemented by a 24-hour cookie, brownie, and coffee service, plus assorted teas, and, in the evening, wine, fruit, and cheese.

What else can you do at Bartels? Let your imagination run wild. One idea is to use the inn's tandem or mountain bikes to pedal to nearby Hennessey Lake. Or think romantic: one groom had the petals of 150 roses delivered to his room, where a "bed of roses" was then prepared for his wedding night. Another couple, celebrating their 45th anniversary, locked themselves up in the library, champagne in tow, for an entire afternoon. No wonder they refer to that part of the house as the "game room."

Hilltop House

9550 St. Helena Road
P.O. Box 726
St. Helena, California 94574; (707) 944-0880

INNKEEPER: *Annette Gevarter.*

ACCOMMODATIONS: *Three rooms, all with private bath; queen-size beds.*

RESERVATIONS: *Six to eight weeks recommended.*

MINIMUM STAY: *Two nights on weekends.*

DEPOSIT: *Half of full amount.*

CREDIT CARDS: *AE, MC, Visa.*

RATES: *Moderate to expensive.*

RESTRICTIONS: *No pets.*

"Guests tell me the view from up here reminds them of the Black Forest in Germany or Tuscany in Italy," says innkeeper Annette Gevarter of the seemingly endless landscape of the Mayacaymus mountains seen from Hilltop's enormous redwood deck. Hilltop House was built on 135 acres of virgin wilderness that Annette's late husband had purchased in 1958 for investment purposes. A long winding road (watch out for deer!) leads you to the seemingly timeless ranch-style home nestled in the contours of the cliff.

The inn itself offers the same feeling of spaciousness as the surrounding countryside: Cathedral ceilings and antique white walls provide a lovely contrast for the dark mahogany furniture in the combination living and dining room. Classic antique pieces like the Duncan Phyfe dining set and curved (clawfoot) glass china closet are complemented by the comfortable Norwegian oak chair and sofa covered in a nubby off-white fabric.

Breakfast is served from 8:30 to 9:30 a.m. on the outside deck. During the rainy season guests convene in the dining room. Each couple has their own table that is set with crystal and fine china. Annette grinds her own special blend of coffee (one day it may be mocha fudge, and the next, hazelnut or vanilla cream) and squeezes fresh orange juice. She also bakes fresh bread and muffins daily. Her blueberry muffins with cream cheese filling elicit guest raves. Warm hard-boiled eggs are offered in Irish Belleek egg cups and fresh fruit with yogurt and granola fills a tall sundae glass.

Each of the three guest rooms (Blue, Vista, and Sunrise) has a breathtaking view that may tempt you out to the deck to soak in the hot tub under the stars. All rooms are furnished with antiques the Gevarters collected over the years. The Vista Room, my personal favorite, is a restful shade of peach. Not only does it have a queen-size brass bed, but an antique daybed covered in a green velvet spread. A cherrywood armoire with mirrored door serves as the closet, and there's also a turn-of-the-century mahogany desk and chair and a sewing table nightstand.

Hilltop House is a magical place, as any past guest will assure you, but Annette has a story to prove it. A few years back a couple planned their second wedding at the inn. Annette was amazed when the two youngest members of the bridal party came dressed in cream colored dresses with maroon jackets. She quickly disappeared into the house and then reappeared with an antique doll wearing an identical outfit. To the delight of everyone, the doll became part of the festivities. "I like to think that the doll was waiting patiently all those years for that wedding," says Annette. Given the love and care that she so obviously radiates towards her guests, I like to think so, too.

The Ink House

1575 St. Helena Highway
St. Helena, California 94574; (707) 963-3890

INNKEEPER: *Ernie Veniegas.*

ACCOMMODATIONS: *Four rooms, all with private bath; queen-size beds.*

RESERVATIONS: *Two to three weeks recommended.*

MINIMUM STAY: *Two nights on weekends May through October and mid-December through mid-January.*

DEPOSIT: *Full amount.*

CREDIT CARDS: *MC, Visa.*

RATES: *Moderate to expensive.*

RESTRICTIONS: *Children discouraged. No pets.*

Theron H. Ink, who built this huge and decidedly Italianate Victorian, operated not one but several vineyards, as well as ranches and a livery stable. He was a landholder in Marin, Sonoma, and Napa counties, serving as a Napa County supervisor for many years.

The Ink House is still very much a private residence. (Guests use the parlor, dining room, third-floor belvedere, and lounge on the wide, wraparound porch.) Owner Ernie Veniegas restored the home to its original colors: pale yellow with soft white, rose, and blue trim. It had been painted dark brown for the 1959 filming of *Wild in the Country* starring Elvis Presley. Double stairways made it possible for Ernie to divide the house in halves, one of which is for guests and the other for himself and friend Jim Annis.

There is a sign on the wrought iron gate outside. Once inside it took me some time to get used to the scale, for the first-floor ceilings are 12 feet high. In adjoining parlors I discovered a concert grand piano as well as an antique pump organ. In the bedrooms are more antiques as well as handmade quilts. My room was decorated in shades of rose and pink contrasted by deep walnut Eastlake Victorian and Georgian style furnishings. The bath housed an early 1900s elephant trunk toilet. The only truly modern touch here was the shower.

Clever Ernie keeps a book in which visitors are encouraged to write down their thoughts while staying at The Ink House. Several entries praise his expanded Continental breakfast that is served buffet-style: eye-appealing platters of decoratively carved fresh fruit; fresh-baked pastries like rhubarb muffins, Swiss cheese and Canadian bacon croissants, or bagels made from scratch; a quiche of some sort (perhaps jalapeño Jack cheese with a hash brown potato crust) or Ink House eggs; orange and cranberry juices, herbal teas, and a Kona-style blend of coffee.

Ernie says his most amusing moment as an innkeeper came when a former Mrs. America who was in the area for a fundraiser booked a stay at the inn. Late one afternoon she came down the stairs adorned in a stunning gold evening gown. One surprised guest who had just arrived and was checking in asked: "Do we all have to dress like that?"

For *your* amusement, The Ink House offers bicycles, a full-sized pool table, in-house Swedish or deep-tissue massage, and movies and televisions with VCRs.

The Ink House (which is listed on the National Register) is a place apart, a fascinating and pleasant curiosity. What makes it interesting is its bold combination of styles. Its monumental scale seems to promise anonymity, yet what it ultimately delivers is warm intimacy. The Ink House is finally a home, not a palace, but then Ernie Veniegas could have told you that.

Oliver House

2970 Silverado Trail North
St. Helena, California 94574; (707) 963-4089

INNKEEPERS: *Richard and Clara Oliver.*

ACCOMMODATIONS: *Four rooms, all with private bath; queen-size beds.*

RESERVATIONS: *Three weeks recommended.*

MINIMUM STAY: *Two nights on weekends.*

DEPOSIT: *First night's lodging.*

CREDIT CARDS: *MC, Visa.*

RATES: *Moderate to expensive.*

RESTRICTIONS: *No pets.*

Just north of the well-known restaurant Auberge du Soleil, on the Silverado Trail, is Oliver House, a three-story Swiss chalet-style home that represents a "dream come true" for its owners, Richard and Clara Oliver. "We met, fell in love, got married, and started talking about what we wanted to do," remembers Clara. "Richard, who had traveled to Switzerland, said he'd love to start a Swiss country inn right here in Napa Valley. He even scrawled out a sketch of his dream home on a little piece of paper. Then two years later, we found it."

Built in 1920, the house features four guest rooms, each with its own bath. Three of the rooms (on the second floor) have French doors that open onto balconies facing acres of vineyards. One also has an ornate 125-year-old brass bed from Scotland, English antiques, and a hardwood floor. Another is filled with English antiques, antique German chairs, and a queen-size oak bed. The largest of the three is replete with an early American oak dresser, a queen-size bed with a mirror that rises from its headboard, a double shower, and a huge walk-around deck. It is also the only guest room in the house with its own stone fireplace with a raised hearth, and numerous windows on three sides of the room all enjoy a wonderful view. The third-floor Alpine Room boasts knotty pine walls, an open-beam ceiling, German antiques, a queen-size bed, and a balcony as well.

Breakfast is a leisurely 9:00 to 10:00 a.m. experience with Richard and Clara's mouth-watering blueberry and bran muffins; rum raisin buns; custard apple rings; banana, pumpkin, and zucchini breads; homemade jams; strawberries from the garden; and blackberries "picked down the road." The Olivers' presentation is so elaborate that photographs of their meals have appeared in magazines both here and abroad. Expect these treats to be served in the sunroom or on the outside deck.

Elsewhere around the house, expect the unexpected. The chunks of glassy, jet black rock you'll find on the Olivers' property are known as obsidian. Prized for jewelry, obsidian is so easy to spot here that the Olivers' hill, Glass Mountain, was once quarried by the Mayacaymus Indians. If obsidian doesn't interest you, all you have to do to discover a genuine archaeological landmark is walk out to the front of the driveway. There next to the road is the original, 400-year-old oak tree the Indians used to sleep under between digs. It is designated California Archaeological Site Number 132.

To round out your stay, stroll to the tasting room of one of Napa Valley's wineries, just a quarter mile away, or drive or walk to any of the seven others that are within two and a half miles of Oliver House.

Shady Oaks Country Inn

399 Zinfandel Lane
St. Helena, California 94574; (707) 963-1190

INNKEEPERS: *John and Lisa Runnells.*

ACCOMMODATIONS: *Four rooms, all with private bath; queen- and king-size beds.*

RESERVATIONS: *Two to three weeks recommended.*

MINIMUM STAY: *Two nights on weekends.*

DEPOSIT: *First night's lodging.*

CREDIT CARDS: *None.*

RATES: *Moderate to expensive.*

RESTRICTIONS: *Children discouraged. No pets.*

For Lisa and John Runnells, finding and turning the property at Shady Oaks Country Inn into a bed and breakfast has been a dream come true. Refugees from what Lisa calls the "corporate hussle" of Southern California, the Runnells knew one thing for sure—they liked people. "We also wanted to raise our daughter in a smaller community," she recalls. In 1986, six months after deciding to move, they pulled up in a 24-foot-long U-Haul, and, without knowing a soul in town, just a week later opened up their first two rooms.

Eight years later, the dash of courage that fortified them for their big adventure is still paying off. Numerous guests have proclaimed in the register that John cooks up "the best breakfast in Napa Valley"; a trio of grandmothers took up a half page each extolling the relaxing charm of the inn's four rooms and the lengths to which Lisa will go to make sure guests have a good time. From supplying menus from every restaurant for miles around to mapping out an itinerary of activities, she makes you think you've brought your own private travel agent along with you. (It's little wonder that some visitors have returned the hospitality. When Shady Oaks' sign was stolen, one guest made a new one that was better than the first—gratis.)

What else draws celebrities like San Francisco Giants great Will Clark here? Besides its strategic location off Highway 29 in the middle of the Wine Country (putting you close to Beringer, Sterling, Phelps, Mondavi, Domaine

Chandon, and a whopping nine other wineries), Shady Oaks is also near Calistoga's mud baths, and, of course, the shops and restaurants of St. Helena. Speaking of wine, the inn itself was a winery from 1883 to 1887 and is still surrounded by vineyards. One building (with a guest room called Winery Retreat) remains, replete with stone walls from the original edifice.

Besides the Retreat, which is behind the main house, there are two splendid rooms (Rose and Country Blue) in the main house and one above Winery Retreat. The smallest is Country Blue, with a white iron antique queen-size bed, double windows, a private bath with shower, several blue and white prints, Priscilla curtains, original '20s wallpaper, and an antique oak armoire Lisa has had since she was 16. At the end of the hall is the Rose Room, with its bevy of beautiful antiques, including a 1926 dressing table, two beaded milkglass lamps with ruffled, dotted Swiss lamp shades, armoire, and 1800s love seat. It, too, has '20s wallpaper, a queen-size bed, and double windows, not to mention a rose bedspread (the walls are also rose), scarlet carpet, and, a special treat: a view of a rope swing.

Outside, past the patio and 100-year-old wisteria, and in the same building as Winery Retreat, is a stunning accommodation called Sunny Hideaway; it faces the vineyards and shady oaks that give the inn its name. This bedroom has a white iron and brass queen-size bed, antique dressing table, white rattan love seat, and its own entrance and balcony. Ready for a good long soak? The bathroom's antique white iron clawfoot tub is perfect for the job.

In addition to the good rooms and service, the food is remarkable. Three entrees (eggs Benedict, whole wheat walnut Belgian waffles, and French toast stuffed with cream cheese and cinnamon-dipped walnuts) are available for breakfast, along with the inn's own Shady Oaks blend of coffee, assorted teas, homemade croissants or other breads, orange and apple juice, and complimentary mimosas. For lunch, the Runnells will make you "a most perfect picnic" if you want. And every evening you can sample cheese and fruit on the patio or in the parlor, plus a beverage that's truly appropriate for a stay in the vineyards: John's homemade Chardonnay.

Zinfandel Inn

800 Zinfandel Lane
St. Helena, California 94574; (707) 963-3512

INNKEEPERS: *Diane and Jerry Payton.*

ACCOMMODATIONS: *Three rooms, all with private bath; double and king-size beds.*

RESERVATIONS: *Eight to ten weeks recommended.*

MINIMUM STAY: *Two nights on weekends and over holiday periods.*

DEPOSIT: *First night's lodging.*

CREDIT CARDS: *AE, MC, Visa.*

RATES: *Expensive.*

RESTRICTIONS: *No pets.*

An English castle in the Napa Valley? It's there. Well, at least a modern-day version. An arched doorway, made from Napa Valley rock and covered with wisteria, frames the two-story English Tudor-style home known as Zinfandel Inn with its wood-shingled peaked roof and turret with in-set pane glass windows crowned by a wrought iron weathervane. "We aren't the only ones who think our residence is a work of art," explains Diane Payton, speaking for herself and partner/husband Jerry. "We often find people sitting out near the fountain with a sketch pad in hand, and once an artist presented us with a watercolor of our place."

The stained-glass windows that grace the home's entryway depict voluptuous vinefuls of ripe zinfandel grapes. The family room also reflects colors characteristic of Napa Valley: dark rich greens and subtle tones of beige. Snuggle up on one of the comfortable forest green couches with sumptuous pillows to watch flames flicker rhythmically in the ageless stone fireplace.

The dining room has a gleaming oak hardwood floor with a hand inlaid pattern that is echoed in the ceiling. A beveled glass and brass chandelier hangs over the graceful pecan dining room table. Ask Diane or Jerry to play one of the antique records on the authentic Queen Anne-style wind-up Victrola. The walls display artwork from local artists who create designs for wine labels. Limited editions of

их works are available for sale at the inn. Breakfast, offered here from 8:30 to 9:30 a.m., includes a fresh fruit
platter; lox and bagels with cream cheese; quiche, eggs
Benedict, or Belgian waffles; and fresh pastries as well as
hot and cold beverages.

In keeping with Napa Valley surroundings, each of the
bedrooms is named to honor a wine varietal: Zinfandel Suite,
Chardonnay Suite, and Petite Sirah. And like the different
flavors of wine, each guest room has its own distinct style.
Petite Sirah, for example, is furnished in 1880s French Victorian. The walnut double featherbed came around the Horn
as a wedding gift for a couple from Amador County. Next to
the bed's seven-foot-tall headboard is a Victorian commode
stand with marble top. The red velvet settee and walnut
makeup table further bespeak this bygone era. The room
overlooks the inn's cobblestone driveway, neighboring vineyards, and the Mayacaymus mountains.

The Chardonnay Suite, situated on the first floor of the
house, has a magnificent brass bed set in a window bay.
Take the chill off the valley's cool evenings with the stone
fireplace blazing at the foot of your bed. A wingback chair
and overstuffed couch are covered in a rich navy blue floral print. The vaulted wood ceiling gives the room the feeling of a stay at a French country inn. French doors open
onto a deck and garden planted in roses, fuchsias, daisies,
ferns, and impatiens. Once outside, you may feel inclined
to stroll over to the gazebo or octagonal aviary to feed the
finches and cockateels.

The Zinfandel Suite also has a private balcony where
you can sip a glass of wine and, through the pepper trees,
catch a glimpse of Mount St. Helena. Or, if you prefer, you
can enjoy this same view from your Jacuzzi-equipped bathroom. The suite is a grand affair with a king-size oak bed,
two overstuffed chairs, a wood-burning stove, and stained-
glass windows.

A leisurely drive down Zinfandel Lane to Highway 29 or
the Silverado Trail will allow you to take in an endless expanse of vineyards, one of the most pleasurable sensory experiences offered by the Napa Valley, particularly in the
spring or fall. If this kind of scenery seems to be soothing,
then Zinfandel Inn is the bed and breakfast for you. Directly across from the Raymond winery, the inn itself is
surrounded by acres and acres of vineyards.

Foothill House

3037 Foothill Boulevard
Calistoga, California 94515; (707) 942-6933

INNKEEPERS: *Gus and Doris Beckert.*

ACCOMMODATIONS: *Four rooms, all with private bath; twin, queen-, and king-size beds.*

RESERVATIONS: *Two months recommended for weekends.*

MINIMUM STAY: *Two nights on weekends.*

DEPOSIT: *First night's lodging.*

CREDIT CARDS: *AE, MC, Visa.*

RATES: *Expensive to very expensive.*

RESTRICTIONS: *Not suitable for children. No pets.*

Foothill House has been given many distinctions by publications and guidebooks through the years, including being honored as one of the top 100 bed and breakfast inns in the United States by *Frommer's*.

Nestled among the western foothills just north of Calistoga, the inn boasts a natural country setting distinguished by lovely old trees and scenic pastoral views. Gus and Doris Beckert spent 10 years looking for such a property, then in 1991 their dream of owning an inn finally came true.

Foothill House is comprised of four luxurious suites, each with private entrance and bath, a fireplace, and a small refrigerator. Interiors are graced by fine antiques and four-poster beds with handsome patchwork quilts. Guests are pampered with a well-chosen, complimentary bottle of wine, a delicious gourmet breakfast (Doris studied at the California Culinary Academy), a late afternoon food and wine pairing, and a miniature cookie jar filled with Sweet Dreams (homemade chocolate chip cookies) by the bedside at turn-down time.

When making your reservation, ask for the inn's Evergreen Suite—canopied bed, whirlpool Jacuzzi tub, and large sun deck with umbrella table and lounge chairs—or totally private Quail's Roost with its king-size bed and double-faced fireplace that looks to both the sitting area and the private bath.

Foothill House is in close proximity to all the Napa Valley attractions. Calistoga itself is justly known for its health spas, mud baths, and mineral pools. Of the over 100 wineries in the valley to try, Cuvaison, Sterling, Chateau Montelena, and Stonegate are all nearby.

ॐ

Quail Mountain Bed & Breakfast

4455 North St. Helena Highway
Calistoga, California 94515; (707) 942-0316

INNKEEPERS: *Don and Alma Swiers.*

ACCOMMODATIONS: *Three rooms, all with private bath; king-size beds.*

RESERVATIONS: *Two to three months recommended.*

MINIMUM STAY: *Two nights on weekends.*

DEPOSIT: *First night's lodging.*

CREDIT CARDS: *MC, Visa.*

RATES: *Moderate.*

RESTRICTIONS: *No children. No pets.*

Don and Alma Swiers originally bought their forested mountain range property in an attempt to run away from the corporate world. Drive up their private road, shaded with walnut, almond, and pear trees, bordering Quail Mountain vineyard, and you find yourself in a wooded paradise far removed from Napa County's tourist whirl. A green and gold wrought iron fence beckons you even further into the twists and turns of Quail Mountain Lane, home to deer, raccoons, squirrels, numerous species of birds, and, of course, the beloved quail for which the inn was named.

The Swiers' cedar home was designed by their son Don and St. Helena's Wayne Leong in the early eighties. Lavish use of floor-to-ceiling glass walls, skylights, and natural wood makes you think that you're staying in the world's most luxurious tree house. A solarium, with an 18-foot glass ceiling and two glass walls, reveals a gardenlike atmosphere. White wicker furniture (with cushions covered in imported Egyptian cotton of a pale blue floral design) adds to the outdoor illusion. You can idle away the hours here with any one of the many games, books, or puzzles that fill a wicker bookcase.

Each of the bedrooms (Forest, Quail, and Fern) has a private deck, a king-size bed covered with a traditional American quilt, and kelly green carpeting that accents the lush green landscape. The most requested of the three rooms is Fern, which is actually a small suite. One wall is painted with a 12-foot-high mural designed to resemble the outdoor forest; the sitting room has an antique daybed covered in pastel blue, and the room's oak floor is covered with an Indian rug. An antique oak table holds a unique alabaster lamp.

Breakfast is served (either in the dining room or the solarium, on the front deck, or near the swimming pool) at 9:00 a.m. Coffee, juice, and the morning newspaper are available around 8:00. The Swiers' half-acre orchard figures prominently in their menu. Japanese persimmons are topped with rum, brown sugar, and sour cream; baked apples that have been cooked overnight in a crockpot filled with orange juice and maple syrup are stuffed with chopped dates and walnuts and topped with low-fat yogurt or whipped cream. One "not to miss" selection is Don's apple pancakes, heaped with slices of homegrown apples, chopped walnuts, and whipped cream and served with Yountville sausages as a side dish. Finally, you'll be wanting to indulge yourself in a second cup of Quail Mountain's own special blend of gourmet coffee.

With its tranquil forest setting and spacious airy rooms, romance seems to flourish at Napa Valley's Quail Mountain Inn. Alma tells of a couple from Portland, Oregon, who stopped over on their way to Reno to be married. "Once they saw what we had to offer, they were hooked. Don and I, with the help of some of our other guests, quickly made all of the arrangements, and they were married right here at Quail Mountain that very afternoon."

Scott Courtyard

1443 Second Street
Calistoga, California 94515; (707) 942-0948

INNKEEPERS: *Joe and Lauren Scott.*

ACCOMMODATIONS: *Six rooms, all with private bath; queen-size beds.*

RESERVATIONS: *Three to four weeks recommended.*

MINIMUM STAY: *Two nights on weekends.*

DEPOSIT: *First night's lodging.*

CREDIT CARDS: *MC, Visa.*

RATES: *Moderate.*

RESTRICTIONS: *Children in bungalows only. No pets.*

Picture a bed and breakfast that blends in perfectly with the surrounding neighborhood and you have an idea of what Lauren and Joe Scott have been "creating," as they like to say, on the edge of Calistoga's historic Main Street district. Their peachy-hued Scott Courtyard, opened in 1990, sprawls over several properties with six two-room suites, a delightful kidney-shaped pool, hot tub, garden area, dozens of fruit trees, and the kind of Raymond Chandleresque, Art Deco, tropical feel to it that makes you think (if you've ever seen the movie *Chinatown*) that you've somehow landed in 1930s Los Angeles.

Further enhancing this motif is the fact that three of the guest rooms are California bungalows, complete with living rooms and kitchens. Also, there's something about the Scotts themselves that adds to the experience. Neophytes in the business from Seattle, Philadelphia, and, later, San Francisco, they never intended to open an inn. But after inheriting a building and buying three adjacent parcels for rentals, one thing led to another and they sort of fell into it.

Because they do not feel bound by the normal "rules" of innkeeping, the Scotts come up with their share of surprises. For example, because the kitchen opens up into the dining room, Lauren encourages guests to chat with her while she cooks breakfast. Unlike other inns, this one does not have a single 19th-century artifact. And where else have you heard of a bed and breakfast that, by this writing, is expected to have an artist's studio where visitors can dabble in painting, sculpting, or making ceramics?

Another "extra": upstairs from the office, where you check in, is an exercise room for light workouts that includes an exercycle, television and instructional videos.

The principal common area, called the social room, just off the pool in the main building (which was built in the '20s), features a Mexican tile floor, 28-foot-high ceiling, floor-to-ceiling brick wood-burning fireplace, Oriental rug, 1930s rattan furniture, and a library of all sorts of interesting coffee table books and volumes for reading. But it also has what is probably the only bed and breakfast "lending library" of books on tape. It's true! "When guests check out they like to take a tape with them to play on the drive home," says Lauren. Afterwards, the readers—in this case, listeners—return them by mail.

All of the guest rooms have queen-size beds, private entrances and baths, air conditioning, and overhead fans. Upstairs from the social area, the Palisades Suite has a separate sitting room with couch, desk, and closets, large tile shower, deck overlooking the pool, and view of the valley and nearby Palisades foothills. At the front of the main house there are two suites: Rose (with entry and living rooms, hardwood floor, burgundy Oriental rug, several hutches, vintage rattan furniture, porch, tub/shower combo, and '20s-style wallpaper inserts known as anaglyphs) and Burgundy (French doors, desk, sitting room, antique clawfoot tub, burgundy tones, garden view). The bungalows (Tropical, Philadelphia, and Hollywood) are spread out off the pool. All have hardwood floors, living rooms, porches, and kitchens with original '20s tile. Lauren's favorite, Hollywood, with a black leather couch, chrome chair, and leopard lamp from the '50s, is the only room with 1950s-'60s ambience.

Breakfast, at 9:00 a.m. in the bistro-style dining room, is a few steps up from the social room, overlooking the pool and a large, showy outdoor aviary of canaries and cutthroat, society, and zebra finches. Expect fresh orange juice, three kinds of cereal, pineapple, melon, or some other fresh fruit, fresh croissants, cinnamon rolls, muffins, or banana bread, coffee, tea, hot chocolate, and a main dish, such as blueberry pancakes, Thai chicken sausage with soft-boiled eggs, or shrimp Dijon quiche. Complimentary wine, cheese, crackers, and fruit are served in the social room after 6:00 p.m.

Silver Rose Inn

351 Rosedale Road
Calistoga, California 94515
(707) 942-9581 or (800) 995-9381

INNKEEPERS: *J-Paul and Sally Dumont.*

ACCOMMODATIONS: *Nine rooms, all with private bath; queen- and king-size beds.*

RESERVATIONS: *Eight weeks recommended for weekends and holidays.*

MINIMUM STAY: *Two nights on weekends.*

DEPOSIT: *First night's lodging.*

CREDIT CARDS: *AE, DC, MC, Visa.*

RATES: *Moderate to expensive.*

RESTRICTIONS: *No children. No pets.*

When you check in at the Silver Rose you are presented with a bottle of J-Paul Dumont's private label cabernet or Silver Rose Cellars' own chardonnay, your choice. But the most difficult decision you might have to make during your stay is: Where to drink it? Perhaps you'll sip the heady wine in the gathering room, with its two-story redwood beamed ceiling filled with plants, as you sink down into one of the large leather couches and gaze at the blazing fire set in the lava stone fireplace. On the other hand, you may want to lounge under the 300-year-old oak tree that shades the deck as you imbibe poolside. You might propose a toast to each other on the balcony overlooking the rose garden just outside your bedroom. It finally doesn't matter where you decide to partake, because Sally and J-Paul will be exhibiting their special talent for making you feel pampered throughout your entire stay at their Silver Rose Inn.

Appreciating fine wines has been J-Paul's passion for over 30 years. A self-styled expert, he stages various wine-related events at his inn: a vertical level tasting, or a blind tasting. Or, he may make his famous wine challenge: During the day couples staying with the Dumonts comb the Napa Valley for a choice bottle of wine and then J-Paul tries to top their selection with a bottle of the same vintage from his wine cellar. The wine challenge is done in good cheer and makes for a fun-filled evening. J-Paul will also arrange a group dinner party at either the Cuvaison or Clos Pegase winery.

Sally will bring her guests breakfast in bed, at the gazebo, near the swimming pool, or anywhere they feel most comfortable. She learned to cook from her Scottish grandmother, a professional baker, and currently makes all of her morning breads from scratch. Hawaiian bread with pineapple, coconut, and carrots is just one variety in her repertoire. A fresh fruit platter, juice, and the house blend coffee complete this simple but delicious meal.

Each of the nine guest rooms at the Silver Rose has a spectacular view of the surrounding hills and vineyards, but the Oriental Suite is the most favored. Gleaming hardwood floors are complemented by Oriental rugs; a beamed ceiling adds drama to the room painted in accent tones of black and mauve. Rattan furniture and shoji screens with matching light fixtures provide an Asian accent. There's also a Japanese lacquered-wood headboard framing a queen-size bed and a balcony decorated with bonsai plants, an ideal spot for watching the sunrise over the Palisade mountains to the east of Napa Valley.

What makes the Silver Rose Inn so special? It's not particularly the resortlike atmosphere with gym (universal equipment and free weights), nor the Jacuzzi, nor the fragrant rose garden. What makes the Silver Rose special is reflected in a photograph printed in the inn's brochure. It shows Sally Dumont standing on the curved walkway in front of the wood-framed home, hands in her apron pockets. Her smile is like a beacon that signals a message of warmth and welcome: We're glad you're here, we've been looking forward to seeing you, won't you come on inside?

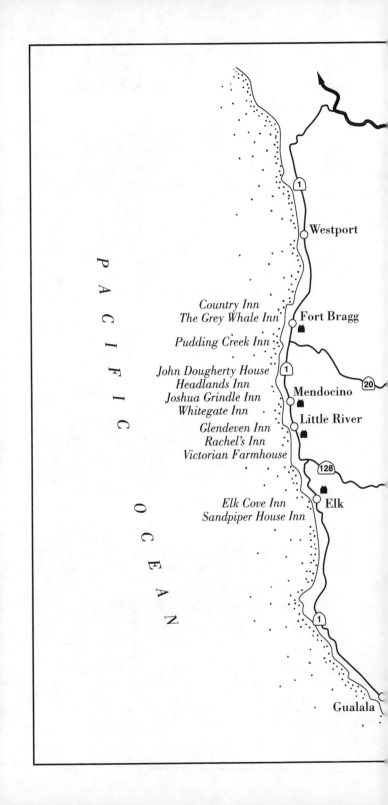

The
Mendocino
Coast

101

Willits

101

20

Ukiah

128

101

Milano Hotel
St. Orres
ale Watch Inn

Cloverdale

N

Old Milano Hotel

38300 Highway One
Gualala, California 95445; (707) 884-3256

INNKEEPER: *Leslie Linscheid.*

ACCOMMODATIONS: *Nine rooms, three with private bath; double and queen-size beds.*

RESERVATIONS: *Four weeks recommended.*

MINIMUM STAY: *Two nights on weekends, three over holiday periods.*

DEPOSIT: *First night's lodging.*

CREDIT CARDS: *MC, Visa.*

RATES: *Moderate to expensive.*

RESTRICTIONS: *No children. No pets.*

In 1905 Bert Luccinetti built a restaurant and pub on a cliff overhanging Castle Rock, alongside what was then a busy railroad and stage road catering mainly to lumbermen. New owners turned it into a resort for fishermen in the 1920s; the 1950s saw it modernized, its Victorian heritage obscured by various layers of ticky-tacky "improvements." Today it is one of the most highly regarded inns on the northern California coast, thanks to the efforts of Leslie Linscheid, a former Macy's employee who put her business and buying skills to work in this impressive blend of old and new (now recorded in the National Registry of Historic Places).

The inn has seven rooms and two cottages. One of the cottages, actually a caboose where the old railroad once ran, has walls of sandblasted wood, a galley, and a red pot-bellied stove. Two brakemen's seats for taking in the sunsets can be reached by a ladder.

Beds, bureaus, tables, lamp shades, quilts, and bric-a-brac have been chosen with loving care. Morris wallpapers, original paintings, redwood wainscoting in the halls, and old-fashioned car-sided ceilings are also featured. A Victorian-era mahogany bed highlights the Master Suite where the Luccinetti family lived. You will also see Eastlake chairs, Tiffany lamps, and a sofa that was the first Riviera bed, made in 1906.

The gracious Wine Parlor is made cheerful by a great stone fireplace. Adjacent are the quieter and more reflective comforts of the Music Room, where aficionados of art books will find a fine collection. One of the more comfortable concessions to modern sensibilities is a hot tub facing the ocean. (It is encircled by an old-fashioned knob-topped fence for privacy.) The staff of the Old Milano will also arrange for you to have a massage by a certified massage practitioner.

Room Four, with its breathtaking ocean view, was my favorite. The wallpaper design is in shades of blue, lilac, pink, and green. A comfortable overstuffed rocker faces the tumultuous Pacific, and an oval wood-framed mirror and fresh flowers in a pitcher complete the feeling of restful privacy.

The complimentary breakfast here is a full American meal: scrambled eggs, quiche, or an omelette with potatoes and fresh fruit; turnovers, poppyseed lemon muffins, or croissants with honey; creamy yogurt; a private blend of coffee; and an assortment of black and herbal teas. Guests may take breakfast in the parlor, on the loggia, or in their room.

The Old Milano's restaurant is in full swing. Wednesday through Sunday night dinner entrees include fresh filet of salmon poached in a cilantro-hollandaise sauce, filet mignon, leg of lamb with spinach and goat cheese filling, and roast duck à l'orange. Best reserve early: seating capacity is only 22.

I left the Old Milano revitalized. Its setting is sensational, but the main ingredients of its success are the good taste of its owner and the delicious taste of its food. There is something dreamlike in its unique compound of the Victorian and the modern. The Old Milano is like an image from art made real, and its restfulness is to a large extent due to its ability to make us feel that we are a part of another, more ordered world.

St. Orres

36601 Highway One South
P.O. Box 523
Gualala, California 95445; (707) 884-3303

INNKEEPERS: *Ted and Eric Black;*
Rosemary Campiformio.

ACCOMMODATIONS: *Eight rooms and 11 cottages,
11 rooms with private bath; double, queen-, and king-
size beds.*

RESERVATIONS: *Three months for weekends.*

MINIMUM STAY: *Two nights on weekends.*

DEPOSIT: *Full amount.*

CREDIT CARDS: *MC, Visa.*

RATES: *Inexpensive to expensive.*

RESTRICTIONS: *Children in cottages only. No pets.*

The windswept isolation and wild charm of this part of the
Mendocino coast are staggering. The environs (not to mention the elements) seem to demand one of two architectural
styles: rigorous simplicity or the same spendthrift abandon
that nature has lavished on her handiwork in the area. Master craftsman Eric Black opted for the latter. The result is a
fantasy, an explosion of fine art, an architectural wonder.

It was just a few years ago that he and another carpenter
bought the remains of the old Seaside Hotel, built in the
1920s, and went to work on it. Oregon red cedar was used
to transform the exterior, topped off by twin domed towers,
deliberately reminiscent of the homeland of the Russian
trappers who settled the area. Is it any wonder that pass-
ersby stop to marvel at this audacious Russophilic beauty
in the wilderness?

The fairy-tale extravagance continues inside. The entrance hall has some very fine Art Nouveau and Edwardian
pieces and highly detailed stained-glass windows. The sitting room is dominated by a castle-size fireplace that looks
like it belongs in Charles Laughton's Henry VIII banquet
scene. There are also six oak doors with stained-glass windows in each. The dining room rises a dizzying three stories
to an octagonal dome above, with row on row of windows
culminating in a single rank of stained-glass panes just
below its copper-domed crown.

The two front rooms have direct ocean views and French doors that open onto a balcony. Except for the cottages, most rooms share baths down the hall—a His, a Hers, and a spacious Ours with tiled tub enclosures and dual shower heads.

A popular accommodation is the Tree House. This experiment in luxury contains a king-size bed, a tile bath with a deep sunken tub, and its own wet bar. As if that weren't enough, there is a Franklin stove with a hand-painted tile hearth; the living room has an ocean view, with French doors leading onto a sun deck.

Other than Rosemary Campiformio's long-standing enjoyment in serving people, none of the three friends (Ted Black is Eric's uncle) had any inn or restaurant experience when they began. This has not handicapped them, however. Their restaurant has achieved a considerable reputation. Fixed-price, three-course dinner entrees offered by the inn range from venison to rack of lamb to quail. The complimentary breakfast is served from 9:00 to 10:00 a.m. and consists of homemade pastries, a hot entrée that changes daily, fresh fruit in season, homemade granola, and fresh-squeezed orange juice. Breakfast is delivered in a basket to the cottage rooms and served in the inn's dining room to the remainder of the guests.

For me the words that best describe St. Orres are magic and wonderful. And perhaps the best part of it is the genuinely reasonable price for rooms located inside the hotel.

Whale Watch Inn

35100 Highway One
Gualala, California 95445
(707) 884-3667 or (800) WHALE-4-2

INNKEEPERS: *Jim and Kazuko Popplewell.*
ACCOMMODATIONS: *18 rooms, all with private bath; queen-size beds.*
RESERVATIONS: *Three to four weeks recommended.*
MINIMUM STAY: *Two nights on weekends.*
DEPOSIT: *First night's lodging.*
CREDIT CARDS: *AE, MC, Visa.*
RATES: *Expensive to very expensive.*
RESTRICTIONS: *No pets.*

Whale Watch Inn, which sits perched on a cliff overlooking Anchor Bay and the southern Mendocino coastline, actually consists of five separate buildings. Hub of the operation is a central hexagonal dwelling with floor-to-ceiling windows on three sides, a central fireplace, and a magnificent view of the ever-changing Pacific Ocean.

The buildings' contemporary architecture has incorporated spacious decks, skylights, and natural-wood interiors. All 18 rooms have ocean views and fireplaces, many have private spas. Five include fully equipped kitchens, and all are supplied with magazines, books, candles, wine glasses, mints, and beach towels.

The Golden Voyage Suite's contemporary furnishings and freestanding Swedish fireplace are framed by the room's many angles and high, beamed ceiling. The Country French Suite's spiral staircase leads to a sitting room where furnishings follow a French country motif. The queen-size bed features a lovely walnut and cane headboard with a matching chest; a chaise longue, upholstered in a rose and teal print, picks up the teal in the carpet and the colorful bedspread. The room also has a fireplace, a wet bar, and a window seat. There's a two-person whirlpool spa that allows you to soak in the tub and look out to sea at the same time, and the deck features yet another fantastic view of the ocean, framed by cypress trees.

Guests of the inn receive breakfast in a decorative basket at the requested hour anytime between 8:00 and 9:30

a.m. A honey-yogurt fresh fruit parfait is accompanied by the main dish of the day (mushroom phyllo turnovers, eggs Florentine, or zucchini casserole); hot breads (muffins, croissants, or scones); fresh orange or apple juice; and coffee, tea, hot chocolate, or milk.

Whale Watch is located at the northern edge of Anchor Bay, a protected inlet with white sandy beaches and calm waters for diving or tidepooling. The site's banana belt weather affords an escape from the usual coastal fog. Sea lions and pelicans, as well as whales, can be seen from both beach and cliffside.

Elk Cove Inn

6300 South Highway One
Elk, California 95432; (707) 877-3321

INNKEEPER: *Hildrun-Uta Triebess.*

ACCOMMODATIONS: *Seven rooms, six with private bath; double and queen-size beds.*

RESERVATIONS: *Two weeks recommended for weekends.*

MINIMUM STAY: *Two nights on weekends.*

DEPOSIT: *First night's lodging.*

CREDIT CARDS: *Not accepted.*

RATES: *Moderate.*

RESTRICTIONS: *No children under 12. No pets.*

This sweet Victorian was built in the early 1890s by the L. E. White Lumber Company. (L. E. built it for his son, who was the superintendent of his mill.) From 1890 to the crash in 1929, the nearby hamlet of Elk was a booming lumber port. Now it is the quintessential sleepy coast village. And this small but charming bed and breakfast inn is the archetypical Mendocino bed and breakfast—provided you come here to get away from everything. Because there is nothing—literally nothing—to do here but walk, read, eat, and sleep. If it is a period of total rest you are looking for, this is definitely the place for you.

Hildrun was born in Germany but was brought to this country early in life; she is a skilled cook, specializing in European cookery. Friendly, folksy, and very amusing, Hildrun has a talent for entertaining that is a central attraction of her operation.

"What I strive for is giving people things they don't do for themselves at home," Hildrun says, "yet in a way that makes them feel like they are at home." Which is, by the way, perhaps the best formula for a successful bed and breakfast.

There are several choices of accommodation at Elk Cove Inn: Two cabins (behind the main house where Hildrun lives) command a spectacular yet ever-changing ocean view; an adjacent two-guest-room addition with bay windows and high beamed ceilings; and, of course, the home's three second-story bedrooms. A path leads from the house to an expansive, secluded beach where egrets, kingfishers, and pelicans provide quite a show.

Breakfast here is a delight. Hildrun is well known for her German egg cakes *(eierkuchen)* with hot plum-raspberry sauce and whipped cream. A chili-cheese quiche or an orange soufflé with sauteed apples and fresh date muffins makes for yet another morning meal. Expect to enjoy these—or any number of other excellent dishes—in the dining room along with coffee and juice (usually orange).

Sandpiper House Inn

5520 South Highway One
P.O. Box 49
Elk, California 95432; (707) 877-3587

INNKEEPERS: *Richard and Claire Melrose.*

ACCOMMODATIONS: *Four rooms, all with private bath; queen-size beds.*

RESERVATIONS: *Four weeks recommended.*

MINIMUM STAY: *Two nights on weekends; three over holiday periods.*

DEPOSIT: *First night's lodging or half total amount.*

CREDIT CARDS: *MC, Visa.*

RATES: *Moderate to expensive.*

RESTRICTIONS: *No children under 12. No pets.*

The romance of flames flickering in a fireplace, the sweet fragrance of garden flowers interlaced with fresh sea air, the timeless beauty of the ever-changing Pacific ocean—Sandpiper House promises all of this, and much, much more.

Built in 1916 by the Goodyear Redwood Lumber Company, this modest gray-shingled home stands as a tribute to the craftsmanship of its era. Hand-fitted redwood paneling is found on walls and ceilings in both living and dining rooms. All rooms are furnished with antiques, but common rooms also have traditional pieces and Oriental rugs, vases, and artifacts. Comfortable chairs, queen-size beds with down comforters, feather pillows, fine linens, and fresh flowers are features that the four guest rooms (Weston, Headlands, Clifton, and Woodland Rose) share.

Richard and Claire Melrose purchased the property in 1987 and went to work on a series of renovation and improvement projects slated to last nearly five years. The first thing they did was lift the house to replace a portion of the foundation and then they built quarters for their personal use. But the work didn't stop there. The raised paneling and coffered ceilings were hand stripped and polished, bay windows were constructed, bathrooms and fireplaces added, and double walls were built for soundproofing. The fruits of their extensive labors are now being enjoyed by people who occupy the household and then spread the word friend to friend. As one past guest noted in a letter he wrote to the travel editor of the *San Francisco Chronicle*: "Claire and Richard Melrose love what they have created, and their own warmth and happiness radiates out into the house and into the hearts of their valued guests."

"We're secure and happy here," Claire wrote me after I had made my first trip to visit the inn. "We love our life in Elk and try to create a peace that fills the house and makes our guests feel like friends. We keep the log fire burning, bake cookies for afternoon tea, put out spiced pecans with the evening sherry, prepare breakfast, and care for each guest personally."

The Melroses' breakfasts are creative two-course menus consisting of an "appetizer" (usually seasonal fresh fruits) followed by an entrée (ongoing favorites are Finnish pancakes topped with sauteed apples and cider sauce, orange French toast served with bananas and pure maple syrup, and lemon soufflé pancakes strewn with raspberry sauce).

Sandpiper's serene location, on the edge of rugged bluffs above Greenwood cove, offers the perfect site for whale watching. (Gray whales make their twice yearly treks between Alaska and Mexico during the months of January, February, and March.) A series of walkways and steps take you to the property's deck which offers a magnificent view of offshore rock formations with wave-hewn tunnels. The path continues to a private beach in the cove just below.

Rachel's Inn

8200 North Highway One
Little River, California; (707) 937-0088
Mailing Address: P.O. Box 134
Mendocino, California 95460

INNKEEPER: *Rachel Binah.*

ACCOMMODATIONS: *Nine rooms, all with private bath; twin and queen-size beds.*

RESERVATIONS: *Three to four weeks recommended.*

MINIMUM STAY: *Two nights on weekends; three over holiday periods.*

DEPOSIT: *First night's lodging.*

CREDIT CARDS: *Not accepted.*

RATES: *Moderate to expensive.*

RESTRICTIONS: *No pets.*

A woman of many talents, Rachel Binah is credited with opening the second bed and breakfast inn ever to hit the North Coast over 20 years ago. (The first was Hildrun-Uta Triebess's Elk Cove Inn; Rachel and her then husband, Jim, had DeHaven Valley Farm up in Westport.) She returned to innkeeping with a property all her own that she simply calls Rachel's. The inn has nine rooms, all exquisitely decorated, and all with private bath and queen-size beds. (Two rooms also have a twin, to accommodate a third person.) Large, fresh flower arrangements fill each room.

Reflecting on her life as an innkeeper, both now and then, Rachel feels that for her the main attraction of DeHaven was "having an extended family—creating a nucleus of people that you could get close to and feel warm about." Her current motivation for running an inn, however, is to "use it as a vehicle to relate to people about issues and ideas."

Rachel is highly visible and involved in the Mendocino community in a variety of ways. She serves as chairperson of the Environmental Caucus for the state's Democratic Party and is on the Central Committee for Democrats in Mendocino County. She's also directly involved in the offshore oil development issues affecting the Northern California coast.

Rachel studied fine arts and did her graduate work in textile construction in Wales. The etchings and tapestries you see throughout the parlors and guest rooms of the house are her very own. In the Garden Room, for example, there's a multicolored wall tapestry that sets off a platform bed. The room also has a fireplace. The inn's Rose Room abounds with frills. It has a hooked tapestry and a white eyelet comforter with matching pillow shams against a background of rose-colored carpeting. The Grey Room has an ocean view, and the Blue Room steps down to a private bath with old-fashioned clawfoot tub. A traditional California barn with a contemporary feel makes available four more fireplace rooms: One has a wheelchair access ramp, and two are suites with balconies and private sitting rooms.

Rachel's breakfasts show off her catering skills. I made my way downstairs just as the cranberry pancakes with maple syrup were being served. An assorted fruit compote with vanilla yogurt, a pot of steaming hot coffee, and bacon and eggs also appeared. The second morning's buffet brought forth an artichoke heart omelette with fried potatoes, home-baked corn muffins, a decadent cinnamon buttermilk streusel coffeecake, and both tomato and orange juice. Rachel caters lunches and dinners for groups who book the entire inn. It's a pity I was there on my own.

Glendeven Inn

8221 North Highway One
Little River, California 95456
(707) 937-0083 or (800) 822-4536

INNKEEPERS: *Jan and Janet deVries.*

ACCOMMODATIONS: *10 rooms, all with private bath; queen-size beds.*

RESERVATIONS: *One month for weekends.*

MINIMUM STAY: *Two nights on weekends; three to four nights over holiday periods.*

DEPOSIT: *Half of full amount.*

CREDIT CARDS: *MC, Visa.*

RATES: *Moderate to expensive.*

RESTRICTIONS: *Children: family suite available. No pets.*

Glendeven was the country home of Isaiah Stevens, who moved here with a group of settlers from Maine. He raised and bred fine horses and cattle on his hundred-acre farm, and in 1867 built a farmhouse for his bride, Rebecca Coombs. It was and is a distinctly New England-style house, typical of the architecture in the Mendocino area; many of the early settlers were from that region.

Jan deVries first saw the home on a visit to the coast in 1962. He returned later as a teacher, married Janet Bell, and the couple then left for Portland. But the rugged North Coast (and perhaps the romance associated with their courtship) continued to exert its pull. When the deVries heard of the impending sale of the house in 1977, they returned to buy it and open it as an inn.

This is the perfect place to get over a bad case of office politics or the blahs associated with the morning headlines. The dominant note here is upbeat, and most certainly up-scale. Antique furnishings sit side by side with contemporary ceramics and works of art; colorful, cheery, abstract paintings hang on the walls. The effect is quite consciously calculated to elevate the mood. And it succeeds admirably.

My favorite rooms are the Garret, a surprisingly large room nestled under the eaves, with a Louis XV queen bed, rocking chair, and a writing desk; and the Eastlin Suite, with its own sitting room, fireplace, and French rosewood bed. Guests in both rooms are invited to breakfast on a tray or to come out and mingle with the other guests. The deVries say that breakfast is "somewhere in between" full and Continental: bread or muffins, coffeecake, hard-cooked eggs, juice, and a variety of fresh fruits including, if you're lucky, their tasty baked apples.

Exploring the sitting room, I discovered a baby grand piano and a row of large-paned windows looking out on tended gardens with an English flavor befitting the inn's name. The light and airy feeling was enhanced by the large original barn in back (which, now remodeled, houses an art gallery and a two-bedroom suite) and the lovely old cypress trees that flank and surround both structures.

Not far from Glendeven, a sense of the forest begins. But it is not Robert Frost's "lovely, dark, and deep" New England woods. Rather, it is a place of laughter, a certain youthful playfulness, and the bright colors of an uncompli-cated childhood. Again it is Frost who expresses this sense of childlike play: "So was I once a swinger of birches. And so I dream of going back to be."

Victorian Farmhouse

7001 North Highway One
P.O. Box 357
Little River, California 95456; (707) 937-0697

INNKEEPERS: *George and Carole Molnar.*

ACCOMMODATIONS: *10 rooms, all with private bath; queen- and king-size beds.*

RESERVATIONS: *Three to four weeks recommended.*

MINIMUM STAY: *Two nights on weekends.*

DEPOSIT: *First night's lodging.*

CREDIT CARDS: *MC, Visa.*

RATES: *Moderate.*

RESTRICTIONS: *No pets.*

This homey inn was built in 1877 by John and Emma Dora Dennen as a private residence, which it still is. A pronounced feeling of privacy is its most striking attribute, but a certain atmosphere of permanence, of stability, runs a close second. One doesn't visit here so much as reside, even if the duration of that residence is only a week or a weekend.

There are several acres and an orchard of apple, plum, and pear trees to ramble around in. I liked the solid triple-hung bay windows in the downstairs parlor, as well as the antique rocking horse, the Regulator clock, and the homey fireplace. Both upstairs guest rooms in the main house have ocean views, while one downstairs has a French wood-burning stove and its own sitting room. Another has an exquisite view of a small private flower garden. Altogether, six of the inn's 10 rooms have fireplaces; quilts from the 1900s to the 1920s adorn all of the beds.

A queen-size brass bed graces the Emma Dora room; there is a white comforter draped with a quilt, white pillow shams, and a ceiling done in a tasteful (and restful) redwood design. I also liked the upstairs sitting room with its view of the rear flower gardens.

Hosts George and Carole Molnar were responsible for the additions to the inn which include the Wicker Room (antique wicker pieces, queen-size bed, ocean view, and open-front Franklin stove) and the Orchard View (pine and oak antiques and an 1815 vintage wood stove). A large wood deck adjoins these two accommodations to allow breakfast outdoors.

Guests are served breakfast in their rooms promptly at 8:30 a.m. Strawberry muffins or poppyseed bread, yogurt with sliced bananas, granola, fresh orange juice, and coffee, tea, or hot chocolate comprise the morning menu. Sometimes guests are served fruit fresh from the orchard outside.

Whatever you are served for breakfast, the fresh ocean breeze in these parts will make it taste better than anything you could eat in the city. The quiet pace and restful environment of this inn are most conducive to concentration and creativity—an excellent place to sort out one's thoughts and prepare emotionally for that big project back in the workaday world.

Headlands Inn

44950 Albion Street at Howard
P.O. Box 132
Mendocino, California 95460; (707) 937-4431

INNKEEPERS: *David and Sharon Hyman.*

ACCOMMODATIONS: *Four rooms and a cottage, all with private bath; queen- and king-size beds.*

RESERVATIONS: *Three months recommended for weekends.*

MINIMUM STAY: *Two nights on weekends; three or four over holiday periods.*

DEPOSIT: *First night's lodging.*

CREDIT CARDS: *Not accepted.*

RATES: *Moderate to expensive.*

RESTRICTIONS: *No children. No pets.*

The Headlands Inn began as a barbershop on Main Street in the town of Mendocino in 1868. Five years later a second story was added for the barber and his family. Afterwards the dwelling was used as a saloon, a hotel annex, and a private residence. In 1893 it was moved to its present location at Howard and Albion streets.

Today, the dwelling is three stories high, with clean, solid lines—most definitely a Victorian with a New England feel. The modern conveniences are not lacking; all five accommodations have private bathrooms and all have wood-burning fireplaces. Guest rooms are named after personages who have figured prominently in the building's history. Two are attic rooms with gable ceilings and window seats, offering the town's best view. (Look particularly for Mendocino's quaint water towers.) One room even comes with a large, private balcony.

My favorite is the Bessie Strauss room, named after a former owner of the home: lace curtain-adorned bay windows facing the ocean, a redwood fireplace, a large mirrored armoire, a full-size comfy sofa, and a wonderful (king-size) bed truly fit for a king (or queen). Yes, that's certainly how these innkeepers make you feel. The Hymans lovingly supply little things like extra bed pillows, and fresh flowers, candy, and fruit.

Breakfast is comprised of two different kinds of home-baked muffins, fresh fruit, a hot entrée that changes daily, and flavored coffees and teas. It arrives on a breakfast tray garnished with fresh flowers. Florentine ham rolls with cheddar cheese sauce, baked pears flavored with ginger and cinnamon, vanilla yogurt, and delicious cranberry and blueberry muffins were part of my morning meal. A copy of the San Francisco newspaper was also delivered to my door. In the afternoon complimentary tea and cookies are served.

Local attractions are many and varied. There is an art center, secluded sandy beaches, tide pools teeming with marine life, hiking (four state parks are within ten miles of Mendocino), golfing, tennis, and canoeing on Big River. But for many, simply walking through Mendocino is enough: It bears an astonishing resemblance to a New England fishing village and has been used as a backdrop for many Hollywood productions.

John Dougherty House

571 Ukiah Street
P.O. Box 817
Mendocino, California 95460; (707) 937-5266

INNKEEPERS: *David and Marion Wells.*

ACCOMMODATIONS: *Six rooms, all with private bath; queen-size beds.*

RESERVATIONS: *Four to six weeks recommended.*

MINIMUM STAY: *Two nights on weekends, three over holiday periods.*

DEPOSIT: *First night's lodging.*

CREDIT CARDS: *AE, MC, Visa.*

RATES: *Moderate to expensive.*

RESTRICTIONS: *Not suitable for children. No pets.*

Soon after Mendocino was founded in 1851, John Dougherty roared into what was then a bustling fishing village and lumber camp. To anyone who's visited Mendocino recently, it's hard to imagine the quiet, little town of 1,000, with its quaint art galleries, cafes, and New England-style residences that are often depicted in movies (*Summer of '42, The Russians Are Coming*) and television shows (as Cabot Cove in *Murder, She Wrote*) as anything but "California mellow."

But in the 1850s and '60s the town's Big River Mill supplied most of the lumber for the construction of San Francisco. Dougherty was the 19th-century equivalent of head trucker of the enterprise; as the chief mule skinner, he was in charge of the mule and oxen-drivers who moved the great timbers from the redwood forests.

Captain John, as he was called, was probably the only captain in the village who never put out to sea. He got his title from the mill. And the only rigging he erected was a two-story Cape Cod Victorian with attached cottage and water tower, at the corner of Ukiah and Kasten Streets in 1867. He married, raised a son and daughter, and died in 1900. Except for a brief stint as a bed and breakfast in the '70s, the house remained a private residence until it was reopened as a hostelry on Valentine's Day 1989.

Before the opening, its new owners, David Wells, a restaurant supply salesman from Los Angeles, and his wife, Marion, a former secretary, lovingly refurbished the property and stocked it with some of the oldest antiques in California.

Pride of the passel is a 19th-century "keeping room," or living room area, with a Primitive-style hutch/cupboard from the 1830s. Each day at 9:00 a.m., breakfast (home-made scones, fresh fruits presented on a 150-year-old platter, granola, yogurt, hard-boiled duck eggs, quiche or frittata, fresh coffee, tea, and locally-made apple juice) is served here on a maple dropleaf gateleg table from the 1700s. In fact, almost all the couple's furniture and "show off" items predate the Civil War. Only the Wedgwood egg cups are "new"; culled by Marion from an antique shop in England, they're just a hundred years old.

Other treasures are scattered throughout the inn's six rooms, particularly in the Captain's Room and Kit's Cabin. The former, which is upstairs in the main house, has an 1840s Boston rocker, along with a private veranda, queen-size bed, deep soaking tub, wood-burning stove, hand stencilled walls, and one of the best ocean views in town. The latter is a two-room suite with a four-poster bed, woodstove, antiques (pine corner cupboard, grain-painted chest, and spongeware pottery), and a delightful garden view.

Next to Kit's is the Water Tower, which is a great place to curl up with a book. Picture an 18-foot beamed ceiling above a four-poster bed, hand stencilled walls, and woodstove, and you get the idea. Adjacent to the main house are a pair of two-room suites (Starboard and Port Cottages) with sitting rooms, private baths, woodstoves, queen-size beds, and ocean views. Last, but not least, is the First Mate's Room, back in the main house, with stenciled walls, private bath, and antique pine furniture.

Want even more history? Spare an hour or two for walking through town, all of which is part of a National Historic Preservation Area. Because of its rugged location on some of the Golden State's most scenic headlands, the community has escaped the urban sprawl that surrounds some landmarks. A short drive away, even more fun beckons: From whale watching spots to lush botanical gardens and even an all-year waterfall, nine nearby state parks bulge with all sorts of attractions.

Joshua Grindle Inn

44800 Little Lake
P.O. Box 647
Mendocino, California 95460; (707) 937-4143

INNKEEPERS: *Jim and Arlene Moorehead.*

ACCOMMODATIONS: *10 rooms, all with private bath; twin and queen-size beds.*

RESERVATIONS: *Three months recommended.*

MINIMUM STAY: *Two nights on weekends, three over holiday periods.*

DEPOSIT: *First night's lodging.*

CREDIT CARDS: *DC, MC, Visa.*

RATES: *Moderate.*

RESTRICTIONS: *No pets.*

Like so many others, the Grindle clan had come to the North Coast from Maine. This lovely Italianate home was built as a wedding present on the marriage of Joshua Grindle and Alice Hills in 1879—a gift from the bride's father. Alice died in childbirth in 1882, but the house remained in the Grindle family until 1967. In 1977 the home was turned into a first-class inn.

The back-East tone of this exquisite bed and breakfast can stand up to the very best New England establishments. And it is a very romantic place; a natural, I would think, for a honeymoon.

The first things I noticed on entering were the early American pieces in the parlor, along with the fireplace and an antique pump organ. Colonial-era furnishings appear extensively throughout the rest of the house. In the dining room I found a pine harvest table dating back to the 1830s, capable of seating 10.

Five guest rooms (the Nautical, Grindle, Library, Treeview, and Master) are located in the main part of the home. In back there is a cottage with two rooms, each with a Franklin stove, wood-beamed ceiling, and a large bath. (Both are also wheelchair accessible.) A recently constructed water tower houses three additional units, two of which have Franklin stoves.

The Grindle has a fine collection of old clocks that will remind you pleasantly of all the time you have to fritter away. I also liked the extensive collection of etchings, oil paintings, and serigraphs. Two of the guest rooms in the main house have fireplaces decorated with handcrafted tiles made in 1870 at Minton's, Stoke on Trent, a factory in England. (The tiles in the Library Room illustrate *Aesop's Fables*.)

Grindle hosts Jim and Arlene Moorehead serve a full breakfast that includes a hot egg dish, fresh fruit, coffee-cake, muffins, popovers, or scones, and tea and coffee. There are always apples and oranges in the parlor for guests, as well as mineral water and a welcome decanter of sherry.

Whitegate Inn

499 Howard Street
P.O. Box 150
Mendocino, California 95460
(707) 937-4892 or (800) 531-7282

INNKEEPERS: *George and Carol Bechtloff.*

ACCOMMODATIONS: *Six rooms, all with private bath; twin, queen-, and king-size beds.*

RESERVATIONS: *Three to four weeks recommended.*

MINIMUM STAY: *Two nights on weekends and throughout the month of August; three nights over holiday periods.*

DEPOSIT: *In full.*

CREDIT CARDS: *MC, Visa.*

RATES: *Moderate to expensive.*

RESTRICTIONS: *Not suitable for children. No pets.*

This house was built in the early 1880s and occupied by Dr. William McCornack, a local physician. He used it as his hospital, and it retained its healing-arts association well into living memory; it was called the McCornack Healing Center before its transformation into a bed and breakfast inn.

Many things have changed in the last hundred years or so, but not the service orientation of the building's succession of owners. Current innkeepers are George and Carol Bechtloff, who acquired the property in June of 1992.

Carol's background as an interior designer and George's former employment as a building contractor have combined to give the Whitegate the enhancements it has so richly deserved for the past several years. This, along with the couple's antique collection gathered over a period of more than 20 years, makes a statement published about the home in 1887 ring true: "(Whitegate is) one of the most elegant and best appointed residences in town."

The Victorian heart redwood home showcases steep gables, fishscale shingles, a symmetrical pair of front bay windows, gilt ceiling moldings, and plaster medallions. The parlor contains Victorian and French settees, a 100-year-old American cut glass lamp, an 18th-century grandfather clock from Huddersfield, England, and a Bardine upright piano with leather-covered hammers. The matching cut glass candelabras in the parlor and dining room are original to the house. A collection of American Civil War memorabilia—a Springfield rifle, $2 Confederate coupons dated May 1861, a lithograph of Robert E. Lee, and a saber—is displayed in the home's entryway.

The Bechtloffs' innkeeping style includes spending as much time as possible with guests while acting as their guide through the North Coast panorama. A trip to a pigmy forest or 47-acre botanical garden, an afternoon of tidepooling at Mackerricher State Park, a horseback ride along the beach, and an evening with the Mendocino Performing Arts Group are some of Carol's "see and do" suggestions. She also makes sure that her guests are aware of the movies and TV shows that have been filmed in the area—from *Johnny Belinda* (1947) to *Murder, She Wrote.* (Keep an eye out for Angela Lansbury when you're in town; the house used in her popular television series is on the corner of Little Lake and Ford streets.) Whitegate itself hasn't escaped Hollywood's notice. It appeared in a Bette Davis movie called *Strangers*, filmed here in the 1970s.

A sit-down breakfast is served in the inn's dining room at 9:00 a.m.; coffee and tea, set out an hour earlier, can be taken back to your guest room or enjoyed on the deck. From the homemade cranberry crunch muffins and cinnamon raisin rounds to the caramel apple French toast or eggs en croute served each morning with fresh fruit, gourmet coffee, and freshly squeezed orange juice, the Bechtloffs' breakfast will leave you as satisfied as their down comforter-covered beds leave you rested.

On the occasion of my first visit to Whitegate Inn I occupied the Cypress Room: bay windows draped with white lace curtains, an Oriental carpet, a rosewood French bedroom set, white crochet coverlet with matching pillow shams, and a Franklin fireplace. The room is sheltered by a lovely cypress tree. The most private accommodation at the inn is the Enchanted Cottage, with its antique French bedroom suite, daybed sofa, Franklin stove, and private bath with clawfoot tub and shower. "A lot of honeymoons are spent here," notes Carol, who also hints of marriage proposals and secret engagement celebrations. Wedding vows are often sealed in the gazebo just outside on the deck.

Country Inn

632 North Main Street
Fort Bragg, California 95437; (707) 964-3737

INNKEEPERS: *Don and Helen Miller.*

ACCOMMODATIONS: *Eight rooms, all with private bath; seven queen- and one king-size bed.*

RESERVATIONS: *Two to three weeks recommended.*

MINIMUM STAY: *Two nights on weekends.*

DEPOSIT: *First night's lodging.*

CREDIT CARDS: *MC, Visa.*

RATES: *Moderate.*

RESTRICTIONS: *No children. No pets.*

We may never know for whom this charming structure was built, but we do know it belonged to the Union Lumber Company. In 1893 it was sold to a Mr. L. A. Moody for $500—a princely sum in those days. (A 1905 edition of the *San Francisco Examiner*, found glued to the redwood wallboards here, advertises overalls at the bargain price of 17¢ each.)

The building has passed through many hands, and lives, since then. But it was in the mid-seventies that Don and Helen Miller first moved to Fort Bragg on the craggy Mendocino County coast. Don was working as a free-lance writer, photographer, artisan, and sculptor (he calls himself a one-man advertising agency). He found himself doing a volume business writing and designing brochures for local innkeepers. It then occurred to the couple that owning their own bed and breakfast inn would be an ideal way to meet people. And so it has been.

This is not one of those bed and breakfasts where one is forever afraid to touch anything for fear it might break. Not that the Millers sacrifice the personal touch. Country Inn is appointed throughout with Don's photographs, sculpture, and watercolors. (The skylight in the parlor not only creates excellent light with which to view them, but accentuates the feeling of comfort and relaxation.) I liked the stairway's redwood banisters and carefully chosen wallpaper; the inn's exterior is entirely done in redwood paneling.

All of the bedrooms have plush carpeting, brass and iron beds, and wallpaper coordinated with sheets and pillowcases. Two of the rooms have fireplaces. The bathrooms are modern (the attic bedroom has a clawfoot tub, however); one is accessible by wheelchair with special facilities for the handicapped.

Helen makes a variety of delicious breads (poppyseed with brandy, sour cream nut, banana, and heavenly chocolate) in addition to her special "surprise" muffins (no, I won't reveal the secret here). Breakfast also includes cheese, fruits of the season, and coffee and orange juice. Don pours complimentary wine in the evening.

Nearby attractions are surprisingly varied in Fort Bragg (a "one-taxi" town). The Footlighter Theater produces locally written musical comedy, usually old-fashioned melodramas in which the audience is encouraged to cheer the fair-haired hero; the villain makes his entrance to boos and hisses. It runs May through August. Fort Bragg is also noted for its many shops, art galleries, gardens, museum, steam train ride through the redwoods—and its award-winning gourmet ice cream.

The Grey Whale Inn

615 North Main Street
Fort Bragg, California 95437
(707) 964-0640 or (800) 382-7244

INNKEEPERS: *John and Colette Bailey.*

ACCOMMODATIONS: *14 rooms, all with private bath; twin, double, queen-, and king-size beds.*

RESERVATIONS: *Two to three weeks recommended for weekends.*

MINIMUM STAY: *Two nights on weekends; three to four nights over holiday periods.*

DEPOSIT: *First night's lodging; in full for holidays and weekends.*

CREDIT CARDS: *AE, DC, MC, Visa.*

RATES: *Moderate.*

RESTRICTIONS: *No pets (local kennel accommodations available).*

Fort Bragg's first (and perhaps its most distinctive) bed and breakfast inn, The Grey Whale, features spacious, comfortable rooms (all with private bath) at very affordable prices. This is an interesting establishment for several reasons, not the least of which is the discriminating staff. I found a genuine desire to please here, and considerable knowledge about Fort Bragg and the Mendocino Coast.

The building itself has long been a landmark, having served from 1915, when it was built, until 1971 as the Redwood Coast Hospital, the North Coast's major healthcare facility. The weathered redwood siding, completely covering the white clapboard, is trimmed with fresh colors. As more than one observer has noted, it looks as though it has always been an inn—a testament to the skill of those who designed the conversion.

John Bailey worked for Alpha Beta markets, Colette at a Veterans Hospital; both wished to go into business for themselves. They spent a year looking in Northern California before they found the right place. (It was advertised in the *Wall Street Journal*.) John enjoys dealing with people in a cooperative, rather than a competitive, way. "One gets positive feedback," Colette says. "The corporate world is a long way from Fort Bragg."

There is a wide variety of rooms here, in terms of size, decor, and views. Hallways are spacious and stairs are easy (guest rooms are on three levels); one bedroom and bath contains accommodations for the handicapped, including ramp access. The Baileys' private collection of art works is displayed throughout the building, with strong emphasis on work by local artists. (The magnificent whale on the front grounds was carved by Byrd Baker, a leader in the "Save the Whales" movement.) A fireplace lounge, mini-conference room, television theater with VCR, and recreation room with a pool table have recently been added to the inn's ground floor.

Guests are encouraged to let the staff know in advance of special dietary requirements. Breakfast is served from 7:30 to 10:00 a.m. each morning in the Breakfast Room. It includes homemade fruit and nut breads or coffeecake, fresh fruit, quiche, an egg casserole (or a hot entrée like crepes filled with fresh asparagus and Swiss cheese topped off with hollandaise sauce), cereal and milk, two selections of juice, the inn's special blend of Thanksgiving-brand coffee, tea, and cocoa. Guests are welcome to take breakfast back to their room.

Those interested in local activities are supplied with a big book listing things to do in the area, easily the most extensive and helpful guide that I saw during my tour. There are a surprising number of attractions: Noyo Harbor with its fishing fleet, state parks and beaches, redwood forests galore, a logging museum, botanical gardens, art galleries, concerts, and even good local opera at certain times of the year. Located just two blocks from the inn is the Skunk Train depot (a 100-year-old steam train ride offering summer day trips through the redwoods). Annual town events include the Whale Festival in March, a salmon barbecue (July), and Paul Bunyan Days in the fall.

This is one of the most successful bed and breakfast inns I have come to know, having been continuously owned and operated by the Baileys now for over 16 years. It accomplishes something that many inns aim for but do not always achieve: It affords the *joie de vivre* of many people gathered under one roof in pleasant surroundings, yet still succeeds—through its conscientious attention to the needs and preferences of the individual, in making each guest feel special.

Pudding Creek Inn

700 North Main Street
Fort Bragg, California 95437
(707) 964-9529 or (800) 227-9529

INNKEEPERS: *Carole and Garry Anloff.*

ACCOMMODATIONS: *10 rooms, all with private bath; double, queen-, and king-size beds.*

RESERVATIONS: *Two to three weeks recommended.*

MINIMUM STAY: *Three nights during holiday periods.*

DEPOSIT: *First night's lodging. In full for holidays.*

CREDIT CARDS: *AE, DC, MC, Visa.*

RATES: *Inexpensive to moderate.*

RESTRICTIONS: *Lodging for children limited. No pets.*

This pretty Victorian was built in 1884 by a Russian count who fled the Old World under a cloud. He did not arrive in the New World penniless, however; some people were even so uncharitable as to suggest that he had departed with money that was not, legally speaking, his own. Ill-gotten or not, he put his spoils to good use, building seven fine homes in the Fort Bragg area.

In deference to the democratic traditions of his new homeland (and for fear of the Russian authorities, no doubt), our hero changed his name to the less aristocratic—and considerably more anonymous—appellation of Mr. Brown. His wedding was the occasion of considerable local interest: His bride wore the first wedding dress advertised in the Montgomery Ward catalog.

Records reveal that an equally anonymous Mr. Woods and Mrs. White later owned and lived in the count's aging home. In the 1970s it was rescued and restored; in 1980 the house opened as a bed and breakfast inn, its hallways presided over by pictures of the count and his wife.

Actually there are two dwellings, both two-story buildings, connected by an enclosed garden court. Breakfast can be enjoyed here in the summer, and in the parlor during wintertime. Breakfast consists of juice, fresh fruit, a hot entrée such as a strata or quiche, homemade coffeecake, and coffee or tea. If the weather allows breakfast on the patio, you can enjoy the many varieties of fuchsias, begonias, and ferns planted in the garden court. A social hour is also conducted here from 5:00 to 6:00 p.m.

There's a total of 10 guest rooms, two of which offer cozy working fireplaces. The Spinning Room is done in yellow and blue, with an old-fashioned spool-design bed and a great old-style bathtub. My favorite is the Interlude Room. Shades of Richard Rogers' *Blue Room:* Everything is blue here (including baby blue), with Priscilla curtains. The king-size bed is pecanwood, and there is a spacious bathroom. Altogether a light and sunny room that I highly recommend.

There are many shops and restaurants near Pudding Creek Inn. Tennis courts, a logging museum, and the Skunk Train depot are only a few blocks away. There is also a Visitors Center in town to familiarize those who are passing through with the many sights and activities in the community.

This inn is a favorite of at least one well-known character actress. It could become your favorite, too. I'm sure the roguish old count who sought refuge in the far reaches of the New World would relish the quiet good taste here—and who could help but applaud the very democratic prices associated with this modern incarnation of his 19th-century hideaway?

Humboldt
County

🐌

PACIFIC OCEAN

*The
Gingerbread
Mansion*
Ferndale

Mattole

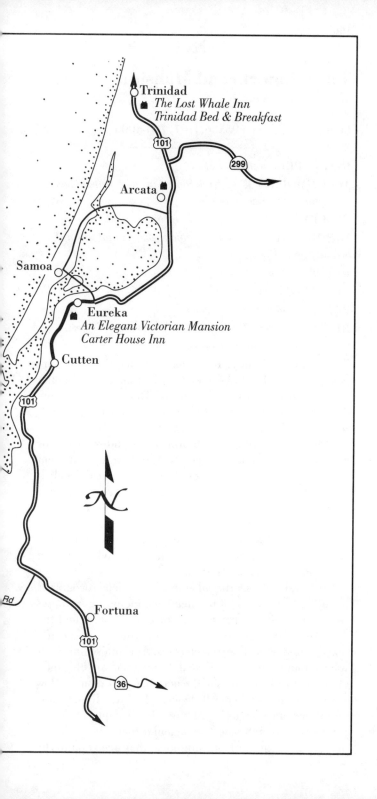

The Gingerbread Mansion

400 Berding Street
P.O. Box 40
Ferndale, California 95536; (707) 786-4000

INNKEEPER: *Ken Torbert.*

ACCOMMODATIONS: *Nine rooms, all with private bath; twin and queen-size beds.*

RESERVATIONS: *Three weeks recommended.*

MINIMUM STAY: *Two nights on weekends and through holiday periods.*

DEPOSIT: *Full amount.*

CREDIT CARDS: *AE, MC, Visa.*

RATES: *Moderate to expensive.*

RESTRICTIONS: *Children over 10 welcome. No pets.*

Watch that 13th step! It's taller than the rest, and purposely designed so to keep evil spirits from ascending the stairway to the upstairs bedrooms. This in strict accordance with Victorian tradition, or rather superstition, carried on to this day at Ferndale's Gingerbread Mansion.

Billed as Northern California's second-most-photographed home, this exquisitely turreted, carved, and gabled mansion with its colorfully landscaped English gardens was originally built as a residence for village physician Dr. Hogan Ring in 1899. It is a visual masterpiece—one of Ferndale's "butterfat palaces" (named for the dairy wealth that built the community), combining Queen Anne and Eastlake architectural styles with an abundance of ornamental trim.

To date The Gingerbread Mansion has been recognized by an impressive list of publications, including *National Geographic*, *Sunset* magazine, *Travel & Leisure*, and the *New York Times*. It was also featured on the cover of a book called *West Coast Victorians*. The inn's nine bedrooms, four parlors, and formal dining room are elegantly appointed with antiques of the period. Guest rooms follow various themes and color schemes (the Lilac Room, Garden Room, and Gingerbread Suite, for example). But surprisingly, two of the most spectacular rooms in the house are the 200-square-foot bathrooms that accompany the

Fountain and Rose suites. One has mirrored walls and ceiling, an elevated clawfoot tub, French bidet, marble-topped dresser, hanging plants, and floral pastel wallpaper with matching stained-glass windows. The other has side-by-side twin clawfoot tubs for his-and-hers bubble baths in front of a fireplace.

The inn's many little extras include nightly turn-down service, hand-dipped chocolates by the bedside, bath-robes, luggage racks in the rooms, bicycles for guest use, a well-stocked supply of information on area activities, after-noon tea and cake, and a generous breakfast featuring homemade muffins and breads, assorted cheeses, fresh fruit, hard-boiled eggs, cold cereals and milk, orange juice, coffee, and tea.

Ferndale, once known as "cream city," is today touted as "California's best-kept secret." The entire village has been designated a state historical landmark. Its well-preserved turn-of-the-century architecture and its Victorian Main Street, offering art galleries, an old-fashioned mercantile store, a blacksmith shop, and even a homemade candy factory, give it an irresistible fairy-tale charm. Among the fairs, festivals, and parades that perpetuate the enchantment are the Scandinavian Fes-tival, the Humboldt County Fair, a Kinetic Sculpture Race, Ice Cream Social, and annual Pet Parade.

Carter House Inn

Third and L streets
Eureka, California 95501; (707) 445-1390

INNKEEPERS: *Mark and Christi Carter.*

ACCOMMODATIONS: *Seven rooms, four with private bath; six double and one queen-size bed.*

RESERVATIONS: *Two to three weeks recommended.*

MINIMUM STAY: *None.*

DEPOSIT: *First night's lodging.*

CREDIT CARDS: *AE, MC, Visa.*

RATES: *Moderate to expensive.*

RESTRICTIONS: *No children. No pets.*

Dear Mom and Dad,

Sophie and I are having a great time up here in Humboldt County. Yesterday we toured the lumber mill at Scotia and drove through the redwoods along the Avenue of the Giants. And you'll never guess what happened. Since we arrived in Eureka earlier than expected, we decided to walk around Old Town and get a look at the Carson Mansion (they say it's the most photographed home in America) before locating the Carter House Inn. We parked the car and were walking down Third Street when we came alongside one of the most magnificent Victorian structures I had ever seen. I turned to Sophie and said: "Now *there* is a place I'd like to spend a night!" As we walked around the corner to get a better look, I just about died. The sign read: Carter House Inn, Bed & Breakfast.

Mark and Christi Carter are just the cutest couple. Mark told us he built this three-story mansion from plans taken from an 1884 San Francisco Victorian designed by Samuel and Joseph Cather Newsom (same architects as the Carson Mansion) that was destroyed in the 1906 quake. By the way, Mark also built the Hotel Carter, just across the street, which is a 20-guest-room incarnation of an 1880 Victorian building that was once known as the Old Town Cairo Hotel. He's so darn talented!

The Carter House exterior is constructed of clear heart redwood; the interior is finished in polished redwood and oak. The first floor serves as a combination contemporary art gallery and common area for the inn. The formal dining room is complete with silver service. There's an ornate wood and marble fireplace; plush velvet upholstered chairs and chaise longues in the parlor; and antiques, pottery, mantel clocks, sculpture, and paintings everywhere. The guest rooms are located on the lower level and the second and third floors. We're sharing the Burgundy Room, which is quite comfortable, but I got a peek at the Pink Room, with its late-1800s European oak bedroom set—my, what a knockout!

We originally planned to go over to the Samoa Cookhouse, a family-style restaurant that used to serve meals to up to 500 lumbermen a day, but the food's so good here there's hardly any room left: wine and hors d'oeuvres at five o'clock; tea, cookies, and cordials scheduled as an after-dinner snack. Then again, we might just stroll over to that divine restaurant in the Hotel Carter lobby and then waddle our way back.

And Mom, Christi said she'd give me the recipe for the pecan phyllo tart she plans on serving at breakfast tomorrow—along with the eggs Benedict, plums with raspberry sauce, bran muffins, smoked salmon platter, orange juice, and coffee. See what I mean? But you and Dad should really get up here sometime yourselves. In the meantime, I'll see you (10 pounds heavier) when I get back.

Love,
Linda Kay

ॐ

An Elegant Victorian Mansion

1406 C Street
Eureka, California 95501; (707) 444-3144

INNKEEPERS: *Doug and Lily Vieyra.*

ACCOMMODATIONS: *Three rooms share three baths; one two-room suite with private bath. Twin and queen-size beds.*

RESERVATIONS: *Three to four weeks recommended.*

MINIMUM STAY: *None.*

DEPOSIT: *Full amount.*

CREDIT CARDS: *MC, Visa.*

RATES: *Moderate.*

RESTRICTIONS: *Not suitable for children. No pets.*

From the *New York Times* ("Opulance, grace and grandeur") and *Sunset* magazine (A "premier architectural treasure") to *California* magazine ("A must see home of Eureka's rich and colorful past"), the critics have raved about this Queen Anne-influenced Eastlake Victorian where governors, senators, entertainers, and tycoons have stayed.

Welcome to the magnificent one-and-a-half-story "cottage," as he called it, that North Coast business magnate William Clark built in 1888. Clark's father, Jonathan, a physician for future General and President Ulysses S. Grant, co-founded Eureka in 1850. When his father died in 1884, William, who had been running the family cattle ranch, moved back into town, took over the Clark banking, brewery, real estate, and mill operations, and erected the town's most opulent Victorian a few blocks away from his father's homestead. Later, as mayor and county commissioner, he entertained such notables as railroad baron A. Leland Stanford, California Senator A. W. Way, and turn-of-the-century theatrical giant Lily Langtry here.

Today, the Clark Estate, which remained in the family until 1942 and continued as a private residence until 1990, is operated as a bed and breakfast by history buffs Doug and Lily Vieyra. Called "the most exciting and eclectic innkeepers on the West Coast" by travel guru Arthur Frommer, the Vieyras greet guests in vintage clothing (Doug plays Jeeves the Butler), guide visitors through the mansion in docent-like fashion, and even keep a croquet game ("The popular sport of the 1880s," says Lily) all set up, with the wickets in place, in the backyard.

A weekend at An Elegant Victorian Mansion is like a romp through the heady times of the late 19th century. Guests enter through an antechamber flanked by a double parlor on the right, with authentically reproduced wallpaper by Bradbury & Bradbury. Many of the trappings, including Belgian tapestries and lace, were collected by Doug and Lily's families. To the left is a library bulging with a floor-to-ceiling gathering of books, games, and flags. Be sure to look for the 48-star U.S. flag that was crocheted by Lily's Flemish family as they awaited liberation from the Nazis.

Four guest rooms with queen-size beds adorn the second floor of the grand old home. Most of them are named after former guests: Lily Langtry's Room (a big, airy space with an oak four-poster bed, 1870-90 Eastlake tables, writing desk, and antique oak dresser); Van Gogh Room (which, along with a separate sitting area, is dominated by the famous painter's works, including an original watercolor, as well as several by Dali); Governor's Room (with country French furniture, Belgian armoire, writing desk, easy chair, 1890s oak sideboard, harbor view, private bath, and connecting room with extra single bed), where Stanford, a California Governor and U.S. Senator, slept; and the Senator's Room (featuring a French Rococo solid brass bed and century-old, marble-topped furniture), where state legislator Way, a buddy of Clark's, frequently lingered.

Even the "service" at An Elegant Victorian Mansion is Victoriana. Instead of wine and cheese, the Vieyras serve lemonade or old-fashioned ice cream sodas in the afternoon. You won't find modern music here but just ask and Doug will show you one of his 150 silent films or early talkies (in the first floor sitting room) or play an old radio show program for you (in the library). Breakfast is lavish and formal, at an 1890s 10-seat dining table filled with fresh croissants, breads, fruits, and coffee, plus hand-squeezed orange juice, tea, and European-influenced egg dishes. When you're sated and ready to see the rest of Eureka's Old Town, ask for a guided tour in one of the inn's antique Fords and Sir Jeeves will comply.

The Lost Whale Inn

3452 Patrick's Point Drive
Trinidad, California 95570; (707) 677-3425

INNKEEPERS: *Lee Miller and Susanne Lakin.*

ACCOMMODATIONS: *Six rooms, all with private bath; queen-size beds.*

RESERVATIONS: *Four to six weeks recommended.*

MINIMUM STAY: *Two nights June through September and weekends year-round.*

DEPOSIT: *First night's lodging or half total amount.*

CREDIT CARDS: *MC, Visa.*

RATES: *Moderate.*

RESTRICTIONS: *No pets.*

From your vantage point on The Lost Whale Inn's private beach, you and your five year old spot a beautiful creature gliding in the cresting waves of the sea. "Look there, it's a whale!" Just off shore, sunning himself on Turtle Rock, a feisty sea lion barks. Vacationing families looking for the ultimate seaside getaway agree that The Lost Whale Inn is *the* place to stay.

A spacious Cape Cod-style dwelling located on four magnificent acres of oceanfront property, The Lost Whale Inn is decorated with simple Scandinavian furnishings complemented by prints with a nautical theme. You won't find any of Aunt Matilda's priceless antique lamps at this child-friendly lodging.

Each guest room reflects the care innkeepers Susanne Lakin and Lee Miller have taken to create a home for folks traveling with (or without) children. The Beluga and Orca Whale rooms have walk-out balconies ideal for taking in the picture postcard perfect scenery. In addition to their queen-size beds, these rooms also boast fully carpeted sleeping lofts accessible by ladder. Couples traveling without small fry will feel most at home in the cozy Humpback Whale room. The Blue and Grey Whale rooms (with their comfortable sitting alcoves complete with table and chairs) are just made for relaxing while watching the crashing ocean waves below. The Agate room contains a kid-size trundle daybed. It is completely carpeted and soundproof—the ideal spot for children age four years and younger. Anticipating your family's needs, the inn is also equipped with cribs and high chairs.

The Great Room is filled with storybooks, challenging puzzles, and games guaranteed to satisfy even the most curious-natured child. Megan and Amara, the innkeepers' daughters, can show your kids where to find huckleberries, blueberries, and strawberries ripe for picking, or introduce your family to the inn's menagerie: ducks, cats, bunnies, goats, and an iguana. After an adventure packed day sleepyheads will nod off as you read aloud the story of "The Legend of the Lost Whale" which is found in a notebook that contains the writings of many children who have been past guests. And after the kids are tucked-in you can stargaze from the outdoor hot tub.

The main dining room affords yet another spectacular view of the rugged Pacific coastline. The salty sea air will whet your appetite for a hearty breakfast of home-baked muffins and casseroles, fresh fruit, and locally-smoked salmon. In the evening, celebrate the sunset from the deck while sipping a complimentary cappuccino.

Don't expect to spend much time indoors, though, with the nearby rhododendron-, azalea-, and fuchsia-covered bluffs beckoning. Visit the inn's private beach; then it's a short hike to Patrick's Point State Park. Take the spiraling steps down to Agate Beach and join local residents who hunt for jade and agates. (Don't forget to bring your camera: The myriad tide pools that magically appear at low tide make wonderful subjects for photographs.) Swim, sail, windsurf, or bicycle up the coast to nearby redwood forests. Spend an afternoon exploring the aptly named Fern Canyon filled with verdant ferns and cascading waterfalls. Deep-sea fishing? If you don't have your own boat you can charter one in the quaint fishing village of Trinidad.

Trinidad Bed & Breakfast

560 Edwards Street
P.O. Box 849
Trinidad, California 95570; (707) 677-0840

INNKEEPERS: *Paul and Carol Kirk.*

ACCOMMODATIONS: *Four rooms, all with private bath; queen- and king-size beds.*

RESERVATIONS: *Three to four weeks recommended.*

MINIMUM STAY: *Two nights on weekends and through holiday periods.*

DEPOSIT: *Full amount.*

CREDIT CARDS: *DC, MC, Visa.*

RATES: *Moderate to expensive.*

RESTRICTIONS: *No children. No pets.*

If you like whales, seals, lighthouses, nature trails, or picnics at the sea then you'll definitely appreciate what the four-room Trinidad Bed & Breakfast, in minuscule Trinidad (population 390 or 410, depending on which local figure you believe), has to offer. Look for it on the coast just north of Eureka, some 80 miles south of the Oregon border, 284 miles north of San Francisco, and, as the Trinidad Chamber Of Commerce likes to relate, "a million miles from the cares and problems you want to leave behind."

Anchored on a bluff overlooking the rugged North Coast with Trinidad's picturesque fishing harbor below and replica of its 1871 lighthouse (complete with a working warning bell, rung yearly on July 4th) across the street, Carol and Paul Kirk's two-story Cape Cod-style home provides travelers with an oasis of rest and relaxation.

Among other activities, you can scope out the whales—in particular, mothers and their babies—in the harbor from March to June (each room has binoculars and a telescope); sit outside on the viewing bench and watch hundreds of harbor seals sunbathing on the rocks of the adjacent beach; go for a walk on the nearby Trinidad Head Trail; visit a museum, 1873 church, or two historic monuments (all within a block of the inn); drive 15 miles north to the crown jewel of the coastal forests, Redwood National Park; or curl up with a good book on the bluffs, in your room, or next to a soothing, wood-burning fireplace in the inn's first-floor living room.

Built in 1950, the red-shingled home with white trim was turned into a bed and breakfast by the enterprising Kirks in 1985. Former San Diegans who were looking for what Carol calls "the peace and calm of a smaller community," the couple operated a local restaurant before adding small hotel management to their list of accomplishments.

The inn's decor is modest yet extremely appealing. You won't find wall-to-wall antiques choking this setting, yet each room has something slightly different to offer. Three have queen-size beds, the fourth, a king. Two are suites, one with a fireplace, and they all have private baths.

Upstairs, the Peach Master Bedroom contains warm, knotty pine paneled walls, a bayview dormer window with a table for two to savor the spectacular sunsets off Trinidad Headland, two bowback chairs, and, of course, calming peach hues.

On the same floor, the Green Window Seat Room, which is slightly smaller than the Peach, has a large, pillow-filled window seat big enough for two people to check the coast for miles. Craggy Indian Beach, considered sacred land because the Tsurai Indians lived here, is directly to the south. (The bay, by the way, was discovered by the Portuguese in 1595, but Trinidad was named and claimed by the Spanish a year before the Declaration of Independence was signed.)

Also on the second floor, the large, all-windowed Blue Bay View Suite has a shower-tub combination, two rocking chairs, a telescope for whale watching, and its own private entrance. Finally, on the first floor, the Mauve Fireplace Suite also has a private entrance, a pair of comfy rockers, and wraparound windows. Two bonuses: this room has a king-size bed and brick fireplace.

After resting up in the Blue or Mauve suites, be ready for breakfast delivered to your door. Otherwise, you'll find Carol's array of homemade muffins and breads, spread of cheeses (made in nearby Loleta, a town even tinier than Trinidad, with only 140 people), seasonal fruits (especially citrus), baked apples, bottomless pot of fresh coffee, juices, teas, and variety of "heart healthy" goodies in the common room downstairs. Hungry for more? Two of the town's four restaurants are located within walking distance of Trinidad Bed & Breakfast.

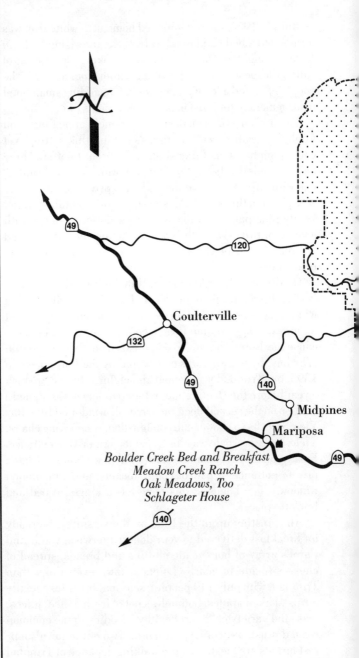

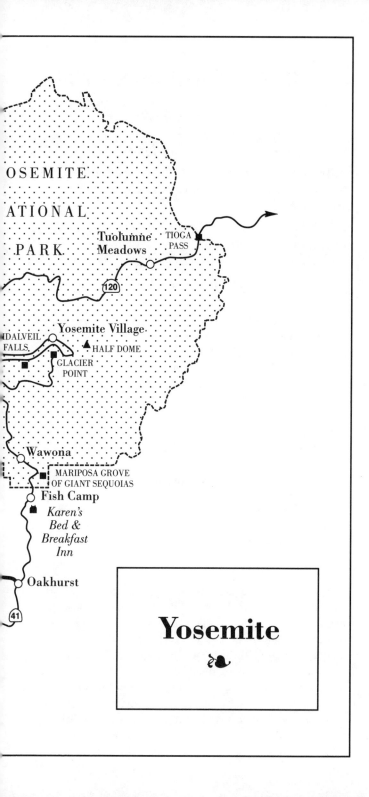

OSEMITE

ATIONAL

PARK.

Tuolumne
Meadows

TIOGA
PASS

120

IDALVEIL
FALLS.

Yosemite Village

▲ HALF DOME

GLACIER
POINT

Wawona

MARIPOSA GROVE
OF GIANT SEQUOIAS

Fish Camp

*Karen's
Bed &
Breakfast
Inn*

Oakhurst

41

Yosemite

Boulder Creek Bed and Breakfast

4572 Ben Hur Road
Mariposa, California 95338; (209) 742-7729

INNKEEPERS: *Michael and Nancy Habermann.*
ACCOMMODATIONS: *Three rooms, all with private bath.*
RESERVATIONS: *One to two weeks recommended.*
MINIMUM STAY: *None.*
DEPOSIT: *First night's lodging.*
CREDIT CARDS: *MC, Visa.*
RATES: *Inexpensive.*
RESTRICTIONS: *Children discouraged. No pets.*

Michael Habermann and Nancy Holst were a love story just waiting to happen. Their meeting came when Nancy, a resident of Huntington Beach, California, embarked on a tour of Germany to research her family history (her grandparents had come to the United States from Tellingstadt, 35 miles north of Hamburg). It was on the last day of her vacation that she met Michael at a Düsseldorf festival. They shared a cup of coffee, walked around town and chatted a bit, then he offered to give her a lift to her hotel before boarding his train back to Hamburg. "Give me a call if you're ever in the United States," Nancy said as she handed him her address and telephone number. Two days later there was a knock at Nancy's door back in Huntington Beach, and, as you may have guessed, there stood Michael. The end of this tale, as in most any storybook romance, is that they married, and have been living together happily ever since.

It was Michael, a jack-of-all-trades kind of guy, who designed and built their little love nest in Mariposa that backs up to Boulder Creek. Acres of meadowlands with white oak, manzanita, redbud, and digger pine trees, deer feeding in the backyard, and huge granite boulders surrounding a dazzling seasonal waterfall all distinguish the environment of their home turned bed and breakfast. The inner realms of this European chalet-style home have an abundance of wood beams and glass. An A-frame living room with 20-foot ceiling is made cozy by a wood-burning stove, a stereo, wood and upholstered rocking chairs, a love seat, and antiques that mingle nicely with the contemporary pieces.

The living room and dining room flow as one continuous space. Around 7:00 a.m. each morning Nancy begins setting the oak dining table with 1939 Century-pattern china, silver, and crystal (bought in Germany) for an 8:00 a.m. breakfast. Once again, it's Michael who is the gourmet chef: He owned a restaurant for eight years prior to meeting up with Nancy. His farmer's breakfast starts off with fresh strawberries and chocolate almond coffee. Glasses of pineapple-grapefruit juice are poured as slices of sourdough bread make their way to the toaster. The pièce de résistance, Michael's farmer's omelette, is stuffed with potatoes and bacon, and topped off with sauteed green onions, carrots, and mushrooms.

The room I nestled up in is the one the Habermanns call their Bridal Suite. Its ornate queen-size iron bed has a pillow-top mattress, down pillows, and white floral comforter. The view from its picture window is of the Sierra foothills. Another guest room, the Blue Room, is also set up with a queen-size bed, this one covered in a patchwork design comforter. A collection of antique teacups, plates, and glasses are displayed in the room's white rattan hutch. The Twin Room, as denoted by its name, has twin beds that make up to a king. The room also has a ceiling fan and an antique smoking stand that houses a collection of old pipes.

Located just two miles from downtown Mariposa (gateway to the Mother Lode) and a 40-minute drive from Yosemite's Arch Rock entrance (the only park road open year-round), the inn attracts visitors interested in both history and nature. Boulder Creek Bed and Breakfast is also just a quarter mile from the California State Mining and Mineral Museum at the Mariposa County Fairgrounds. This museum houses over 100 Mother Lode gold specimens, an assay office, mine tunnel, mineral collection, and gift shop.

Meadow Creek Ranch

2669 Triangle Road
Mariposa, California 95338
(209) 966-3843 or (800) 955-3843

INNKEEPERS: *Bob and Carol Shockley.*

ACCOMMODATIONS: *Four rooms, one with private bath; twin and queen-size beds.*

RESERVATIONS: *Four weeks recommended.*

MINIMUM STAY: *None.*

DEPOSIT: *Half of full amount.*

CREDIT CARDS: *AE, MC, Visa.*

RATES: *Moderate.*

RESTRICTIONS: *No children under 12. No pets.*

Down the road, a brown dog romps with two cats. Gray squirrels scurry into holes as a red-tailed hawk soars overhead. And a horse whinnies next to a two-story, western farmhouse that looks like it hasn't changed much in the last hundred years or so.

This is Meadow Creek Ranch. Located some 11 miles "out of town" (Mariposa is just to the north), the ranch wasn't always so placid. Built as a stage stop in 1858, it offered weary stagecoach riders a place to stay overnight. One of them, Jessie Fremont, wife of General John C. Fremont, slept in the barn, which, in 1859, she called "a haven of rest." The structure has also served as home to some of the first ranch families of California's fertile Central Valley. In later years, a lumber mill clanked away on the sprawling grounds.

Today the stagecoach and mill are gone and a four-guest-room bed and breakfast inn stands in their place. Started in 1983, the inn was bought in 1985 by antique collectors Bob and Carol Shockley. "We'd always wanted a fine house, a repository for our collectibles, and a business where we could serve the public," said Bob. "We wanted to work together, too. Running a bed and breakfast fulfills all these goals."

Within these walls the Shockleys have made some great changes. They've placed many small period pieces throughout, but they're proudest of an antique you'll find in the very first room you enter. As you come into the big, airy, country living room, look for the 125-year-old French carousel horse above the stone and brick fireplace. By the time you've had a chance to admire it, Carol will probably have slipped a nice, cold beverage in your hand.

Your tour continues to the upstairs bedrooms. Decorated with a queen-size, step-up bed, an oak armoire, and lots of house plants, the Meadow Breeze Room's tone is warm and friendly. Bright patchwork quilts cover two twin-size iron beds in the Sunrise Room. The Wildrose Room, whose most prominent feature is a century-old, European leaded-glass window, is also pleasant. It has a queen-size bed on a simple frame against the window. All three rooms share the downstairs bath.

For total privacy, you may want to stay in what was once the chicken coop of the old ranch—don't worry, the hens are long gone. Transformed over the years into a bunkhouse for hired hands and a rental unit, this cottage next to the barn has been repainted, recarpeted, and filled with amenities by Carol and Bob. Among them: a queen-size, canopied bed made of hand-carved Austrian mahogany; a private bath with a two-person, clawfoot tub; and sitting area with a propane fireplace and a Queen Anne drop-top desk.

The dining room of the main house has its own comfortable ambience. Guests are seated around a long, sturdy trestle table for meals which are prepped by Bob and then cooked by Carol. One morning you might be served French toast, ham, orange juice, coffee or tea, and a big bowl of strawberries, cantaloupe, and apples. The next day, light, fluffy pancakes, baked eggs, bacon, and applesauce may be offered.

Well sated, you'll be ready to take a stroll on the ranchland to check out its pastoral vistas or use the inn as a jumping-off point for trips to Yosemite National Park or the Badger Pass ski resort. Great summer rafting is available on the Merced River. All these attractions are less than an hour's drive from the inn.

Oak Meadows, Too

5263 Highway 140 North
P.O. Box 619
Mariposa, California 95338; (209) 742-6161

INNKEEPERS: *Don and Francie Starchman.*

ACCOMMODATIONS: *Six rooms, all with private bath; twin, queen-, and king-size beds.*

RESERVATIONS: *Three to four weeks recommended.*

MINIMUM STAY: *None.*

DEPOSIT: *First night's lodging.*

CREDIT CARDS: *MC, Visa.*

RATES: *Inexpensive to moderate.*

RESTRICTIONS: *No pets.*

A few years ago I took a cursory glance at Oak Meadows, Too while staying at another bed and breakfast in Mariposa and decided that it looked (and felt) too much like a motel to include within the pages of this book. On my last trip down Highway 140 to Yosemite I stopped by again and was pleasantly surprised by not only a new, very personable resident innkeeper, but also by the many changes that had occurred within.

My first clue to the transformation was a beaming group of Europeans that were sharing a breakfast of scrambled eggs with Canadian bacon, blueberry muffins and banana bread, coffee, tea, and orange and apple juice, on the inn's newly constructed, enclosed front porch.

The parlor with its stone fireplace and guest bedrooms had been redecorated (or perhaps merely upgraded) to a refreshing ambience that was nothing short of homey. Beds sported brass headboards and colorful handmade quilts. New wallpapers brightly complemented turn-of-the-century antiques. Each room also boasted the central heat and air conditioning so necessary for the cold winter nights and hot summer days that are typical of this area. Another bonus of the early American colonial-style inn is its very agreeable prices, some of the lowest to be found in all of California: starting at $59.

Although Oak Meadows, Too still has the motel-like exterior and sits just off the all-weather thoroughfare to

Yosemite National Park, it has been "warmed" since its opening in 1985 by more than just central heating. Other amenities include fresh flowers and chocolate mint candies in each of the guest rooms. Pleasant, clean, and friendly are adjectives now worthy of the Oak Meadows, Too bed and breakfast experience.

Schlageter House

5038 Bullion Street
P.O. Box 1202
Mariposa, California 95338; (209) 966-2471

INNKEEPERS: *Lee and Roger McElligott.*

ACCOMMODATIONS: *Three rooms, all with private bath.*

RESERVATIONS: *Three weeks recommended.*

MINIMUM STAY: *None.*

DEPOSIT: *First night's lodging.*

CREDIT CARDS: *Not accepted.*

RATES: *Inexpensive.*

RESTRICTIONS: *No pets.*

For many, the small town of Mariposa is a pleasant respite from the crowds encountered at Yosemite National Park. A scenic 40-minute drive from the park's Arch Rock entrance, Mariposa offers travelers the choice of several small inns, gift shops, and restaurants, and opportunities to tour a museum and history center, a mining and mineral exhibit, as well as many other historic sites in and around town that are quiet reminders of the gold-seeking way of life of 1849.

Built in 1856, Schlageter House is itself a monument to the Gold Rush era. Its broad porches are characteristic of a Carpenter Gothic architectural style. Sycamore trees frame the walk to the home's front entrance, and day lilies, rose bushes, pansies, and petunias adorn manicured lawns that lie just behind a white picket fence.

While entertaining his bed and breakfast guests, Roger McElligott speaks fondly of his days growing up in the area. "When the hard-rock miners from southern England settled here, they introduced meat pasties to us American folks," Roger told me. "We play up this heritage in our inn operation with a breakfast pasty recipe we developed."

A Schlageter House breakfast pasty includes bacon and eggs spiced with parsley, onion, and garlic, baked in folded pastry dough. The hand-held pasty is accompanied by sliced fresh fruit, coffee, and home-baked corn or cinnamon swirl muffins.

Compared to the seeming formalness of the home itself, Roger McElligott and wife Lee are very casual in manner and innkeeping style. For openers, guests can have their breakfast served just about anytime they want it. "We also offer an afternoon glass of wine or cold soft drink," Lee comments. "I might be inclined to bake a cake or a pie, or, if we're barbecuing, we may even invite guests to join us for dinner."

With three guest rooms, a "full house" only consists of six people. For the most privacy, the downstairs bedroom is your best bet. Tucked away in a corner, it holds a lace canopy four-poster and an antique wardrobe. Just off the bedroom is an old-fashioned porch equipped with a comfortable rocking chair and a private bath that has a modern shower and pull-chain toilet. The two upstairs bedrooms each have a private bath. Set under the roof's eaves, one room has a blue and white decor with wicker bed, settee, and dressing table. The other, twin-bedded room, is done in pink and peach tones. It has a ceiling fan, antique dresser, and lounge chair.

When Lee's not busy serving breakfast, working in the yard, or cleaning house she can usually be found painting landscapes in her art studio in the backyard woodshed. Many of her original works grace the walls of Schlageter House, particularly the living room. Also part of this room's furnishings are a Victorian settee and side chair, fireplace, television and VCR, numerous books, and games (like checkers, dominoes, cribbage, and Trivial Pursuit), all for the guests' amusement.

Karen's Bed & Breakfast Inn

1144 Railroad Avenue
P.O. Box 8
Fish Camp, California 93623; (800) 346-1443

INNKEEPER: *Karen Bergh.*

ACCOMMODATIONS: *Three rooms, all with private bath; twin and queen-size beds.*

RESERVATIONS: *Three to four weeks recommended.*

MINIMUM STAY: *Two nights over holiday periods.*

DEPOSIT: *First night's lodging or half of full amount.*

CREDIT CARDS: *Not accepted.*

RATES: *Inexpensive.*

RESTRICTIONS: *No pets.*

Located just three minutes from the entrance to Yosemite National Park and five minutes from the Mariposa grove of giant sequoias and Sugarpine narrow-gauge railroad, guests of Karen's Bed & Breakfast Inn will find themselves at a driving advantage when it comes to getting around this vast range of scenic natural forest. Other nearby attractions are the Wawona Pioneer Village and nine-hole golf course (a 15-minute drive), Bass Lake recreation area (20 minutes), and Badger Pass ski resort (only 40 minutes from Karen's).

In summer, rock climbing, hiking, waterskiing, trout fishing, and river rafting are recreational activities afforded by this area. Besides downhill skiing, winter also brings opportunities for cross-country skiing or ice skating at an outdoor rink. Whatever time of year you choose to visit, Karen's offers yet another plus: Her home is open and welcoming all year, unlike some of the other inns around Yosemite that close their doors off-season.

Built with bed and breakfast in mind, this two-story wood frame home is painted a bright blue. (It was Karen's father, a realtor, who sparked the idea of her becoming an innkeeper.) The homey living room is a virtual guest entertainment center, with its television, stereo, piano, and quaint Regency stove. Blue wall-to-wall carpeting and white vertical blinds set off the room's twin upholstered rocking chairs and blue and gray patterned contemporary sofa.

Guest rooms are named and coordinated by color. The Rose Room has twin daybeds of white iron and brass with pink and white comforters and matching pillow shams. A white wicker chair and desk provide a bright contrast to the room's plush rose carpeting. The modern, private bath (one of three) offers both tub and shower. The Blue Room, also on the second floor, holds a queen-size bed with blue and white comforter and throw pillows. It has baby blue carpeting and bedside tables and lamps. Blue print Priscilla curtains cover windows that look out to towering pine trees and rustic oaks. The Peach Room has a false canopy over its queen-size bed that is covered with a peach bedspread. Reading is made easy by two peach-colored bedside lamps.

A full American breakfast starts off as early as 7:30 or as late as 8:30 a.m. (guests' choice) with a platter of fresh fruit, coffee (or tea) and hot cider, homemade muffins or coffeecake, and scrambled eggs with cottage fries, creamed eggs over toast points, or waffles (or pancakes) hot off the griddle.

Light refreshments (iced tea, lemonade, coffee, and black or herbal teas; home-baked oatmeal cookies; and cheese and crackers) are served from 4:00 until 6:00 p.m. Menus from local restaurants and sightseeing brochures are stored in the living room for guest perusal.

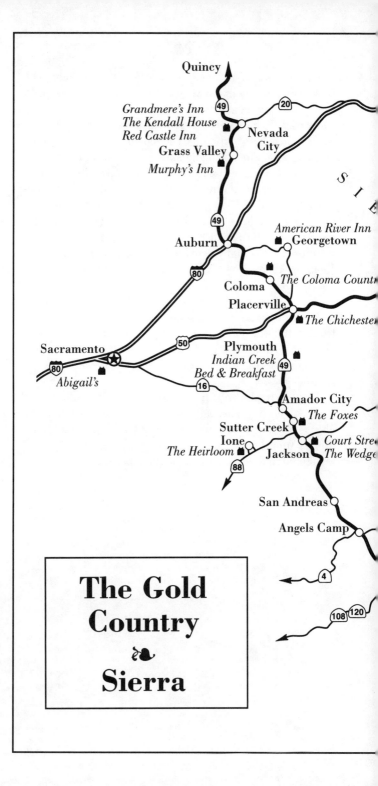

Quincy

(49) (20)

Grandmere's Inn
The Kendall House   Nevada
Red Castle Inn   City
Grass Valley

Murphy's Inn

S I E

(49)

American River Inn
Auburn   Georgetown

(80)
Coloma   *The Coloma Countr*
Placerville
The Chicheste

Sacramento   (50)   Plymouth
(80)   *Indian Creek*
Abigail's   *Bed & Breakfast*   (49)

(16)
Amador City
The Foxes
Sutter Creek
Ione   *Court Stre*
The Heirloom   Jackson   *The Wedge*

(88)

San Andreas

Angels Camp

(4)

(108)(120)

The Gold
Country
❦
Sierra

Chaney House
Mayfield House

89

28

Tahoe City

*Rockwood
Lodge*

Homewood

*LAKE
TAHOE*

89

**South
Lake
Tahoe**

50

Kee House

NEVADA
CALIFORNIA

*R
A*

n

N   E   V   A   D   A

*n
d Inn*

4

Dunbar House, 1880

Murphys

108

Tuolumne

Sonora   ○   *Oak Hill Ranch*

*Llamahall Guest Ranch
The Ryan House, 1855*

Chinese Camp

120

49

Abigail's

2120 G Street
Sacramento, California 95816; (916) 441-5007

INNKEEPERS: *Susanne and Ken Ventura.*

ACCOMMODATIONS: *Six rooms, four with private bath; queen- and king-size beds.*

RESERVATIONS: *Two to three weeks recommended.*

MINIMUM STAY: *Two nights May and June weekends, and during Thanksgiving and Christmas holidays.*

DEPOSIT: *First night's lodging.*

CREDIT CARDS: *DC, MC, Visa.*

RATES: *Moderate.*

RESTRICTIONS: *No children under five. No pets.*

While other San Francisco residents head to the beaches, mountains, and surrounding countryside for their holidays and weekends, I frequently make my great escape to Sacramento. The special appeal of California's capital city is evidenced in its wide, tree-lined residential streets, gorgeous architecture (Victorian and Arts and Crafts-style homes), one-of-a-kind cafes and boutiques, and friendly, down-home people.

It was on a recent visit, over Labor Day weekend, that I "discovered" Abigail's. A cube-style Colonial Revival mansion built in 1912, Abigail's is painted white with turquoise trim and set in a designated historical preservation park area.

An eclectic mix of furnishings fills Abigail's double living room: an Edwardian parlor table, a Belgian-made Oriental-style carpet, two floral print traditional sofas, wingback chairs, and Tiffany and Art Deco-style lamps. A separate game room is stocked with a piano and brass music stand, an oak game table, an English oak buffet, a Victorian lady's boudoir chair, and built-in corner curio cabinets, as well as a variety of puzzles and games. A large informational bulletin board details what's happening around Sacramento.

Second-floor guest rooms sport family member names: Albert, Margaret, Rose, and Anne. Dressed in shades of maroon and gray, the masculinely decorated Albert holds a queen-size mahogany bed covered in a white spread; wall-paper is pin-striped. There's also a double oak wardrobe and matching pull-down top desk. An upholstered wingback chair and matching ottoman afford a pleasant spot for reading, but plentiful light is also provided by bed-side tables and lamps. Albert's private bath has a marble floor and large shower.

Anne's color scheme is antique white and Wedgwood blue. The room's king-size bed is nicely complemented with a double armoire, a mahogany desk, and Chip-pendale-style chair. Bedside tables with pretty fabric skirts hold Oriental-motif lamps. The private bath, papered in a floral print, has both tub and shower.

On weekdays, breakfast is offered as early as 7:30 a.m.; eight o'clock on weekends. Fresh fruit, sour cream swirl coffeecake, and vegetarian cheese strata or jam-stuffed French toast dusted in powdered sugar are examples of items on a typical morning menu served around the 14-seater teak dining room table. Accompanying bever-ages include the usual coffee, tea, and orange juice. Guests can help themselves to lemonade and sodas stocked in the kitchen refrigerator. Hot tea and home-baked cookies are set out on the upstairs sideboard later in the day.

Sacramento itself offers so many things to see and do throughout the year. There's the State Capitol and Governor's Mansion tours, as well as the Crocker Art Museum. Old Town (the original downtown) has the re-markable California State Railroad Museum. Sacramento has a symphony, and in summertime, an outdoor Music Circus housed under a tent (recent productions have in-cluded *Peter Pan* and *The Boyfriend*). Annual events also include a Dixieland Jazz Festival held over Memorial Day weekend; the California State Fair (which runs through the month of August into the first week of September), a Camellia Festival in March each year, a Blues Festival and Old House Tour (popular events in September), and the California Marathon (December).

Grandmere's Inn

449 Broad Street
Nevada City, California 95959; (916) 265-4660

INNKEEPERS: *Doug and Geri Boka.*

ACCOMMODATIONS: *Seven rooms, all with private bath; queen-size beds.*

RESERVATIONS: *Three to four weeks recommended.*

MINIMUM STAY: *Two nights on weekends and holidays April through December.*

DEPOSIT: *First night's lodging.*

CREDIT CARDS: *MC, Visa.*

RATES: *Moderate to expensive.*

RESTRICTIONS: *One room accommodates children. No pets.*

Nestled on a hill above the old downtown section of Nevada City is a white, Colonial Revival home with restrained Victorian gingerbread known as Grandmere's Inn. This seven-bedroom inn is listed in the National Register of Historic Places, not just because it was built back in 1856, but because it was originally the home of Aaron Augustus Sargent, one of California's most powerful politicians. Also a lawyer, miner, and newspaper editor, Sargent rose to become a congressman, senator, and U.S. ambassador to Germany. He was a champion of the bill that created the transcontinental railroad, succeeding where others had failed for a decade. And it was Sargent who authored the 1878 women's rights law called the Anthony Amendment that was finally passed some 40 years later, with no change in wording.

An influential suffragist of her time, Aaron's wife, Ellen, was a close friend of Susan B. Anthony, who was often a guest in this house. (When Ellen died in 1911, flags in San Francisco were lowered to half-mast for a woman for the first time in the city's history.)

Today, the home looks much the same as it did in 1856 on the outside, but it has been considerably brightened and polished within. Gray and white marble floors grace the entry at the bottom of a curving stairway. A floral-patterned Victorian-style sofa, two Queen Anne chairs, and antique oak side tables warm up the cozy living room. Kitchen tiles are made from molds designed by Julia Morgan (one of the architects of Hearst Castle).

Upstairs, Dawn's Room holds an antique walnut bed with carved headboard, round nightstands covered by green tablecloths, vases of silk flowers, a big, mirrored armoire, white wicker armchairs, a double-size hideaway sofa bed, and French doors that open to a sunny, glassed-in sitting room with a fine view of the garden.

The Master Suite is comprised of a bedroom, parlor, veranda, and private bath. It has a double-size sleeper sofa, twin pine dressers, and an oak four-poster. Mama's and Papa's Room, with a mahogany four-poster, also has a sitting room and private bath with shower and oversized tub. Kelli's Room has a pole pine bed; Danny's Room, a queen bed with pine head- and footboard. Gertie's Room boasts a queen-size white wicker bed as well as its own garden entrance. The least expensive room, at the rear of the house on the second level, is Maggie's Room with its pineapple-motif carved four-poster.

If the heart of Grandmere's is its history, then the soul is its food. Guests gather around one of two big, rectangular tables starting at 9:00 a.m. The "serve-yourself" sideboard includes such delectables as corn soufflé, Grandmere eggs, or stuffed French toast served with homemade applesauce or fresh fruit compote. The bread pudding is topped with a nutmeg-flavored sauce; otherwise expect quick breads or croissants.

The area has many activities to sample as well. From an annual bluegrass festival and teddy bear convention to a Father's Day bicycle race, November quilt show, or Victorian Christmas, the Gold Rush town of Nevada City just blossoms with excitement. But perhaps nothing can top the thrill of staying in a historic home in the heart of this area that boasts such a colorful past.

The Kendall House

534 Spring Street
Nevada City, California 95959; (916) 265-0405

INNKEEPERS: *Ted and Jan Kendall.*

ACCOMMODATIONS: *Five rooms, all with private bath; queen-size beds.*

RESERVATIONS: *Three to four weeks recommended.*

MINIMUM STAY: *Two nights on weekends.*

DEPOSIT: *First night's lodging.*

CREDIT CARDS: *MC, Visa.*

RATES: *Moderate to expensive.*

RESTRICTIONS: *Limited accommodations for children. No pets.*

In 1991, a physician and his wife turned the pre-Victorian California farmhouse they'd been living in for 15 years into a majestic bed and breakfast just two blocks from downtown Nevada City. Surrounded by redwoods, oaks, pines, cedars, and fruit trees on two peaceful acres, the dwelling is still occupied by Jan Kendall, who's known for her down-home Arkansas country cooking, and her husband, Ted, who still practices right in town. "Ever since we moved to the Gold Country, people have been coming to stay with us," says Jan, a former bookkeeper. "We just decided to make what we were used to doing into a business."

The Kendall House is full of surprises, including its own mysterious past. Nobody knows who built the home, or when, only that, according to city records, it dates to at least 1869 and may go back to the 1850s. Even the contour of the facility—two floors in the front and three in the back—is as unexpected as the amenities within. Entering the large wood-paneled living room, which doubles as a game room, you'll discover chess and other games, a library of leather-bound books, and paintings and sculptures fashioned by several of Dr. Kendall's patients. There's also a workout room with a weight machine and exercycle.

Four guest rooms are in the main house, and one is next door. All of them have queen-size beds and, according to Jan, reflect her "eclectic" taste. "I don't particularly like antiques," she explains. "Besides, everything I have will *eventually* be an antique." The home's Guest Room has country French chairs and other furniture, air conditioning, and a private bath with shower. If you like waking up to morning light, it's a "must try." Also upstairs in the main building is Leslie's Room, where the Kendall's daughter (now 22 and married) grew up. Highlights include white wicker furniture, private bath with tub, air conditioning, a reading nook, and a 19th-century chair, lamp table, and chaise longue.

Ted's old waiting room has been converted into the Garden Room. With a private entrance, deck, and even a partially draped platform bed, it has an almost secretive quality. Standouts here include a custom-made armoire and, right in the bedroom, an antique clawfoot tub. But the most elegant room is the Master Bedroom, on the main floor. In addition to a massive, built-in four-poster bed, guests will find a picture window sitting area, overhead fan, gas fireplace, private entrance, and extra large bathroom.

Outside in its own building next to the inn's spacious pool is a real treat. Called The Barn, what is now a guest room was built in 1923 to hold a cow belonging to the village's Cicigoni family. Today, though, instead of bovines or poultry, The Barn has its own kitchen, living room, second queen-size sofa bed and bedroom, wood-burning stove, air conditioning, and fan.

The main garden, above the pool area, is shaded by a large Scarlet oak and several nut trees. As for the pool itself, if you relish cool, invigorating water on a hot summer day, then just dive in.

Breakfast (two kinds of juice, apple crepes or other fruit, fresh breads, coffee, and tea, plus such offerings as banana nut pancakes, eggs Benedict, scrambled eggs with sausage or bacon, crustless quiche, or French toast) is served 8:30 to 10:00 on summer mornings, and 9:00 to 10:30 in winter on the enclosed veranda or in the dining room.

The Kendalls are equally spontaneous in their dealings with guests. They sometimes pop up complimentary popcorn in the evening. Some visitors, especially newlyweds, are rewarded with bottles of champagne. But everybody gets something special on the way out: a hug from Jan. "It's my way of saying I want you to come back," says the cofounder of one of California's most delightful inns.

Red Castle Inn

109 Prospect Street
Nevada City, California 95959; (916) 265-5135

INNKEEPERS: *Conley and Mary Louise Weaver.*

ACCOMMODATIONS: *Seven rooms, all with private bath; double and queen-size beds.*

RESERVATIONS: *Four weeks recommended.*

MINIMUM STAY: *Two nights on weekends (April through December) and over holiday periods.*

DEPOSIT: *First night's lodging.*

CREDIT CARDS: *MC, Visa.*

RATES: *Moderate.*

RESTRICTIONS: *Children discouraged. No pets.*

Imposing is the word for this baronial structure high on Prospect Hill, overlooking the historic Gold Rush town of Nevada City. Four stories high, it is also one of the few classic examples of Gothic Revival—as opposed to the more popular Carpenter Gothic—to be found in the Western states. (Gothic Revival was an architectural fashion in the United States from 1835 to 1880; the Red Castle was built in 1859-1860.) Extensive gardens and a pond enhance the castlelike effect; a pathway on the grounds winds to the town below.

At 2,800 feet, Nevada City was one of the first towns set up by the forty-niners, who came from all parts of the world looking for the legendary quick strike in the Mother Lode. (The Spanish called it the *Veta Madre*, and the name stuck.) Some in fact did make their fortunes in gold; others prospered by furnishing the Argonauts—the name by which the gold seekers were most frequently known in the 19th century—with basic goods and services. One man who did both was Judge John Williams. Crossing the plains in 1849, he stayed in the booming new city long enough to become a well-known businessman, mine owner, civic leader, and finally, judge. After two false starts he succeeded in erecting this monument to his industry. The Red Castle stands today as a reminder of the dreams of glory that motivated all who came to this near wilderness and stayed to carve out a new state.

Shortly after its 100th anniversary, the Red Castle was restored and turned into an inn. Conley and Mary Louise Weaver took possession of it in 1986. Conley, an architect by profession, not only appreciates the historical detail of the home but strives to preserve its romantic past as a registered state landmark.

The proprietors have followed a middle course in furnishings: authentic, but comfortable. The bathrooms retain the old-fashioned washbasins, but stall showers have been added. The original pine floors, grain-painted doors, and ceiling moldings are exactly as Judge Williams installed them; antiques of the period have been carefully selected for each room. Guest accommodations on the second floor are parlor suites, each containing a small sitting area as well as a bedroom and private bath. Rooms on the first floor open up onto a veranda, and there is a tastefully appointed parlor, complete with an 1880 Storey & Clark pump organ.

Breakfast is a full buffet served on weekends between 8:00 and 10:00 a.m.; weekdays at 9:00. Included are quiches, frittatas, and soufflés; hot and cold cereals; breads, muffins, and biscuits with homemade jam; and fruit dishes. After breakfast on Saturday, guests can take a horse-drawn carriage into town. The ride includes a capsule tour of the historic district along with Nevada City lore.

Nearby attractions include plenty of gold mines, as well as community theater, and river rafting trips. Classical music and bluegrass festivals (in neighboring Grass Valley) are presented each year. Both Tahoe National Forest and Soda Springs, a popular ski area and resort, are nearby as well.

Smithsonian magazine calls the Red Castle a "perfect restoration," and the Daughters of the Golden West have named it an important point of historical interest. It is an ideal spot to revel in the gingerbread facade and icicle trim of another era's architectural imagination, but also to relax in the comforts its present-day owners have given it.

Murphy's Inn

318 Neal Street
Grass Valley, California 95945; (916) 273-6873

INNKEEPERS: *Tom and Sue Myers.*

ACCOMMODATIONS: *Eight rooms, all with private bath; queen- and king-size beds.*

RESERVATIONS: *Four to six weeks recommended for summer weekends.*

MINIMUM STAY: *Two nights on weekends and over holiday periods.*

DEPOSIT: *First night's lodging.*

CREDIT CARDS: *AE, MC, Visa.*

RATES: *Moderate.*

RESTRICTIONS: *Children: negotiable. No pets.*

Murphy's Inn was originally the opulent estate of gold baron Edward Coleman, owner of the North Star and Idaho mines. Today, this showplace of the northern Gold Country, an 1866 Colonial Revival house, looks almost as it did in century-old etchings. Ivy still pours from baskets on the huge, wraparound veranda. Vines still twine up the porch's stately white columns. And a majestic sequoia tree still stands sentinel-like in the front yard.

Crossing the threshold of the two-story home, you'll find two sitting rooms with marble and antique tile fireplaces and cherrywood and oak mantels. The pride of the three guest rooms downstairs is Theodosia's Suite, which, for honeymooners, comes with a complimentary bottle of champagne. If you arrive on a cold night, you'll be impressed to notice the fireplace already lit. The window seat holds a treasure trove of old magazines, such as a 1929 *Harpers* and a 1948 *Life*. Together with an antique vanity and a large library arranged by topic, the suite even has a king-size brass bed surrounded by lace curtains.

Of the four upstairs rooms, the guest favorite is the spacious East Room, which features a mahogany four-poster bed, platform rocking chair, antique dressing table and, best of all, a skylight right in the shower. Would you prefer having an entire penthouse to yourself? Then you might consider staying in the inn's Donation Day House. The sprawling top floor of the house includes French doors that separate a private sitting area from the bedroom with its king-size white iron bed and wood-burning stove.

Following a toasty night in the Gold Country, you may not even feel like leaving your room. One whiff of the inn's country breakfast, however, should be enough to lure you out. Fresh orange juice; freshly ground coffee; coddled eggs, omelettes, or eggs Benedict with hollandaise sauce; sausage; fresh fruit compote; homemade lemon or poppyseed bread; and blueberry muffins are just some of the palate-pleasers to expect.

After breakfast, if you're in the mood for a little exercise, put on your walking shoes for a historical tour of Grass Valley or take a short drive to do the same thing in nearby Nevada City. The area bulges with fine restaurants, saloons, museums, and monuments, such as Empire Mine State Park and the Malakoff Diggings.

Upon your return, you'll want to laze the rest of the day away, dividing your time between a rest in the inn's hammock, or, if it's hot outside, a dip in the 16-foot-long modern swim-spa. At night, it doubles as a hot tub that will leave you so relaxed they may have to come and fish you out.

American River Inn

Main and Orleans streets
P.O. Box 43
Georgetown, California 95634; (916) 333-4499

INNKEEPERS: *Will and Maria Collin.*

ACCOMMODATIONS: *25 rooms, 19 with private bath; twin and queen-size beds.*

RESERVATIONS: *Two to three weeks recommended.*

MINIMUM STAY: *None.*

DEPOSIT: *First night's lodging.*

CREDIT CARDS: *AE, DC, MC, Visa.*

RATES: *Moderate.*

RESTRICTIONS: *No children under 10. No pets.*

Georgetown is one of those Gold Country villages that seem to exist in more than one time, the modern starkly accented by visible reminders of the Old West. Cars are parked along the main street—part of which still has the old wooden sidewalk—but it isn't unusual to see a horse tethered in front of a saloon. It was once a place of quick (if not particularly easy) money, supported by the Woodside Mine, estimated to have brought in $2 million in gold by the spring of 1853. Directly behind the mine was a spacious rooming house for miners, later a pleasure house with gambling and ladies of the night. Lola Montez, the legendary "spider dancer," once entertained here, according to local history.

The rooming house was also used as a way station by stagecoaches on the Wentworth Springs route to Tahoe. First finished in 1853, the house suffered at least three fires that razed the town during the 1880s, never quite succumbing but requiring partial renovation each time. In recent years it was a private residence and was allowed to decline.

Restoration of this historic structure turned out to be more difficult than anyone could have predicted. Will and Maria Collin only managed to finally finish it with help from their friends. The exterior has now been painted ivory with Wedgwood blue trim, and a redwood deck was added on. Inside, the red-fir floors have been stripped and refinished, and a floor-to-ceiling rock fireplace was built from native stone. Four cramped rooms downstairs were turned into two; upstairs guest rooms have been furnished with wainscoting, crown moldings, and ornamental mopboards. Victorian antiques, including brass beds and massive armoires, fill all guest rooms.

Breakfast at the American River Inn is always a treat. Maria makes it a point never to serve any guest the same breakfast twice. The morning I was there I was privileged to receive quiche Lorraine, Canadian bacon, blueberry muffins, orange juice, and cinnamon-flavored coffee.

Guests may relax in either the dining room or the parlor with its Franklin stove and player piano. Outside is an aviary, a vegetable garden, a swimming pool, and a heated Jacuzzi. The inn offers both croquet and horseshoes; also available for guest use are bicycles and an outdoor barbecue.

Nearby attractions include 12 lakes "up country," good fishing, white-water rafting, and gold panning. But this is essentially a place to get away from activities, not to pursue new ones. Let's just say that if you're feeling lost, the American River Inn is a place where you can begin to find your way back.

The Coloma Country Inn

345 High Street
P.O. Box 502
Coloma, California 95613; (916) 622-6919

INNKEEPERS: *Alan and Cindi Ehrgott.*

ACCOMMODATIONS: *Seven rooms, five with private bath; double and queen-size beds.*

RESERVATIONS: *Four to six weeks recommended.*

MINIMUM STAY: *Two nights through holiday periods.*

DEPOSIT: *First night's lodging or half total amount.*

CREDIT CARDS: *None.*

RATES: *Moderate.*

RESTRICTIONS: *No pets.*

It's been a long time since I got the goosebumps, but such was the case as I drove down California's Highway 49 through a portion of the 300-acre Coloma Gold Discovery State Historic Park. It was here at Sutter's Mill in 1848 that the cry "Eureka, I've found gold" rang out. Today, the quaint village of Coloma is a shadow of its former self, but it still retains working blacksmith, gunsmith, and tinsmith shops, a one-room schoolhouse, historical museums, and a re-creation of the old-time mill.

Situated on the south fork of the American River, and smack-dab in the middle of all this, is The Coloma Country Inn bed and breakfast. What a location! The inn lends itself to the perfect romantic tryst or full-fledged family vacation. Innkeepers Alan and Cindi Ehrgott provide afternoon refreshments—iced tea and lemonade—in the garden gazebo and bicycles for guests who disdain quieter pastimes like feeding the ducks or catnapping on the front porch.

Alan is a certified hot air balloon pilot with 10 years' experience lifting people out of their doldrums to dizzying heights of up to 2,000 feet above the spectacular American River canyon. If arising at dawn isn't your cup of tea, consider a thrill-a-minute one- or two-day white-water rafting trip. Your host will be happy to make these arrangements for you in advance of your stay.

Built in 1852, The Coloma Country Inn is decorated with American antiques, primitives, handmade quilts, and old-fashioned stenciling. Five guest rooms contained in the New England-style country farmhouse have antique beds and private sitting areas; three have private baths with old-fashioned clawfoot tub/showers. Two newly constructed suites (ideal for families) are located in a circa 1890 carriage house.

If you neglect to mention that you would like breakfast served to the room, simply join the others in the dining area with its view of the pond. The inn's late checkout allows you to linger over fresh fruits in season and homemade baked goods, scrambled eggs or cheese omelettes, orange juice, and French roast coffee. Use any spare time to browse through Coloma Country Inn's extensive collection of "Gold Rush days" pictures and books.

🐌

The Chichester-McKee House

800 Spring Street
Placerville, California 95667
(916) 626-1882 or (800) 831-4008

INNKEEPERS: *Bill and Doreen Thornhill.*
ACCOMMODATIONS: *Three rooms, each with half-bath; twin and queen-size beds.*
RESERVATIONS: *Three to four weeks recommended.*
MINIMUM STAY: *None.*
DEPOSIT: *First night's lodging.*
CREDIT CARDS: *AE, DC, MC, Visa.*
RATES: *Moderate.*
RESTRICTIONS: *No pets.*

Though the glittering gold mines of California attracted fortune seekers by the thousands, not many of them were easily lured to a spot with a name like Hangtown. So Hangtown, where some of the ore was found right in the dry ground (and, hence, did not require much work to extract), changed its name to Dry Diggins. Unfortunately, more than one adventurer thought this meant the local mines had gone "dry." It was a smart developer who soon came up with an even better title for the budding municipality: he dubbed it Placerville.

As the name stuck, Placerville's luck began to change. Miners started flocking to it by the hundreds. Millions of dollars worth of the shiny yellow metal was taken out of the Goldbug Mine alone, one of more than 200 claims within an easy walk of today's Chichester-McKee House.

But even more money was to be made right in town, by selling goods and supplies to the ever-burgeoning tide of humanity. In the summer of 1892, D. W. Chichester, a partner in the S. G. Beach Company Mill and Lumberyard, built this impressive, two-story Queen Anne Victorian for his wife, Caroline. As it was being constructed, the *Mountain Democrat* newspaper predicted it would surely be "the finest residence in Placerville."

Today, you can not only relive Hangtown's Gold Rush era by staying in the Chichester mansion, which is surrounded by many other stunning Victorians, but also, incredibly, enjoy some of the "improvements" that

Chichester, one of the area's most prosperous business-men, brought to his city. The house still has the town's first footed tub, its first hand-held shower, and its first indoor sink, as well as its own plant-filled conservatory and a library with a built-in seat for reading and nook where you could place your candle (now occupied by a potted plant).

Welcome to the abode of innkeepers Doreen and Bill Thornhill, who have their own amazing story to tell. In 1990, the two vacationing Kansans were driving along Highway 49 when they spied the pretty yellow house with a "For Sale" sign on it. They stopped by, intending to ask for a floor plan to copy. But when Doreen turned to Bill and said, "There's no way we could build something like this," he replied, "Then I guess we'll have to buy it."

In addition to the conservatory, library, cozy parlor room (with a native Mariposa slate, wood-burning fireplace), antique "storybook doll collection," and the century-old tulip tree in the yard, the Chichester-McKee offers three treasures.

Guests can stay in the McKee Room which boasts carved wood furniture in the Eastlake style, an English armoire, cranberry Oriental rug, and a crocheted bedspread over a cranberry comforter; the Carson Room, with a brass bed, handmade Mennonite quilt in a peach and blue Lone Star pattern, English armoire, and an Illinois hotel combination dresser/washstand; or Yellow Rose Room, where Flossy, an old-fashioned Wolf dressform with an early 1900s dress, will greet them. The room also has an Amish oak bed with a handmade fishnet canopy, oak dresser, and bay window. All the rooms have queen-size beds and half-baths; the Yellow Rose also has a twin bed and a sink from a 1930 Pullman train.

For breakfast (8:00 to 9:00 a.m. in the dining room) expect eggs Benedict, spinach-mushroom crepes, or ham and asparagus quiche; coffeecake; four kinds of muffins; fresh fruit (or, in the cold months, baked apples or fruit compote); orange, grapefruit, or mixed juices (plus, in fall, locally made apple cider); hot chocolate, tea, and Bill's special blend of coffee. After dinner (your best bet is to stroll a block and a half to historic downtown Placerville) check for Doreen's scrumptious caramel brownies, a homemade specialty. She usually brings them out after everyone has gone off to explore "Hangtown" restaurants. "I love surprising people," she admits, "but no, I won't give out the recipe."

Indian Creek Bed & Breakfast

21950 Highway 49
Plymouth, California 95669
(209) 245-4648 or (800)-24-CREEK

INNKEEPERS: *Geof Denny and Jay Cusker.*

ACCOMMODATIONS: *Four rooms, all with private bath; queen-size beds.*

RESERVATIONS: *One month recommended.*

MINIMUM STAY: *None.*

DEPOSIT: *First night's lodging.*

CREDIT CARDS: *DC, MC, Visa.*

RATES: *Moderate.*

RESTRICTIONS: *Not suitable for children. No pets.*

In 1932 Hollywood producer Arthur Hamberger built this beautiful log home for his newly-married son and bride, Margaret Breen, a former Ziegfeld Follies girl. Hollywood's elite—Ginger Rogers, John Wayne—would gather here for relaxing weekends in the country. While a log house might bring to mind images of rustic country living, in its own right, this "humble" abode could rival many a Beverly Hills mansion.

Evocative of another era, Indian Creek has walls of pine logs and floors of highly polished fir. Interior spaces are an eclectic blend of Southwestern-style furnishings mixed with Asian appointments. In the main room a pair of Japanese carved wood temple statues stand guard near a massive floor-to-ceiling quartz rock fireplace; the room itself is nearly 60 feet long with an awe-inspiring 25-foot ceiling with majestic log beamed rafters. The dining room's log ceiling is arranged in a spoke pattern design which is echoed in a brass accented wagon wheel chandelier. The room's English refectory table and Windsor chairs sit poised on a Southwestern area rug. A dramatic fir splitwood staircase with manzanita wood railing leads the way to a sweeping balcony and the inn's four guest rooms.

Reflecting the personalities of the women they were named for, each of the bedrooms has its own distinctive character. The Joan Elaine (named for innkeeper Jay Cusker's mother) is a creamy white sea of Battenberg lace with a draped ceiling and Victorian wicker furniture. One full wall is a painted aspen grove trompe l'oeil. A pine fireplace completes this bedroom's romantic appeal. The Juli Ann (Jay's sister) is like a breath of fresh air with its rag-rolled walls in three shades of lavender. The bedspread is covered with violet nosegays, and completing the theme, decoupage violets grace the bathroom walls. The Elizabeth Ann honors Geof Denny's sister's love of horses. Hunter green walls provide a rich background for the demi-canopied brass bed covered with a rose-embellished bedspread. Matted hunting scene prints and hand-painted furniture give the room an elegant sporty feel. The Jami Beth (Jay's sister) is the inn's secret rose garden. A pink haze of sponge-painted walls provide a perfect backdrop for the bed's pale green wrought iron headboard. The cozy room reflects the owners' sense of whimsy: a Suffolk sheep doll is perched on an antique Belgian chair busily knitting her own wool.

Ever the perfect hosts, Geof and Jay believe that breakfast should be served to accommodate their guests' schedules. A typical menu might include eggs Benedict or lemon soufflé pancakes, rosemary potatoes, fresh seasonal fruit (pears, bananas, apricots), and one of Geof's special home-made muffins (chewy orange with raisins are a favorite) served with dark rich coffee or your choice of herbal teas. Your breakfast menu is carefully recorded to ensure that on your next visit you are served a new fare.

After breakfast, the Victorian-style sunroom, filled with plants and fresh herbs, is an ideal lazy-time spot. Snuggle in the clawfoot overstuffed cabbage print sofa while you read one of the books from the inn's collection. Later in the afternoon refreshments are available: ice-cold lemonade or iced tea served with irresistible hot artichoke dip.

The inn, which sits on the site of a former gold mine, is situated on 10 wooded acres lush with California oaks, digger pines, live oak, and manzanita trees. The wet set will appreciate the outdoor hot tub and swimming pool. After a dip in the pool, take a stroll to the Japanese rock garden or one of the two fish ponds.

The Foxes

77 Main Street
Sutter Creek, California 95685; (209) 267-5882

INNKEEPERS: *Pete and Min Fox.*

ACCOMMODATIONS: *Six suites, all with private bath; queen-size beds.*

RESERVATIONS: *Three months recommended for summer weekends.*

MINIMUM STAY: *Two nights over weekends and holiday periods.*

DEPOSIT: *First night's lodging.*

CREDIT CARDS: *DC, MC, Visa.*

RATES: *Moderate.*

RESTRICTIONS: *No children. No pets.*

This is one of those places that, at first glance, reminds you of the European bed and breakfast spots. But it's more than just a couple of spare rooms; these are luxury suites, each intended to accommodate two people.

This charming two-story Victorian was once known locally as the Brinn House. It was built in 1857 and purchased by Morris Brinn and his brother in 1865. Like so many who prospered during the Gold Rush, they sought their fortunes not in mines and gold pans, but in supplying the miners with the basic necessities of life in a gold camp. They owned a dry goods store in Sutter Creek, and a fairly large one at that. Their fine home has a definite New England flavor to it, typical of many of the old homes in this area and reflecting the origins of many of the settlers.

What is remarkable is that this quintessential Gold Rush Victorian was allowed to stand vacant for 25 years. In the 1960s it was rescued by a couple who began its restoration; later it was owned by another couple who continued the work and served lunch in a luncheon room in the building. The Foxes have now had it for 14 years, and the old Brinn residence has never looked better in its 137 years.

A typical accommodation at The Foxes is exemplified by the Victorian Suite, which consists of a sitting room, a bedroom, and a private bath. The bed in this particular room has an amazing nine-foot-high headboard, and there is a matching marble-topped dresser, also nine feet tall, of walnut and walnut burl, circa 1875. The hand-crocheted bedspread is coordinated with an antique floral-stripe wallpaper and ecru eyelet drapes. There is a Queen Anne love seat in the sitting room; another Queen Anne piece— a fine writing desk—doubles as a breakfast table.

Breakfast arrangements with the Foxes are quite flexible. "Since there are only six couples to consider," Min says, "we can talk about it once they get here." Usual breakfast fare might include juice, fresh fruits, eggs with ham or bacon, sourdough French toast or Swedish pancakes, and a hot beverage of your choice.

Both Min and husband Pete come from Orange County. They got into the bed and breakfast business almost by accident. Pete had been in real estate for many years and envisioned the Brinn place as a possible office. The couple selling the house liked the Foxes' plan to open an antique shop there, but also spoke glowingly of the possibility of furnishing and renting a suite upstairs.

It was a natural. Min Fox remembers her first customer well. A neighboring innkeeper called to say that a honeymoon couple had reserved a room with her, but in the bustle and rush of wedding arrangements had forgotten to mail their deposit. Could the Foxes put them up for a night? They could and did. The next morning the bride and bridegroom watched the annual Italian Picnic Day parade from the Foxes' porch. "They got very emotional when they left," Min recalls. "They came back for their first wedding anniversary, and have been back every year since."

There is nothing like a bed and breakfast inn to launch a new marriage—or to invigorate one that has been around awhile. And there is no inn that I would recommend more highly for this than The Foxes.

Court Street Inn

215 Court Street
Jackson, California 95642; (209) 223-0416

INNKEEPERS: *Janet and Lee Hammond; Scott and Gia Anderson.*

ACCOMMODATIONS: *Seven rooms, three with private bath; double and queen-size beds.*

RESERVATIONS: *Three to four weeks recommended.*

MINIMUM STAY: *None.*

DEPOSIT: *First night's lodging.*

CREDIT CARDS: *MC, Visa.*

RATES: *Moderate.*

RESTRICTIONS: *No pets.*

The main part of this house was built in 1870 by Edward Muldoon, a mine owner, saloon keeper, and rancher on what was then called Corral Hill. Muldoon sold the home to the Isaac Peiser family in 1874, and just three short years later, Mr. Peiser and his young son died, victims of diphtheria. The remainder of the Peiser family continued to reside here until around 1900 when the house was again sold, to George and Emily Blair (who owned the Jackson Water Works) and their daughter Grace Blair Depue.

The Miwok Indians in this area were frequently unable to pay their water bills in cash, so they made payments in the form of baskets and other artifacts. Grace Depue kept the collection in a brick house in the Blairs' backyard (now called the Indian House, where two of the inn's guest rooms are located). In her will she donated the collection to the University of California at Berkeley; at the time of her death it was appraised at $90,000. In this way a priceless collection of Miwok folk art was preserved for the enjoyment of all Californians.

Janet and Lee Hammond appreciated Court Street Inn's colorful history when they first heard it because they are also voracious art and antique collectors. For over 20 years Lee Hammond gathered items in anticipation of opening an old-fashioned country store. Instead, his six-foot, glass-fronted oak deli case now serves as a wine rack, the 1920s grocery store scale holds a welcome decanter of creme de menthe, and a vintage brass cash register and 1910 coffee grinder act as dining room accent pieces at the Hammonds' and Andersons' bed and breakfast inn.

In the parlor there's a unique 1910 baby grand player piano and an Indiana Amish country trunk full of antique piano scrolls. The unusual tin ceilings in the parlor, as well as the dining room and hallways, are original to the home.

Down comforters and pillows adorn antique beds situated in each of the inn's seven guest rooms. Additionally, all of the rooms are air conditioned in summer, and most have ceiling fans. My favorite accommodation at Court Street, which is now on the National Register of Historic Places, is undoubtedly the Peiser Room. It has its own sun porch and sitting area, as well as a half canopy queen-size bed, oak vanity and mirror, turn-of-the-century cast-iron shoeshine stand, and antique dental chair.

Along with their valuable collection of antiques, the inn-keepers are heralded for their delicious full breakfast. Crab custard casserole or seafood stuffed pastry rings are accompanied by cheese and sour cream potatoes, a fruit compote, and fresh pork sausages or Canadian bacon. A one-time-only seating is scheduled in the dining room at 9:00 a.m.

At 6:00 p.m. it's back to the dining room again, only this time for hot stuffed mushrooms, fresh artichoke spread, Brie cheese, or sweet and sour meatballs, crackers, and zesty crab dip.

The fabulous food is made especially enjoyable by the friendly companionship of your innkeepers (an extended family group), and even sometimes the inn's reputed ghost. Janet tells an eerie story about wanting a cup of tea one afternoon. "When I walked into the kitchen, my cup was sitting out and the teakettle was already turned on! For a long time I thought it was probably Mrs. Blair's ghost. But then we had a woman who stayed overnight in the Peiser Room. She claims to have heard a little boy crying. Aha, I thought, it must be Mr. Peiser's four-year-old son, Abby." Haunting questions—and ones that may never be answered. But that's not to say they shouldn't be mulled over when guests convene for a glass of iced tea on the inn's front porch.

The Wedgewood Inn

11941 Narcissus Road
Jackson, California 95642
(209) 296-4300 or (800) 933-4393

INNKEEPERS: *Vic and Jeannine Beltz.*

ACCOMMODATIONS: *Six rooms, all with private bath; queen-size beds.*

RESERVATIONS: *Three to four weeks recommended.*

MINIMUM STAY: *None.*

DEPOSIT: *First night's lodging.*

CREDIT CARDS: *MC, Visa.*

RATES: *Moderate.*

RESTRICTIONS: *Not suitable for children under 12. No pets.*

Distinguished as one of the top 50 inns in America by *Inn Times'* annual guest survey, the Wedgewood is a pristine country Victorian replica set on five wooded acres just 10 minutes east of Jackson.

Owners Vic and Jeannine Beltz were on an extended vacation through the New England states when the idea of bed and breakfast took hold. "Vic was working for IBM, but he wanted to take an early retirement," Jeannine mentioned. "As a former stay-at-home mom with a lifetime of entertaining behind me, I figured that innkeeping was not really much different than what I had already done.

From Vic's handcrafted stained glass to Jeannine's stylish Victorian lamp shades, the Beltzes' newly constructed Queen Anne is the perfect showcase for their creative talents. Needlework that appears in pictures, pillowcases, tapestries, quilts, and afghans is illustrative of what Jeannine does to occupy her spare time. Home furnishings here are primarily European and American antiques; the Austrian grand piano that dominates the front parlor frequently inspires guest sing-alongs.

A stroll through the richly landscaped and carefully tended grounds reveals a rose arbor and Victorian-style gazebo. Benches, hammocks, and a porch swing also provide plenty of opportunity to relax out-of-doors. A carriage house, with south side showroom, holds "Henry," the couple's 1921 Model T Ford. The north side of the carriage house is a guest cottage which displays four generations of family heirlooms: portraits, clothing, and childhood dolls and toys. The suite also has a carved walnut canopied bed, walnut game table, love seat sofa, old-fashioned rocker, and wood-burning stove.

I selected the Wedgewood Cameo room for my overnighter. Its bay window looks out to the wooded hillsides and gardens below. French and English carved wood furnishings and marble top tables are accented by white eyelet and Wedgwood blue fabrics. As the evening was a bit chilly, I particularly enjoyed the warmth of the room's wood-burning stove.

There is also a newly installed woodstove in Granny's Attic. This room, with sky blue and peach accents, has a vaulted ceiling and skylight. Furnishings include a four-poster bed, walnut writing desk, gentleman's armchair, and spindle rocker. The popular Victorian Rose room is elegantly appointed with an English bedroom set, round walnut table, and tapestry-covered chairs. Country Pine's antique iron scroll bed faces bay windows with a forest view; a finial scroll four-poster characterizes the Heritage Oak room.

The Wedgewood's policy of providing fresh-ground Colombian coffee to the upstairs hall table two hours prior to the 9:00 a.m. breakfast is a godsend to coffee addicts like myself. The candlelit morning meal begins with a blessing. The first course is dessert: usually fresh fruit topped with raspberry sorbet or a baked apple with cinnamon-coated walnuts and a scoop of French vanilla ice cream. Eggs a là Wedgewood (a crustless quiche filled with bacon or broccoli) are served with homemade banana pecan muffins or almond poppyseed cake. Between 3:00 and 6:00 p.m., Jeannine offers a complimentary beverage and cheese and fruit platter.

The Heirloom

214 Shakeley Lane
Ione, California 95640; (209) 274-4468

INNKEEPERS: *Patricia Cross and Melisande Hubbs.*

ACCOMMODATIONS: *Four rooms, two with private bath; twin, double, queen-, and king-size beds. A two-guest-room adobe cottage, each room with private bath.*

RESERVATIONS: *Two to three weeks recommended.*

MINIMUM STAY: *None.*

DEPOSIT: *First night's lodging.*

CREDIT CARDS: *Not accepted.*

RATES: *Inexpensive to moderate.*

RESTRICTIONS: *No pets.*

Part of California's fascination is due to the diversity of its people. This is reflected in its variety of architectural styles—particularly in the Gold Country, where people from many parts of the country converged at once. A good example of this is The Heirloom, a bed and breakfast inn in Ione. Obviously built by a Southerner, this two-story brick colonial mansion with an antebellum arch replicates perfectly the prevailing fashion in the South before the Civil War.

Built in 1863 by a Virginian, who also built another Southern-style mansion in Ione, the structure was soon purchased by Dr. Luther Brusi, who in 1870 was a veteran of the Confederacy. He must have felt very much at home in this lovely dream house, with its stately columns, verandas, and white-wood balconies. Some time later it was sold to James and Catherine Browning (Catherine remained here until 1923); James was associated with the famous Browning rifle company.

The house was purchased by Patricia Cross and Melisande Hubbs in 1980. Both had been looking around Sonoma and Carmel for a dwelling appropriate for a bed and breakfast, when they heard of this place. Ione is somewhat off the tourist track: It was never a boom town but served as a supply center for the mining camps. Yet when they saw this undeniably breathtaking structure, they knew it was the right one for them.

All windows are deep-set in the Southern style. (The house and garden are completely hidden from public view by shrubs and trees.) The front entrance boasts a fan transom. The living room is completely paneled in wood painted off-white, as was the custom in early days. The high ceiling and paneled windows draped in gold brocade, stained pine floor with area rugs, and colonial staircase and mantel are an elegant background to the antique furnishings in this very livable mansion.

One of the pieces Pat and Melisande are most proud of is their grand piano, once the possession of Lola Montez, famed Gold Rush queen of Grass Valley. This instrument has an offset keyboard and heavy, beautifully carved rosewood legs.

The rooms are named for the seasons. The Winter Room has a fireplace; burgundy and pale blue tones predominate. The Spring Room, in yellow and green, has lovely handmade quilts, a wingback upholstered chair, and a nice Queen Anne desk. The Autumn Room has a brass bed, a comforter, and pillow shams with matching duet ruffles. The Summer Room features pink rose wallpaper and a double Eastlake walnut bed. (This room also has a private bath.) Guest rooms in the handcrafted adobe cottage offer the campfire aroma of a wood-burning stove and the romance of moonbeams dancing across the skylights.

Pat and Melisande are quite flexible toward guests; one is not encumbered with a surfeit of rules and regulations here. "I like to see the tension melt out of people's faces after they've been in the country awhile," says Melisande.

Refreshments are served in the afternoon, and guests find fresh flowers, fruit, and candy in their rooms. Breakfast is full—and very generous. On a typical morning you will receive fresh-squeezed orange juice, crepes with fresh fruit topping, popovers and croissants, Brie cheese, and gourmet coffee. In keeping with the Southern theme, Pat and Melisande usually serve breakfast wearing long aprons and skirts, adding to the sense of calm and antebellum luxury that is so much a part of The Heirloom.

Dunbar House, 1880

271 Jones Street
P.O. Box 1375
Murphys, California 95247
(209) 728-2897 or (800) 225-3764,
ext. 321

INNKEEPERS: *Bob and Barbara Costa.*

ACCOMMODATIONS: *Four rooms, all with private bath; queen-size beds.*

RESERVATIONS: *Five weeks recommended.*

MINIMUM STAY: *Two nights on weekends.*

DEPOSIT: *First night's lodging.*

CREDIT CARDS: *MC, Visa.*

RATES: *Moderate.*

RESTRICTIONS: *No children under 10. No pets.*

This lovely Italianate Victorian with its white siding and blue shuttered windows, wraparound veranda, and white picket fence reminds one of a set from an old Western and was, in fact, used in filming the television version of MGM's *Seven Brides for Seven Brothers*. It reflects the character of Willis Dunbar, a man of means who built the home for his bride, Ellen, in 1880. Dunbar was a prominent citizen in the community, a superintendent of the water company, and at one time served a turn in the State Assembly. Murphys was a boom town then, a magnet drawing fortune seekers who discovered some of Calaveras County's richest placer gold claims here. Today historical Main Street, just steps from the inn, affords seekers of a different sort a well-preserved glimpse into the past of this Queen of the Sierra.

For Bob and Barbara Costa the flight to Murphys killed two birds with one stone. They wanted to live in the Gold Country and, having inn-hopped their way around the world, wanted to own a bed and breakfast. When this property, which was already an inn, came up for sale, they couldn't say no. Bob is active with the Murphys Fire Department, and Barbara is president of the Calaveras County Lodging Association. Both are interested in preserving the historic heritage of their newly adopted hometown.

The four guest rooms here have country antiques and treasured family pieces. Flowers and doilies are much in evidence; beds are turned down while guests are out to dinner. Down comforters and wood-burning stoves will keep you warm here in winter; there is air conditioning throughout the inn for that hot summer weather. Handicrafts and original watercolors scattered around the house show off the talents of local artists. Books, games, and a stereo are located in the parlor (guest rooms are now furnished with televisions and VCRs). Old photographs of the Dunbar family and of historical events pertinent to the house grace the walls of the entryway.

Breakfast is served between 8:30 and 9:30 a.m., but the coffee is always ready an hour earlier. Egg dishes—from crepes to frittatas—are accompanied by fresh fruit, home-baked quick breads or muffins, juice, and coffee or tea. Guests have the option of being served in their room, the dining room, on the porch, or in the garden.

A side table full of brochures advertising area attractions sits by the door. Pick up a few on your way out, as I'm sure you'll want to get a good start on the day. I'd recommend a couple of hours at Calaveras Big Trees State Park; stop at the Quyle Kilns on your way up to buy some local pottery. Moaning Cavern and Mercer Caverns offer guided tours; six wineries in the area now have tasting rooms; downhill and cross-country skiing is just 45 minutes away; antique and gift shops, as well as fine dining, are just a block's walk. Annual celebrations include St. Patrick's Day, the Murphys Homecoming in July, an Oktoberfest, and performances by the Black Bart Players in April and November.

Llamahall Guest Ranch

18170 Wards Ferry Road
Sonora, California 95370; (209) 532-7264

INNKEEPER: *Cindy Hall.*

ACCOMMODATIONS: *Two rooms, each with private bath; twin and queen-size beds.*

RESERVATIONS: *Two to three weeks recommended.*

MINIMUM STAY: *Two nights over holiday periods.*

DEPOSIT: *First night's lodging.*

CREDIT CARDS: *Not accepted.*

RATES: *Moderate.*

RESTRICTIONS: *No pets.*

Now *here* is a stay with a difference—Llamahall Guest Ranch, home of Cindy Hall, her son, and their twenty-some pet llamas.

There is so much to be said about this bed and breakfast's wholesome country environment: the quiet, the lovable llamas (which guests are encouraged to feed, play with, and pet), a barbecue pit, a hot tub and sauna, a piano and a guitar, fishing and gold panning on the creek that borders the property, a virtually untraveled road for jogging, and horseshoes and volleyball. Several cats, croaking frogs, and a host of other animals (squirrels, gophers, lizards, ducks, and geese) are around to keep you company. A red-tailed hawk lives here and blue heron frequent the pond. And you can not only bring the kids, you're encouraged to. Need I say more?

Guest rooms are on the lower level of the house, ideally situated for a family vacation. Each has its own private entrance, private bath, and both queen- and twin-size beds. Flora, the room that faces the garden, is papered with a deep green raspberry-bramble pattern. Its ceiling fan revolves at a snail's pace, and the tub was especially sculptured for two. Fauna, the room I spent the night in, had a brass bed with a white eyelet comforter and matching pillow shams, a marble-topped table, chairs, and an armoire. The bath featured a clawfoot tub with brass fixtures and shower head. Long-range plans call for two additional upstairs guest rooms.

This all-redwood ranch house, built only 20 years ago, is a showpiece of area craftsmanship. Its living room, which is open to overnight guests, is stocked with puzzles, games, and books as well as toys, musical instruments, and a stereo. There is a rocking chair and a fireplace; oak paneling and a beamed ceiling complete the warm, homey scene.

The substantial ranch-house breakfast consists of granola, eggs, bran muffins with butter, jam, and cream cheese, and a fresh fruit plate. Beverages include coffee, tea, and freshly squeezed orange juice.

Cindy can arrange to get you theater tickets or put together a weekend ski package; her expertise is also handy for personalizing your Gold Country sightseeing tour.

The Ryan House, 1855

153 South Shepherd Street
Sonora, California 95370; (209) 533-3445

INNKEEPERS: *Nancy and Guy Hoffman.*

ACCOMMODATIONS: *Four rooms, all with private bath; queen-size beds.*

RESERVATIONS: *Three to four weeks recommended.*

MINIMUM STAY: *Two nights over holiday periods and some special event weekends.*

DEPOSIT: *Full amount.*

CREDIT CARDS: *MC, Visa.*

RATES: *Moderate.*

RESTRICTIONS: *No pets.*

Have you ever wondered if *everybody* lived in elegant, grand Victorians back in the 1800s? If you're a bed and breakfast fan, then you can find the answer to the question in the town of Sonora, where there's a wonderful inn that is very historic—it dates to 1855—but cannot be considered "stately." Part of the delight of staying in The Ryan House, just three blocks from downtown, is that it "feels" authentic: as if an average, well-off citizen lived here rather than a tycoon.

The other great thing about the home, which has housed three generations of the Ryan family, is that it seems bursting with original artifacts. From the 144-year-old roses outside (look for the bush with the gnarly trunks, and yes, they are still baring) to son Joe Ryan's 1883 junior high school notebook (in those days it was called a "journal") with a history lesson ("The Persian army . . . was defeated with arduous slaughtering") in the library parlor, innkeepers Nancy and Guy Hoffman have been keeping "living history" alive and well in the Gold Country.

For example, while a modern dishwasher is carefully hidden in the kitchen, the Hoffmans have been careful to preserve the Ryans' original handmade windows (none of which match), the home's original square nails, and the cement slab with the names of the Ryan children still inscribed.

Visitors step back in time as soon as they come through the front door into first the kitchen and then the front parlor, one of three in the house. (In addition to the library parlor, the upstairs suite has one.) The pellet-burning stove and carpet are new but the chair and love seat (from the 1870s), together with the rest of the furniture, are Victorians.

Walk up the stairs and you'll come to the suite, which features a cherry and maple table from Vermont that's been in Nancy's family for more than a century, a Primitive-style pine cradle with bonnet top, white iron queen-size bed with brass trim, and private bath with a soaking tub that's big enough for two. From the suite's parlor, complete with its own pellet stove, you can see St. Patrick's Catholic Church (from 1863), another bit of Sonora history that, like Ryan House, withstood several fires that ravaged the town during its early years.

Downstairs, there are three bedrooms, each with brass queen-size beds and private baths, including antique pedestal washbasins. The Lavender Room, which is actually burgundy, has a four-poster bed; English Oak Barley Twist-style tables, side chair, and dresser; and one of the oldest objects in the house, an 1850 English armoire. The Mae Kelly Room, named after the last member of the Ryan clan to live here (she was the city librarian for 28 years), holds a hand-carved walnut bed and walnut furniture, including a dresser with brown marble top and another English armoire dating back to the last century. And the Colonial Room, done in shades of blue in the back of the house off the dining room, sports a stunning Bentwood armchair, as well as yet another 1800s English armoire.

As for the wake-up meal, look for it in the dining room about 9:00 a.m. A recent example of the full sit-down extravaganza included eggs Florentine, two homemade coffeecakes (fruit and oatmeal), fresh orange juice, a bowl of cut melons and peaches, fresh coffee, an assortment of 12 teas, and Nancy's delicious scones. In the afternoon, the Hoffmans put out sherry and port, soft drinks, and iced tea.

The area also sizzles with many fun activities. Ryan House is just three miles from both Columbia State Historic Park and Railtown, an 1897 state historic park; 30 miles from Dodge Ridge Ski Resort; and a two-hour drive from Yosemite National Park.

Oak Hill Ranch

18550 Connally Lane
P.O. Box 307
Tuolumne, California 95379; (209) 928-4717

INNKEEPERS: *Sandy and Jane Grover.*

ACCOMMODATIONS: *Five rooms, three with private bath; double and queen-size beds.*

RESERVATIONS: *Three to four weeks recommended.*

MINIMUM STAY: *Two nights over holiday periods.*

DEPOSIT: *First night's lodging.*

CREDIT CARDS: *Not accepted.*

RATES: *Moderate.*

RESTRICTIONS: *No children. No pets.*

A visit to Oak Hill Ranch is like living a day in the life of an old television classic—"Lassie," for instance—without having to do any of the chores. In fact, segments of "Little House on the Prairie" were shot just a mile away from this yellow farmhouse that only looks like it is a century old. Its saga began in the 1950s when Sandy Grover, who was then a school counselor, and his wife, Jane, a teacher, dreamed of building their own Victorian-style home. For 20 years, they scoured old houses as far away as Canada for anything that someday might be useful as vintage detailings—a turn-of-the-century mahogany fireplace, Victorian turn-posts, ornate stairs, redwood doorways, railings, balconies, and other relics.

This is one dream that came true. In the late '70s Jane, Sandy, and their son, Don, began building the four-bedroom house from the ground up on the site of a dairy ranch. Because of all the paint stripping that had to be done on the salvaged parts, it was a job that would take two long, painstaking years. But when they were through, the Grovers had themselves a nearly exact replica of a Western farm from 1880 crowning an oak-topped hill.

Still unabashedly devoted to 19th-century traditions, the Grovers love to surprise guests at breakfast time by dressing in vintage clothing. They also own an antique car—a 1908 two-cylinder Maxwell.

Genuinely nice people, the innkeepers, as much as their inn, exude peace and warmth. And when you are surrounded by this much country, it's hard not to feel like you are "down-home." Rimmed by 56 acres of pines and a view of the snowcapped Sierra Nevadas, the ranch house features fireplaces in the sitting room and den, both with 120-year-old gingerbread mantels, plus a wonderful Victorian pump organ. If you're longing to hear old-time music but can't play it yourself, look to the player piano just off the front hall.

There are three bedrooms upstairs. The Canopy Room has a canopied maple double bed, an armoire, and a balcony that looks over two duck ponds. The balcony sports a white wicker love seat, table, and chair. This room shares a bath with the Calamity Jane Room, which houses a white iron and brass antique bed, a wicker rocker, and an Eastlake dresser; from the room's window is a lovely garden view. The Eastlake Room, which brims with a queen-size bed, an armoire, and other Eastlake-style pieces, has a private bath complete with an old-fashioned clawfoot tub and a marble-top basin.

Downstairs is the romantic Rose Room furnished with a queen-size Eastlake bed with matching dresser, nightstand, and elegant armoire. A fifth bedroom is in the cottage down the knoll from the main house. Called Cow Palace, it used to be a milking barn. Today, it holds a slate fireplace, a full kitchen, and enough beds—two queens and two rollaways—to sleep six.

In *their* kitchen Jane and Sandy make a full gourmet breakfast: eggs fantasia, crepes Normandy, a River Ranch soufflé, or an omelette with ham, bacon, or sausage; fresh orange juice; banana, blueberry, or pecan muffins; biscuits with homemade jelly; coffee and tea; and melon or other fresh fruit.

Fueled by such a feast, you'll be ready to explore the surrounding countryside. The ranch is an excellent stopping-off point for Yosemite National Park, some 60 miles away; Pinecrest Lake, 30 miles distant; or, just a 12-mile drive, the Railtown 1897 State Park. With its miles of hiking and horseback riding trails and its frequent rodeos and fairs, Tuolumne County is sure to keep you occupied.

Rockwood Lodge

5295 West Lake Boulevard
P.O. Box 226
Homewood, California 96141
(916) 525-5273 or (800) LE-TAHOE

INNKEEPERS: *Connie Stevens and Lou Reinkens.*

ACCOMMODATIONS: *Four rooms, two with private bath; double and queen-size beds.*

RESERVATIONS: *One month recommended for summer weekends.*

MINIMUM STAY: *Two nights.*

DEPOSIT: *Full amount.*

CREDIT CARDS: *Not accepted.*

RATES: *Moderate to expensive.*

RESTRICTIONS: *No children. No pets.*

"This, you think, is the way a mountain chalet ought to be, the way it always looked in your dreams," brags *Ski* magazine about the Rockwood Lodge's three stories of knotty pine and stone that were crafted by Austrian carpenters and stonemasons back in the 1930s. Complete with a roof that slopes at a 60-degree angle, Rockwood looks as though it was suddenly plucked out of the Swiss Alps and magically moved to Northern California. But then, its transformation into a bed and breakfast inn also seems to be a tale right out of a storybook.

Connie Stevens, a flight attendant, and Lou Reinkens, an aerospace consultant, were looking for a vacation home when they spotted a for-sale sign on a house that was only 100 feet (not yards) from Lake Tahoe on the area's elegant west shore. "We put down a silly bid, and much to our surprise, the owners said yes to it. So we had to decide what to use this big house for," remembers Lou. Because the property came with its own business license, the couple opted to start a bed and breakfast lodge.

Like they say, the rest is history. As Lou and Connie soon found out, Rockwood is imbued with the spirit of Old Tahoe. Part of *The Godfather Part II* was filmed just down the road at the Kaiser Estate. Across the street is historic

Obexer's Marina, where plush yachts of the rich and famous have docked. Some 17 ski resorts ring the area.

The sprawling, Craftsman-style house was built in 1939 for Carlos Rookwood, a wealthy dairyman from Vallejo who used it as a summer home. In the '40s, the retreat became a guest lodge. In 1949 the new owners decided the name Rookwood was too hard to remember, so they cut the lodge's iron "o" into a "c" and renamed it Rockwood. By the time Lou and Connie found it, the house was being used as a real estate agency.

For nine months after their purchase, this married couple sandblasted walls, cleaned ceilings, tiled bathrooms, and put new carpets on the floor. Finally, they filled the lodge with European and early American antiques.

Guest raves include the warm atmosphere, the hand-hewn pine beams and panels that have been restored to their original golden color, and the Laura Ashley fabrics used throughout the decor.

Each guest room is named after a different location along the lake: Carnelian Bay contains an 18th-century American woodworker's bench, an antique armoire, and a queen-size feather bed. Rubicon Bay sports a queen-size four-poster. Emerald Bay harbors a feather bed, an antique nightstand, and a pleasant view of the lake and woods. Upstairs is Zephyr Cove, the only bedroom on the third floor—so high up you feel like you're in a tree house. A stately white fir stands just outside the window. This room has a double-size feather bed.

Still, the main draw of Rockwood isn't its history or decor. It isn't even the food, which you can partake of in the dining room or on the outside terrace. (Breakfasts include juice and fruit, a selection of muffins and croissants, granola, yogurt, and special entrees ranging from Lou's Dutch babies to Connie's fresh fruit crepes.) The biggest attraction is the pampering you get at Rockwood. Special touches like hors d'oeuvres, sweets, and cordials, down comforters and pillows, complimentary bubble bath and shampoos, and terry bathrobes hanging right in the closet are just waiting for the two of you.

Chaney House

4725 West Lake Boulevard
P.O. Box 7852
Tahoe City, California 96145; (916) 525-7333

INNKEEPERS: *Gary and Lori Chaney.*

ACCOMMODATIONS: *Four rooms, two with private bath; queen-, and king-size beds.*

RESERVATIONS: *Three to four weeks recommended.*

MINIMUM STAY: *Two nights on weekends and over holiday periods.*

DEPOSIT: *Half of full amount.*

CREDIT CARDS: *Not accepted.*

RATES: *Moderate.*

RESTRICTIONS: *Children discouraged. No pets.*

The historic Vikingsholm on Emerald Bay is a must-see for anyone traveling to Tahoe. In the late 1920s the same Italian stonemasons who created that home also built the Chaney House. And what a house it is! Eighteen-inch-thick stone walls, detailed carved woodwork, arched doorways, beamed cathedral ceilings, and a huge stone floor-to-ceiling fireplace give you the illusion that you are staying in an Italian count's villa in the Alps.

The beautiful exterior stone walls are also the home's interior walls. Craftsmen worked for four years to create the intricate patterned stonework. In the living room (decorated in warm tones of rust and green), the stone fireplace is nothing short of breathtaking, reaching to the full height of the second story. Lori Chaney calls her furnishings Old Tahoe: A tapestry covered tuxedo couch, a turn-of-the-century cherrywood bench, and her great-grandfather's veterinarian work chest that now serves as a table bear her out.

Like the living room, the dining room has a beamed ceiling the color of ash trees. A chandelier hangs over a walnut dining table that can accommodate eight people. The rust and green tapestry pattern found in the living room also adorns the windows and dining room chairs.

Chaney House bedrooms reflect the same warmth. The small room downstairs (facing one of three outdoor patios) has a double brass bed covered in a handmade quilt made by local artist Wendy Moon. The room has the characteristic stone walls with antique accents as well as a cherrywood basin with mirror and crystal lamps. Two adjoining rooms, upstairs, have private commodes, but share a shower. Formerly maids' quarters, the rooms have been converted into delightful accommodations, each with its own color scheme and decor. The most requested room at the inn is the Honeymoon Hideaway situated over the garage. It is an intimate apartment complete with kitchen, breakfast nook, and sitting area (the futon couch can be used as a second bed). The bedroom's double bed sports a quilt that captures Lake Tahoe's forest greenery and crystal blue skies.

A buffet breakfast (served from 8:00 until 10:00 a.m.) is offered in the formal dining room, or, weather permitting, on the patio with its splendid view of Lake Tahoe. Some guests like to take a tray and wander down to the pier to watch the seaplanes take off. Wherever you dine you are bound to return for seconds of Lori's scrumptious breakfast spread. Fresh-ground French roast coffee, orange juice, apple cider, hot cocoa, and an assortment of teas are your choices of beverages. Each day of the week Lori offers something different for the entrée. Mexican scrambled eggs with green chilies topped off with black olives, salsa, tomatoes, and three cheeses, and Grand Marnier French toast stuffed with cream cheese and covered in homemade hot blackberry sauce with crème fraîche are just two of her to-die-for creations.

Chaney House is located on Tahoe's North Shore and is a winter and summer sports lovers' paradise. The inn has its own secluded beach and an idyllic private pier for watching the waterskiers and sailboats on Lake Tahoe. Ask Gary or Lori to arrange for a mountain bike rental so you can explore the forested bike paths or for a surreylike covered paddleboat that seats three for a leisurely cruise around the lake. After the first winter blizzard you can head for one of the 18 ski resorts within a short drive from the Chaney House. Many guests like to cross-country ski to Homewood, just a mile down the road. Ice-skating and snowmobiling are other cold weather sports available just minutes from the inn.

Mayfield House

236 Grove Street
P.O. Box 5999
Tahoe City, California 96145; (916) 583-1001

INNKEEPERS: *Bruce and Cynthia Knauss.*

ACCOMMODATIONS: *Five rooms with shared baths; twin, double, queen-, and king-size beds.*

RESERVATIONS: *Two to three weeks recommended.*

MINIMUM STAY: *Two nights on weekends.*

DEPOSIT: *Half of total amount.*

CREDIT CARDS: *MC, Visa.*

RATES: *Moderate.*

RESTRICTIONS: *No pets.*

This reasonably priced and very special bed and breakfast began as the private residence of Norman Mayfield, who built it in 1932. The rooms reflect its history as a residence: Julia's Room commemorates Julia Morgan, a frequent visitor; the Mayfield Room, the builder himself; and the Den, the Study, and Mrs. Hinkle's Room are remembrances of the first principal of a local school who lived here while she pursued her teaching and administrative career.

The idea of using this warm and stylish home as a bed and breakfast was a good one. The furnishings are mostly original to the house. None are Victorian, but there are some striking Queen Anne and oak pieces, as well as some handsome Empire Revival ones. There is a large stone fireplace and, in winter, an ample supply of wood. There are no telephones or televisions in the rooms, but you will find beamed ceilings and plenty of rare stonework. Each room has its own library; and down pillows and comforters, fresh flowers, and brass and copper accents are the rule. The original watercolors are by Margaret Carpenter. One touch I especially appreciate are the His and Hers terrycloth robes.

This inn caters to both summer and winter activities; in fact, its proximity to skiing is one of the features that make it distinctive. Both tennis and golf are possible in season just across the street, and guests are within 30 minutes of 15 downhill ski areas and 10 Nordic ski areas. In the summer guests are just a half block from Lake Tahoe and Commons Beach, as well as within walking distance to fine shops and restaurants. There is gambling at the state line.

Breakfast at the Mayfield House is exquisite—and different every day. The day I was there, that "something different" was Portuguese toast (sweet bread, pan-fried, with fresh peach sauce), freshly squeezed orange juice, freshly ground coffee, tea, and milk. Mayfield House is also known for its Belgian waffles, sweet potato muffins, and Finnish pancakes with sour cream and strawberry topping. A newspaper accompanies breakfast—a small but very accommodating extra.

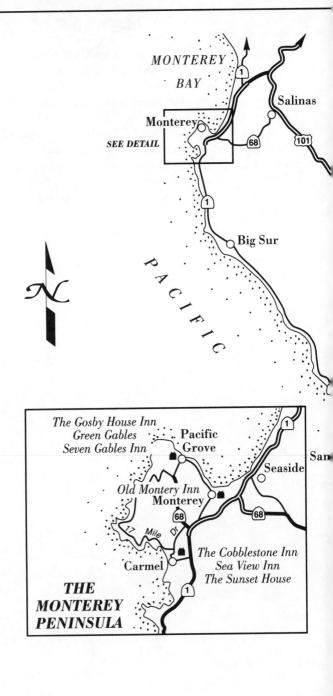

The Central Coast

PINNACLES
NAT'L MON

King City

198

101

HEARST
CASTLE

ón.

The J. Patrick House
Olallieberry Inn

Pasa Robles

Cambria

46

Templeton

Country House
Inn

Atascadero

Morro Bay

1

Garden Street Inn

101 San Luis Obispo

Arroyo Grande

1

OCEAN

The Gosby House Inn

643 Lighthouse Avenue
Pacific Grove, California 93950; (408) 375-1287

INNKEEPERS: *Roger and Sally Post; Shelley Post-Claudel.*

ACCOMMODATIONS: *22 rooms, 20 with private bath; double and queen-size beds.*

RESERVATIONS: *One week for weekdays, six weeks for weekends recommended.*

MINIMUM STAY: *None.*

DEPOSIT: *First night's lodging.*

CREDIT CARDS: *AE, MC, Visa.*

RATES: *Moderate.*

RESTRICTIONS: *No pets.*

The Gosby House Inn, which like Green Gables is owned by Roger and Sally Post, is one of those fascinating places that have been inns right from their inception. The founder of this inn was one J. F. Gosby, an industrious native of Nova Scotia who made his way to the sunnier climes of California in 1853. He had learned the shoemaking trade at an early age and soon became the town's only cobbler. In the meantime he kept his eyes open for the big break—which came in 1875, when the Methodist Church established religious conference grounds in a secluded area near the ocean. The shrewd Gosby, a Methodist himself, decided that an inn was needed to house the visitors and participants in the many religious and cultural activities that took place there.

So in 1887 Gosby built this comfortable, rambling inn and began almost immediately renting rooms to visitors attending the various meetings sponsored by the church. Civic-minded and gregarious, Gosby was a member of many lodges and a town council member from 1892 to 1896. Meanwhile the Southern Pacific railroad extended its tracks to Monterey and built the beautiful Del Monte Hotel, also during the 1880s (building the smaller El Carmelo Hotel to handle the overflow). This brought even more visitors.

Just as the area had become firmly established as the place of choice for vacations and religious retreats, the Del Monte burned to the ground. The demand for accommodations was now overwhelming; Gosby's fortunes soared. He added a round corner tower and bay windows in the late 1890s, as well as electric wiring, indoor plumbing, and connecting doors in the early 1900s. In the 1920s the irrepressible cobbler changed the name of his inn to the El Carmelo Hotel, no doubt to take advantage of the more famous caravansary's name.

From 1930 onward the inn changed hands several times and was finally purchased by the present owners in 1976. It has now been rehabilitated in a manner that reflects its original glory, and is once again called by its original name. Fresh paint, brass fixtures, marble sinks, and antique furnishings throughout reflect the over 12,000 hours necessary for restoration.

Look for the rare doll collection in the entry parlor when you arrive and the old photograph of Mr. Gosby in front of his shoe shop. Teddy bears are also part of the welcoming committee. Complimentary tea, sherry, wine, and hors d'oeuvres are served in the late afternoon. But the real distinction of the Gosby is in the many extras not often found in a bed and breakfast. Shoes left outside your room door are shined by the Boots (shades of an English inn). The morning newspaper arrives with your breakfast. A hall porter will arrange theater tickets and dinner reservations. Bicycles are available for riding along the Pacific Grove shoreline. (Watch for migrating gray whales from December to March, plus sea otters, pelicans, and other shore birds.)

Breakfast here is a bountiful feast sure to please any palate. Special services at the Gosby include an iron and ironing board, a sewing kit, alarm clocks, and a very thoughtful policy of celebrating special occasions such as birthdays, anniversaries, or weddings.

Green Gables

104 Fifth Street
Pacific Grove, California 93950; (408) 375-2095

INNKEEPERS: *Roger and Sally Post.*

ACCOMMODATIONS: *11 rooms, seven with private bath; double and queen-size beds.*

RESERVATIONS: *Two to three months recommended.*

MINIMUM STAY: *None.*

DEPOSIT: *First night's lodging.*

CREDIT CARDS: *AE, MC, Visa.*

RATES: *Moderate to expensive.*

RESTRICTIONS: *No pets.*

William Lacey of the prominent Monterey Laceys created this Queen Anne-style mansion in 1888, right by the water's edge. A Judge Wilbur used it as a summer home in the 1890s. In this century the Gerrard family was responsible for the intelligent and systematic improvements that have kept Green Gables in mint condition. Always an impressive residence, with its wide-angle view of Monterey Bay, this relatively small but elegant dwelling has been an inn since 1958.

Roger and Sally Post were living in Pasadena when they first stayed here on a visit to the area. They told their astonished hosts that they would like nothing more than to buy it; and sure enough, when it was finally put on the market, it was to the Posts that the owners first turned. "It was one of those things that just happens," Sally says. "Call it luck—or Providence."

They add that Pacific Grove has many of the advantages of a small town, but isn't isolated: The Monterey Peninsula has all the activities and attractions of any large metropolitan area. Shopping, tennis courts, boutiques, golf courses, bike paths, swimming, and the world-famous 17-Mile Drive are all close; many are within walking distance.

The inn's living room features cozy blue and mauve print love seats by a fireplace, a gay carousel horse, and silk flowers. In the formal dining room there is a panoramic view of the coastal shoreline. Here also there is a fireplace, a crystal chandelier, and several fine Oriental rugs. Photos of the inn grace the stairway.

Guest accommodations consist of five upstairs bed-rooms, a two-room suite downstairs, and a five-guest-room carriage house. Each room is supplied with fresh flowers and fruit, antique furnishings, and cozy quilts. The Garret Room has a gabled roof, floral wallpaper, and an iron bed—an appealing little hideaway. The Balcony Room has a delightful closed-in balcony with a stupendous view of the ocean. The Gable Room contains a queen-size bed, a large desk, and blue and white wallpaper; the bed has an eyelet lace comforter.

Breakfast is a full buffet including quiche or poached eggs, fresh fruit, granola, homemade bread or croissants, juice, and coffee or tea served in the dining room from 8:00 until 10:00 a.m. There are fine gourmet restaurants situated in other historic homes in Pacific Grove; the Posts or their manager are more than happy to help with directions or reservations.

Seven Gables Inn

555 Ocean View Boulevard
Pacific Grove, California 93950; (408) 372-4341

INNKEEPERS: *John, Nora, Susan, and Ed Flatley.*

ACCOMMODATIONS: *14 rooms, all with private bath; queen-size beds.*

RESERVATIONS: *Six to ten weeks recommended.*

MINIMUM STAY: *Two nights on weekends.*

DEPOSIT: *Full amount.*

CREDIT CARDS: *MC, Visa.*

RATES: *Moderate to expensive.*

RESTRICTIONS: *No pets.*

Perched on a rocky promontory overlooking scenic Monterey Bay, the three-story Seven Gables Inn was one of a parade of large, showy homes built in the area around the turn of the century.

Completed in 1886 for a Mrs. Page of Oakland, the structure was sold in 1906 to Henry and Lucie Chase, who added the gables and a sun porch. Their fond memories of their Salem, Massachusetts, roots led them to name the house after Nathaniel Hawthorne's multigabled home and classic novel, *The House of Seven Gables.*

But it wasn't just this house that was so unusual. Lucie was quite a character herself. A generous philanthropist, she amazed civic leaders by plunking down $20,000, a small fortune in the 1930s, to help build the Museum of Natural History in Pacific Grove. She also liked to purr around town in one of Monterey's first electric cars. Her nephew inherited the house and in 1971 sold it to John and Nora Flatley.

Today, Lucie's old home bubbles not only with history, but also with the hospitality of a family-run operation. When John and Nora decided to restore and refurbish the home with their collection of elegant antiques and open it to the public, they gave their adult children a chance to participate too. Daughter Susan handles personnel matters as well as the bookkeeping and promotion work, son Ed does the yardwork and repairs, Nora is the guest reception-ist and cook, and papa John is supervisor of all this activ-ity, or, as he describes himself, Chief Drone.

Filled to the brim with French furniture, crystal chandeliers, and Persian and Oriental rugs, the home also has a sun porch with a marble pedestal honoring the Three Graces and a parlor loaded with antiques. The latter features a Victorian chaise longue, a French mantel clock, and a sampling of the fine art glass collection from the 1860s to 1880s that is scattered throughout the house.

Each of the seven guest rooms in the main house is also decorated in an eclectic but pleasing mix of Victorian-era pieces and antiques from as far away as Europe, China, and Brazil. Of the five upstairs rooms, my favorite is the Breakers, which holds a queen-size ceiling canopy bed, an armoire of seashell-carved wood design, a Federal-style bull's-eye mirror, a small refrigerator, and, over by the bay window, a marble-topped table and two chairs.

Some of the nicest rooms are to be found in the Guest House. Its four bedrooms (Cypress, Ocean Mist, Victoria, and Mayfair) all have modern baths and built-in refrigerators. All of the inn's guest rooms feature exceptional ocean views.

Also special at the Seven Gables is the 8:00 to 10:00 a.m. breakfast that's served around the inn's ten-seater dining table: It includes a piping-hot egg dish accompanied by platters of fresh fruit, yogurt, gourmet croissants (cinnamon walnut, apricot, or blueberry) and muffins (mincemeat, cream cheese-pumpkin, or buttermilk bran), strawberry shortcake or apple cobbler, fresh orange juice, and freshly brewed coffee or tea. The presentation is on antique serving pieces from the family treasure trove. Afternoon high tea commences at 4:00 p.m. Among the goodies usually included are delicious homemade and imported cookies, dried fruits, candies, nuts, and Nora's homemade fudge.

Would Lucie Chase be proud of the job the Flatleys are doing? You bet she would. I'm sure even Nathaniel Hawthorne would take note. He would probably rechristen this friendly, family-oriented place The House of the Four Flatleys Inn.

Old Monterey Inn

500 Martin Street
Monterey, California 93940; (408) 375-8284

INNKEEPERS: *Ann and Gene Swett.*

ACCOMMODATIONS: *Nine rooms and a cottage, all with private bath; twin, queen-, and king-size beds.*

RESERVATIONS: *Two to three months for weekends.*

MINIMUM STAY: *Two nights on weekends.*

DEPOSIT: *In full.*

CREDIT CARDS: *MC, Visa.*

RATES: *Expensive to very expensive.*

RESTRICTIONS: *Not suitable for children. No pets.*

No doubt about it, the Old Monterey Inn is special. The only word that works here is elegance. And what a pleasure it is—particularly because the elegance is achieved without a hint of ostentation! Located in a quiet area near the heart of Monterey, the inn is surrounded by lovely gardens that create the illusion of an English country house. Architecturally it is in fact English Tudor, and owners Ann and Gene Swett have given it many of the characteristics of the finest English and Scottish inns.

The dwelling was built in 1929 by Carmel Martin, a former mayor and civic leader of Monterey. After passing through several hands, it was purchased and restored by the Swetts and used exclusively as a private residence until the last of their six children flew the nest. A visit to the Sutter Creek Inn caused the Swetts to consider the possibility of creating a country-style bed and breakfast inn in the heart of Monterey. They have most definitely succeeded—to the lasting delight of the hostelry's many regular guests, including visitors to the world-famous Monterey Jazz Festival.

Typical of the careful architectural detail to look for at this inn are the huge timber beams and posts in the vestibule. Hand-carved designs on the stairs were done by August Gay, an artist in the community who is also responsible for the window valances.

Besides its sensational setting, it was the extras that won me over at the Old Monterey Inn. The beds aren't just beds—they're experiments in total relaxation. There are soft and firm pillows for each guest, and European goose down comforters. Free soft drinks and juices are stored in a refrigerator on the second floor. Breakfast is served on fine china. In the bathroom medicine cabinet I discovered the following: shampoo, nail polish remover, toothpaste, a razor, safety pins, hairspray, and deodorant; a hair dryer, a curling iron, and electric rollers are also available (ask if you need them). Rose petals from the garden are used to make potpourri that guests may take with them as a gift.

Branches from an old oak tree frame an enchanting view from the window of the room called Brightstone. Guests in the Library Room enjoy both a sun deck and a fireplace in this book-lined hideaway that was once actually a library. Visitors in the Dovecote Room can relax by a fireplace in shadows cast by a skylight. The Cottage features a sitting room with stained glass; it also has a cozy seat in the bedroom bay window with a view of the garden.

Breakfast here is generous—and very good. The day I was there the following was served: fresh fruit, orange juice, a delicious artichoke frittata, home-baked muffins, as well as coffee, tea, and brewed decaffeinated coffee. Those who wish may have their morning meal delivered to their room or served to them in bed. On pleasant mornings breakfast is available in the garden, a perfect setting for daydreaming or romancing. Complimentary wine is served every afternoon at 5:00 p.m.

The Swetts are firm believers in a quote from Boswell's *Life of Johnson:* "There is nothing which has yet been contrived by man by which so much happiness is produced as by a good tavern or inn." This is one of those rare places that delivers this total serenity and pleasure. It is also one of the few that must be experienced to be believed.

The Cobblestone Inn

Junipero between 7th and 8th
P.O. Box 3185
Carmel, California 93921; (408) 625-5222

INNKEEPERS: *Roger and Sally Post.*

ACCOMMODATIONS: *24 rooms, all with private bath; queen- and king-size beds.*

RESERVATIONS: *Four to six weeks recommended.*

MINIMUM STAY: *None.*

DEPOSIT: *First night's lodging.*

CREDIT CARDS: *AE, MC, Visa.*

RATES: *Moderate to expensive.*

RESTRICTIONS: *No pets.*

The Cobblestone, which offers 24 rooms, all with fireplaces and their own "adoptable" teddy bears (details to follow), is one of the Four Sisters Inns that dot the California coast. They were created by Roger and Sally Post and named for their four daughters: Kimberley, Shelley, Jennifer, and Stefanie.

These romantic small inns and hotels began when the Post family moved to Pacific Grove, into the Green Gables, a Victorian mansion by the sea. Their innkeeping adventure started as a summer experiment, with each of the girls helping with the effort. Today, there are seven inns in the family, including this country hideaway that is just eight blocks from the beach.

Built around a courtyard of slate and colorful flowers, it's hard to believe that, until 1984, this was the home of the Hideaway Motel. The Posts completely changed the look and feel of the structure—first, by covering it with cobblestones from the Carmel River (giving it its name), and second, by adding warmth and appeal.

Just off the main lobby is a living room with large stone fireplace, soft rose and pale green carpeting, overstuffed chairs and sofas, country antiques, and fresh flowers. All the guest rooms—12 are on the first floor, 12 on the second—have country pine furniture, refrigerators stocked with complimentary soft drinks, and a television tucked discreetly away. Five have king-size beds, showers, and tubs; the others have queens and showers; two are suites. Top picks are the Honeymoon Suite, with a four-poster king, a great window seat, and an oversize tub; and Room 18, a large, particularly quiet upstairs room with king-size bed that also comes with a view of the Santa Lucia Mountains.

Still, probably the best thing about the Cobblestone is its continuing feast of food. Between 4:30 and 6:30 p.m. the inn serves an array of hors d'oeuvres, including Brie, smokey sharp cheddar, and Swiss cheeses, gourmet crackers, and salmon dip; plus a homemade hot soup (especially clam chowder or tomato); and dessert. The buffet breakfast from 8:00 to 10:00 a.m. in the dining room (or, for $5 extra, brought right to your bed!) is changed daily. It always features a main dish, such as eggs, quiche, or pancakes; fresh bread and homemade muffins (like blueberry, pecan, or a house favorite, gingerbread); sour cream coffeecake; granola and other cereals; and fruit. Coffee, tea, and cocoa are always available.

Bear and breakfast? It's a reality at the Cobblestone, where teddy bears, more than a hundred at a time, are everywhere. Indeed, guests can barely (no pun intended) believe the sea of cuddly creatures: one's atop an antique carousel horse in the lobby, 30 or so are in an antique wagon, 50 more in a sled, three antique teddies are behind the front desk, and, each night when your bed is turned down, you'll find a teddy tucked into the sheets, next to chocolates and a long-stemmed rose.

The bear bonanza began when the Posts initially bought several, hoping to sell them as gift items. When they put them on the beds, people started asking if they could sleep with and keep them. Each "beddy" bear is available for "adoption" (i.e., purchase), and comes with adoption papers, a poem, and a recipe for one of the establishment's gourmet goodies. If you just can't bear it, here's another idea: head back to the lobby and check out the inn's display of a dozen or so antique dolls.

Sea View Inn

Camino Real between 11th and 12th
P.O. Box 4138
Carmel, California 93921; (408) 624-8778

INNKEEPERS: *Marshall and Diane Hydorn.*

ACCOMMODATIONS: *Eight rooms, six with private bath; queen- and king-size beds.*

RESERVATIONS: *Three weeks recommended.*

MINIMUM STAY: *Two nights on weekends and holidays.*

DEPOSIT: *First and last night's lodging.*

CREDIT CARDS: *MC, Visa.*

RATES: *Moderate.*

RESTRICTIONS: *No children under 12. No pets.*

Here's an economical bed and breakfast where one can park the car and take it from there on foot. (It's three blocks from the beach; five from Ocean Avenue, Carmel's main street.) This country-style Victorian, built in 1906, is one of the oldest guest houses in this artist-colony-by-the-sea. Yet it is well out of the tourist crush. In this residential neighborhood there are no traffic noises or other distractions associated with congested downtown areas.

The Sea View is popular as a honeymoon haven; don't be surprised if you meet guests returning for their anniversaries. It is also patronized regularly by visitors to the Jazz and Bach festivals, both annual events in Monterey and Carmel, respectively. (Book a room early if you are attending either; accommodations are hard to get during festival time.)

Proprietors Marshall and Diane Hydorn first visited Carmel looking for a vacation home. (Marshall was flying for TWA and Diane was occupied as a homemaker, raising the couple's children.) More as a joke than anything else, they asked the real estate agent if there were any "little inns" for sale. "As a matter of fact, there is one," was the sobering reply. The Hydorns were hooked as soon as they saw it and have now been innkeeping for over 10 years.

This is an adult hideaway where privacy is everything, but children over 12 are allowed as long as they are reasonably well-behaved. The Sea View is furnished with antiques blended in with newer pieces. A great many belongings of the hosts are to be found around the house, too, adding to the personal feeling of the inn. The Hydorns try to give their guests as much attention as possible. They are well-informed about local happenings and attractions, including good local restaurants.

The Continental breakfast is served in the living room, before the fireplace, and varies from day to day. When I visited there were assorted cold cereals, juice, fresh fruit, whole-grain toast, and muffins. (And, of course, a choice of hot drinks: tea, coffee, herb tea, and cocoa.) A tasty coffeecake is served other mornings, and on certain Sundays Diane has been known to make quiche as a special treat.

Sunset House

S.E. Camino Real between Ocean and 7th
P.O. Box 1925
Carmel, California 93921; (408) 624-4884

INNKEEPERS: *Camille and Dennis Fike.*

ACCOMMODATIONS: *Three rooms, all with private bath; king-size beds.*

RESERVATIONS: *Four to six weeks recommended.*

MINIMUM STAY: *None.*

DEPOSIT: *First night's lodging.*

CREDIT CARDS: *None.*

RATES: *Moderate to expensive.*

RESTRICTIONS: *No pets.*

While Sunset House has lots to brag about, the most remarkable thing is its location: just two blocks from Carmel Beach. From here, you can leave your car in the inn's complimentary parking area, saunter to the sand, soak up some rays, and still have plenty of time left over for a leisurely walk back up Ocean Avenue to inspect the intriguing shops of this arts-and-crafts community. Of course, Carmel has more going for it than shores and stores. Don't forget to partake of its fine restaurants, occasional music festivals, and nearby scenery-studded 17-Mile Drive.

After either a lazy day at the beach or a full menu of activities, there's one last "must do" to perform at the three-room bed and breakfast. True to its name, Sunset House is an ideal locale for watching the sky change from sea blue to orange, pink, and red.

The North Room, upstairs in the two-story, stucco and wood, almost Danish seeming building, is the best place to toast the arrival of evening with some complimentary wine (just ask) from the inn's gracious hosts, Dennis and Camille Fike. The view of the ocean from here isn't complete but it definitely captures the last gleaming of twilight. Another surprise: Hans Christian Andersen is said to have slept in the room's king-size bed, which came from Denmark's Royal Hotel. The Fikes extended its side rails so it could accommodate a California king mattress.

Also in the North Room are three large windows with Plantation shutters, a sitting area around a wood-burning fireplace, a hide-a-bed love seat that can hold a third person, Queen Anne dressing table, and Martha Washington sewing stand from the 1800s. All of the units have private bathrooms with showers. The other two also have kings and wood fireplaces.

On the same floor as the North Room, the South Room offers a filtered view, through some majestic pines, of the blue Pacific. A hand-forged California king iron bed, Victorian twin daybed, and century-old dresser are some of the standouts. Downstairs, the West Room combines a 19th-century French armoire and washstand, Plantation shutters, and country French decor with a cathedral beam ceiling, private entrance, and two overstuffed chairs that form a cozy sitting area around the fire.

Dennis and Camille, former contractors and furniture shop operators from Lafayette, California, can be justly proud of the antiques and upgrades they've added to the property, which was built as an inn in 1960. The Fikes, who arrived in 1991, purchased it from a former guest who'd been so pleased with his stay that he bought the house.

One bonus of visiting Sunset is that the innkeepers are never intrusive. They live nearby but return each morning to serve up a healthy breakfast of fresh orange juice and coffee, muffins and croissants, granola or oatmeal, yogurt, and fresh fruits. On the day of my sojourn, I savored mangoes, strawberries, bananas, apricots, grapes, and cantaloupes. Then I went out for yet another stroll on the beach.

The J. Patrick House

2990 Burton Drive
Cambria, California 93428; (805) 927-3812

INNKEEPER: *Molly Lynch.*

ACCOMMODATIONS: *Eight rooms, all with private bath; queen- and king-size beds.*

RESERVATIONS: *Three to six weeks recommended.*

MINIMUM STAY: *None.*

DEPOSIT: *Full amount.*

CREDIT CARDS: *MC, Visa.*

RATES: *Moderate.*

RESTRICTIONS: *No pets.*

For good reason, Jerry Hulse, longtime travel editor of the *Los Angeles Times*, called The J. Patrick House "without question the prettiest bed and breakfast on the entire Central California coast." Woodsy and tucked away in a grove of fragrant pines, the log cabin-style inn offers warmth, hospitality, soothing American country furnishing, and a great locale just six miles south of Hearst Castle.

But above all, it's the proprietress who makes this inn come alive. Vivacious yet gentle, Molly Lynch has infused a good dose of her own personal style into her inn. From the music she plays on the phone recorder ("Greensleeves") to the name of her hostelry (which honors her Irish dad), Molly's inn is as Irish as Irish can be.

Each of the eight bedrooms (all with wood-burning fireplaces and all nearly the same price) is christened after an Irish County: there's Galway, Tipperary, Dublin, Limerick, Donegal, Kerry, Kilkenny, and Clare. Decorated with pine antiques and willow reproductions, the spacious living room is where you check in and, if you wish, partake of the complimentary wine and snacks (a recent serving was loaded with three cheeses, fresh vegetables and dip, ham and cheese rolls, smoked almonds, crackers, cherries and strawberries, as well as soft drinks) from 5:30 to 6:30 p.m.

Both the living room/parlor (with its willow-branch chair, navy and coral floral print sofa, braided, heart-shaped rug, dried flower wreaths, and modest library) and the dining room/sun porch (with tables covered by gay blue and white checked tablecloths) are unpretentious and inviting. "We're not filled with sterling silver and major antiques; we strive to make our guests comfortable," professed Molly as she served a visitor some mineral water.

The Clare, which is located upstairs in the front of the main house, contains a king-size bed, log walls with a brick fireplace, pale blue carpets, and windows that overlook stately conifers. The path to other guest rooms passes through a colorful garden. It includes thick plantings of pungent lavender and a long, flowing passionflower vine with scarlet flowers instead of the usual yellow and white mix.

Of the seven rooms in this cedar-sided lodge behind the main house, the Limerick and Kilkenny are the real items. The former has a reproduction of an Amish willow rocker, a queen-size bed with willow headboard, a brick fireplace, and a window seat covered in brown and white plaid. The latter is dressed in three patterns of pale blue wallpaper and also has a tile-front fireplace, a willow rocker, and a willow headboard for its queen-size bed.

For the 7:30 to 9:30 a.m. Continental breakfast on the sun porch, Molly serves up a bowl of fresh fruit, two types of baked goods, such as apple bread and oatmeal-coconut muffins with jam centers, fresh juice, yogurt, granola, teas, and freshly brewed coffee. A don't-miss for vacationing chocoholics looking to indulge their sweet tooth is Molly's plateful of homemade chocolate chip cookies, featured nightly in the kitchen pantry.

Refreshed and unhurried, you'll leave this pseudo-Irish roadside inn with a twinkle in your eye and a smile on your lips. Farther up the coast is Big Sur, farther down is Morro Bay. Also beckoning are nearby beaches great for seashell hunting and tidepooling, hiking trails at Las Padres National Forest, a local berry farm that sells pies and homemade jams, and lots of little wineries.

Olallieberry Inn

2476 Main Street
Cambria, California 93428; (805) 927-3222

INNKEEPERS: *Peter and CarolAnn Irsfeld.*

ACCOMMODATIONS: *Six rooms, all with private bath; queen- and king-size beds.*

RESERVATIONS: *Three to four weeks recommended.*

MINIMUM STAY: *None.*

DEPOSIT: *First night's lodging.*

CREDIT CARDS: *MC, Visa.*

RATES: *Moderate.*

RESTRICTIONS: *Not appropriate for children. No pets.*

When Peter and CarolAnn Irsfeld say that "time stands still" at their Olallieberry Inn bed and breakfast, they mean that—literally. You see, they purposely never wind any of their prize collection of antique clocks.

The Greek Revival home was originally built on the banks of Santa Rosa Creek by Cambria's Manderscheid brothers in 1873. A few years later the Manderscheids planted a tree out on the front lawn. Today, the scene is exactly the same, with the exception of the size of this 100-year-old Coastal Redwood.

The Olallieberry offers six guest rooms—three upstairs and three down. Each claims a private bath, although three of these are actually detached from their bedrooms, with the worst-case scenario being Santa Rosa's bath, which is located down the home's long front hall. On a more positive note, the innkeepers provide bathrobes.

The Santa Rosa room itself is decorated in deep forest green and burgundy and contains an antique-style four-poster made of brass. Moiré and lace frame the queen-size bed in Cambria; this first-floor room also has a raised fireplace and attached bath with oversized sunken tub. San Simeon is the third downstairs room, furnished with a king-size bed with burl maple headboard and matching armoire and nightstand.

Upstairs, Harmony takes the afternoon sun through its eyelet lace curtain-covered windows; the room's queen bed has a ceiling canopy. Decked out in blue, white, and lavender is the romantic Olallieberry with its lace canopied bed and ball and clawfoot tub. Room at the Top is done up in blue, rose, and white; its brass and iron bed and wicker chaise look to a cozy fireplace.

Guests of the Olallieberry Inn visit over a breakfast of poached apple crepes with brandy cream sauce, fresh fruit with olallieberry yogurt, homemade peach almond muffins, and granola and milk in the sunny Gathering Room. In the early evening the parlor is the setting for locally produced wines and fresh-squeezed lemonade served with roasted garlic and goat cheese, a vegetable platter with lemon dill dip, and focaccia bread.

One of the few historic buildings left in Cambria, the Olallieberry enjoys a Main Street location in the East Village, which is easily accessible by foot to shops, galleries, and restaurants.

Country House Inn

91 Main Street
Templeton, California 93465; (805) 434-1598

INNKEEPER: *Dianne Garth.*

ACCOMMODATIONS: *Seven rooms, five with private bath; queen- and king-size beds.*

RESERVATIONS: *Three to four weeks for weekends recommended.*

MINIMUM STAY: *Two nights on holiday weekends.*

DEPOSIT: *First night's lodging.*

CREDIT CARDS: *DC, MC, Visa.*

RATES: *Moderate.*

RESTRICTIONS: *Children by arrangement. No pets.*

The smell of Mexican quiche and zucchini bread hot out of the oven, along with the sight of cups of caramel custard and baked peaches with raspberries and cream, filled my senses as I popped my head in the back kitchen door of the Country House Inn. Apparently I was just in time for breakfast. "Sit down and make yourself comfortable," said Dianne Garth as she offered me a choice of orange juice or coffee. Dianne had bought Country House just a year before my visit (it was already an inn) after previewing the property in an edition of *Country Living* magazine.

Built in 1886 by C. H. Phillips, founder of the town of Templeton, the house's Victorian country charm was clearly in evidence even though it was in the throes of a complete face lift the day I stopped by. Now, the exterior has been painted a light gray and white with rose trim; interiors are in a country French style.

Of the seven guest rooms my preferences ran to Garden View—with its bay window with rose-patterned window seat, crystal chandelier, nice wardrobe, and king-size bed smothered in a white and pink floral comforter—and Scarborough, formerly servants' quarters, done in yellow, blue, and white Laura Ashley prints. A quilt wall-hanging and braided heart-shaped rug basket caught my eye as did the queen-size bed with brass headboard and bright, white walls.

Having worked as an interior decorator, Dianne describes herself now as "homebody, mother of three children, and inn proprietor." She has her degree in art and also once owned an art gallery. "It's quiet here, restful you might say. Of course, there's wine tasting in the area, and hot air balloon rides. But most people who stop here are on their way to Hearst Castle, just a 40-minute drive."

A good place to relax, the living room at Country House holds a fireplace and a blue and white patterned sofa. Peachy pink walls are accented by a blue border. Games like Monopoly and backgammon are on hand. French double doors in the inn's dining room open onto a deck. White lace curtains frame the windows and a quilt hangs on the wall. The pecan wood table and chairs are occupied by guests gathered for a communal breakfast anytime between 8:00 and 10:00 a.m. Dianne named French toast and baked apple pancakes with sausages as other main dishes she serves. Oh well, that's another day—maybe on my way back up the coast.

Located halfway between Los Angeles and San Francisco, Templeton is an old Western town with many finely restored buildings. Templeton's Country House Inn is a Designated Historic Site.

Garden Street Inn

1212 Garden Street
San Luis Obispo, California 93401; (805) 545-9802

INNKEEPERS: *Dan and Kathy Smith.*

ACCOMMODATIONS: *13 rooms, all with private bath; queen- and king-size beds.*

RESERVATIONS: *Three to four weeks recommended.*

MINIMUM STAY: *Two nights on summer and special event weekends as well as over holiday periods.*

DEPOSIT: *First night's lodging.*

CREDIT CARDS: *AE, MC, Visa.*

RATES: *Moderate to expensive.*

RESTRICTIONS: *No children under 16. No pets.*

The early history of Garden Street Inn is the tale of two families—the Goldtrees and the McCaffreys. Merchants who were also successful in land transactions, railway enterprises, and winemaking, the Goldtree clan, specifically Morris and Helene Goldtree, built the 1887 vintage structure in which the Garden Street Inn abides on land that was once part of the city's Mission Vineyard Tract. The Goldtrees uprooted at the turn of the century to return to their native Germany, only to depart again at the onset of the Holocaust. Goldtree grandsons, now in their 70s, have been guests of today's Garden Street Inn.

The second phase in the life of 1212 Garden Street dates to 1898 when the home was acquired by Patrick and Elizabeth McCaffrey. They built on the dwelling's second level and divided the property into four flats. The McCaffrey family name is connected with one of the first breweries founded in San Luis Obispo. Enter Dan and Kathy Smith, modern-day owners; in 1989 they renovated apartments into guest rooms and gave birth to their idea of the perfect bed and breakfast inn.

Garden Street's nostalgic surroundings are fashioned by antiques of the era, fireplaces, and historical memorabilia. Bookshelves in the Goldtree Library brim with volumes ranging from biographies to the classics. An exterior photo of the home when it was still only one story appears above an 1893 Vose & Sons upright grand piano. In the

McCaffrey Morning Room guests socialize over a breakfast of individual crab soufflés or asparagus frittatas, spicy pear muffins, fresh fruit and juice, and vanilla nut coffee. (On occasion Dan takes a notion to wind up his 1904 woven wood horn gramophone.) Stained-glass windows in the bay alcoves are original to the home.

Five downstairs and eight upstairs guest rooms have been devoted to historic personages, cherished family members, and artists, authors, and composers. They include The Lovers (a suite themed around the Picasso print of the same name that hangs on the south wall of the sitting room), Emerald Isle, Valley of the Moon (echoes of Jack London), Walden, Dollie McKeen (honoring another former owner of the structure), Our Town (Thornton Wilder), Close To Home (a suite dedicated to accomplished women and named after Pulitzer prize-winning columnist Ellen Goodman), Ah Louis (shades of the Chinese labor movement that played a major role in the development of the Pacific Railroad), Cocoon (themed around Kathy's butterfly collection), Field of Dreams (a memorial to Kathy's father who was a newspaper sports editor), Edelweiss (Dan's mother was born in Austria), Amadeus, and Concours d'Elegance (your host is a vintage car buff). Each accommodation features a spacious private bath and queen- or king-size bed.

Los Alamos

Union Hotel
Ballard

The Ballard Inn

101

Bath Street Inn
Blue Quail Inn
The Old Yacht Club Inn
Simpson House Inn

Summerland

Santa Barbara

Inn on Summ

101

La Mer

Ventura

Southern California

❧

Union Hotel

362 Bell Street
P.O. Box 616
Los Alamos, California 93440; (805) 344-2744

INNKEEPER: *Dick Langdon.*

ACCOMMODATIONS: *13 rooms, three with private bath; twin, double, and king-size beds. Six-room Victorian house annex.*

RESERVATIONS: *Three to six weeks recommended.*

MINIMUM STAY: *None.*

DEPOSIT: *Full amount.*

CREDIT CARDS: *AE, MC, Visa.*

RATES: *Moderate to expensive.*

RESTRICTIONS: *No children. No pets.*

J. D. Snyder was a New Yorker who came West to make his fortune—and succeeded. In the 1880s he owned the way station in tiny Los Alamos for the stagecoach route between Santa Barbara and San Francisco. In addition to being the local agent for Wells Fargo, he was also involved in farming and a variety of other business ventures in Santa Barbara County. One of them was the Union Hotel, where stage passengers could eat, stay overnight, and wet their whistles before continuing the arduous overland journey.

Fire destroyed the hotel, however, as it did so many other wooden structures of that time. In 1915 it was rebuilt with Indian adobe. Thereafter it was used as a hotel, a rooming house, and a pool room, after which it was boarded up and forgotten. Until it was discovered by Dick Langdon, that is. It became his dream to rehabilitate—or rather re-create—this old Western hotel based on original sketches of the Union. Wood from 12 dismantled barns was used to replicate the original exterior, with various craftspeople in the area contributing their talents. The result is a work of art that has attracted comment from Western buffs and bed and breakfast enthusiasts alike.

Antiques here are imaginative and provocative: 200-year-old Egyptian urns, a pair of swinging doors from a New Orleans house of ill repute, dining room furniture from a Mississippi plantation, an 1880 Brunswick pool table. My room was a masterpiece of whimsy, containing a ceiling fan, an antique trunk, hats hanging from a coatrack. Some of the most innovative (though expensive) guest rooms are found in Dick's recently completed Victorian-house annex. A case in point: In the Fifties Drive-In accommodation, the bed is situated in a 1956 Cadillac.

Overnight guests dine together at 7:00 p.m.; the home-cooked meal is served family style. Then everyone gathers in the old saloon for an evening's worth of entertainment: There's a Rockola jukebox full of old 78s, a Ping-Pong table, shuffleboard, and a collection of old radio tapes.

One of the most interesting architectural and design triumphs of this inn is the swimming pool. There were no such conveniences in the 1880s, so Dick concealed this one in the guise of an old-fashioned reflecting pond. The grounds also include streetlights, park benches, flower gardens, and manicured lawns. There is a lovely Victorian gazebo with a secret Jacuzzi inside, large enough to accommodate a dozen guests.

A full breakfast is served, and it is as special as everything else about the place. It has been known to include such diverse delights as gingerbread cake, chocolate chip cookies, pound cake, and brandy. After breakfast guests are treated to a tour of Los Alamos in a 1918, 15-passenger touring car.

The Victorian annex rooms are available for bed and breakfast any day of the week, but the distinctive adventure in dining and lodging at the hotel is only open on Friday, Saturday, and Sunday. "Three days a week is fun," Dick is often quoted as saying. "After that, it becomes work."

The Ballard Inn

2436 Baseline Avenue
Ballard, California 93463
(805) 688-7770 or (800) 638-2466

INNKEEPERS: *Steve Hyslop, Larry Stone, and Kelly Robinson.*

ACCOMMODATIONS: *15 rooms, all with private bath; twin, queen- and king-size beds.*

RESERVATIONS: *Three to four weeks recommended.*

MINIMUM STAY: *Two nights on weekends and over holiday periods.*

DEPOSIT: *First night's lodging.*

CREDIT CARDS: *AE, MC, Visa.*

RATES: *Expensive to very expensive.*

RESTRICTIONS: *No pets.*

Northern California's famed Napa and Sonoma wine country is rivaled in the south by the Santa Maria, Los Alamos, and Santa Ynez valleys, all located inside of Santa Barbara County. Here some 10,000 acres of vineyards support 30 wineries, most of which welcome the public year-round. Nearly all produce Chardonnay, but the region is also known for its Pinot Noir, Riesling, Sauvignon Blanc, Syrah, Merlot, Gewurztraminer, and Cabernet Sauvignon.

The most widely recognized tourist town in the Santa Ynez Valley is Solvang, a Danish community that was settled in the early 1900s. Just two miles from Solvang is tiny Ballard, population 320, with its charming one-room schoolhouse, quaint country chapel, and spectacular 15-guest-room Ballard Inn.

Manicured lawns, flower gardens, and a white wicker rocker on the gray and white inn's front veranda heighten anticipation for a tour of the elegant accommodations within. Check-in precedes a late afternoon tasting of locally produced wines and a hot and cold hors d'oeuvres spread.

The antique- and quilt-filled bedrooms each offer a private bath and queen- or king-size bed; seven of the accommodations have wood-burning fireplaces. My three personal favorites are the Vineyard Room (unique bent willow bed headboard and matching cushion-covered chairs), the country-style Farmhouse Room (pine furnish-ings), and the cozy Mountain Room (warm autumn colors, fireplace, and balcony).

Breakfast, which commences at 8:00 a.m. and runs un-til 10:00, starts off with a buffet of fresh fruits, muffins, toast, and cold cereals. The entrée, cooked to order, can be selected from any one of four daily choices. A typical menu might include oatmeal pancakes sided by fresh applesauce, smoked trout and egg scramble, Irish oatmeal, or Danish sausage or Kentucky country ham served with eggs any style. Breakfast is served in the inn's stately din-ing room with its green Italian marble fireplace.

Twenty-five year veterans of the hospitality industry, owners Larry Stone and Steve Hyslop are experts when it comes to arranging recreational activities and special tours for their guests, including private tours of wineries that don't have visitor facilities or are not usually open to the public. Among their other offerings are horse-drawn carriage rides through Ballard and the surrounding area, bicycle tours that include a lunch stop at one of the win-eries, and dinner or brunch cruises in nearby Morro Bay or Santa Barbara.

Things to explore on your own are the art and antique shops in Los Olivos, glider plane rides at the Santa Ynez airport, the miniature-horse farm outside Ballard, and area horseback riding, hiking, and golf. Always popular with lovers of fine wine is the annual Vintners' Festival held each April and the Harvest Celebration in the fall.

Bath Street Inn

1720 Bath Street
Santa Barbara, California 93101; (805) 682-9680

INNKEEPER: *Susan Brown.*

ACCOMMODATIONS: *10 rooms, all with private bath; twin, queen-, and king-size beds.*

RESERVATIONS: *Six weeks recommended.*

MINIMUM STAY: *Two nights on weekends.*

DEPOSIT: *First night's lodging or half the full amount for longer stays.*

CREDIT CARDS: *AE, MC, Visa.*

RATES: *Moderate to expensive.*

RESTRICTIONS: *No pets.*

From the time Vizcaino entered the harbor on the eve of Saint Barbara's Day in 1602 (and so, appropriately, named the channel for her), Santa Barbara has been a magnet for adventurers, visionaries, entrepreneurs, and most of all, people irresistibly attracted to its mild climate and scenic beauty. Both newcomers and old Santa Barbara hands have found the Bath Street Inn ideally located for maximum enjoyment of the city's rich cultural and resort activities.

Bath Street Inn began as a private residence in 1873, and was called the House of the Three Sisters by local residents. When Susan Brown found it with the aid of a realtor, the old dwelling was badly in need of some sisterly attention. And it got it—with the help of a local architect who supervised much of the renovation.

A common theme among owners of bed and breakfast establishments is a desire to leave an environment of cutthroat ambition and enter a service-oriented world. Susan, a personnel manager in Anaheim for 10 years, was no exception. This charming and intelligent woman pronounced herself "somewhat disillusioned" with the business world. Or at least its most competitive (and least reflective) aspects.

This Queen Anne Victorian has three stories with a small second-story eyelid balcony in front and is larger inside than it appears from the street. In fact, the third floor, where the guest common area is located, feels like an entire house itself. The rooms are decorated with a nice mix of antiques that enhance the 1873 atmosphere of the original dwelling.

A full breakfast is served outdoors on the porch or patio when weather permits—which it usually does in Santa Barbara. It consists of homemade breads and granola, egg dishes, pancakes or French toast, fresh fruit in season, juice, and a choice of coffee, tea, milk, or cocoa. In the evening, light refreshments are also provided.

Blue Quail Inn

1908 Bath Street
Santa Barbara, California 93101
(805) 687-2300; (800) 549-1622 (in California)
or (800) 676-1622 (outside California)

INNKEEPER: *Jeanise Suding Eaton.*

ACCOMMODATIONS: *Nine rooms, all with private bath; queen- and king-size beds.*

RESERVATIONS: *Three to four weeks recommended.*

MINIMUM STAY: *Two nights on weekends.*

DEPOSIT: *First night's lodging; in full for weekends.*

CREDIT CARDS: *MC, Visa.*

RATES: *Moderate to expensive.*

RESTRICTIONS: *Children in cottages only. No pets.*

Most bed and breakfasts offer a cozy retreat in quaint, homelike surroundings, and that's true of the Blue Quail Inn's turn-of-the-century California Craftsman-style bungalow. But, innkeeper Jeanise Suding Eaton offers something more—seven antique-filled guest rooms in self-contained cottages surrounded by lush gardens overflowing with rose bushes, impatiens, ferns, and avocado trees. The garden's birdbath attracts a constant flurry of blue jays and hummingbirds, and a quaint winding brick pathway leads from the front of the house to backyard patio areas where a persimmon tree shades white wrought iron lawn furniture.

Jeanise attempts to assure her visitors' comfort in every way. Guests are presented with their own key to the main house and are free to come and go as they please. The home's living and dining room areas are decorated in English country style. The living room's cream-colored couch is as inviting as its two rose-colored wingback chairs. A television set is hidden away in an antique pine chest and an abundant bouquet of fresh cut flowers is always on display. The dining room's window seat, which is home to Quincy the teddy bear, looks out on the flower-fringed walkway. A Queen Anne dining table and antique English pine buffet give the room a European flavor.

Breakfast is a formal affair (with tablecloths and bone china), served in an informal patio setting under the shade of the persimmon tree. Fresh-ground mocha java coffee, a selection of teas (presented in a woven basket), and fresh-squeezed orange juice comprise the selection of beverages. A typical breakfast may consist of a spinach and cream cheese omelette served with a boysenberry coffeecake and a mixture of fresh fruit (cantaloupe, grapes, and bananas) topped with yogurt sauce and piled high in a parfait glass. Popovers are a house favorite served piping hot with butter and strawberry or apricot-pineapple jam. Besides the scrumptious breakfast, Jeanise offers her guests an early evening snack of wine and hors d'oeuvres (crab and shrimp dip and an assortment of cheeses and crackers) from 5:00 to 7:00 p.m. And, after dinner in one of the nearby restaurants in downtown Santa Barbara, savor a homemade brownie or a few chocolate cookies with a mug of hot spiced apple cider that Jeanise serves until 10:00 p.m.

Guest rooms are named for birds you might catch sight of while staying at the inn: the Wood Thrush, Whippoorwill, Hummingbird, Cardinal, Mockingbird, Nightingale, and Oriole. All the rooms have antique furnishings (Jeanise's mom owns a local antique store) and most have queen-size beds. The Whippoorwill is furnished in a friendly English country manner. A queen-size iron bed with rose patterned duvet and antique daybed with rose throw pillows make the room ideal for families. The Nightingale Suite is decorated in warm peach colors with a tempting white rug placed in front of the white brick fireplace. The queen-size canopy bed is covered in a stunning peach and cream comforter.

Most people realize their ambition of owning an inn when they have retired or made a midlife career change. "I made my dream come true years sooner than I thought possible," says thirty-something innkeeper Jeanise Suding Eaton. After graduating from Loyola Marymount with a business degree, Eaton decided to go into business for herself. Lucky for us that we didn't have to wait too long for Jeanise to open this delightful bed and breakfast.

The Old Yacht Club Inn

431 Corona Del Mar
Santa Barbara, California 93103
(805) 962-1277; toll free (800) 549-1676 (in California)
or (800) 676-1676 (outside California)

INNKEEPERS: *Nancy Donaldson, Sandy Hunt,*
and Lu Caruso.

ACCOMMODATIONS: *Five rooms, all with private bath;*
queen- and one king-size bed. The Hitchcock House (next
door) is operated as part of the inn with four rooms, all with
private bath; queen- and king-size beds.

RESERVATIONS: *Four to six weeks recommended*
for weekends.

MINIMUM STAY: *Two nights on weekends.*

DEPOSIT: *First night's lodging.*

CREDIT CARDS: *AE, DC, MC, Visa.*

RATES: *Moderate to expensive.*

RESTRICTIONS: *No pets.*

Take three independent career women. Add a historic
structure crying out for tender loving care. Stir in a need to
try something new and different, and you have the highly
successful ingredients of one of Santa Barbara's most hos-
pitable bed and breakfast inns.

The Old Yacht Club Inn was built in 1912 as a private
residence on Cabrillo Boulevard overlooking the beautiful
Pacific. In the 1920s Santa Barbara's yacht club was completely destroyed by a disastrous storm. The present structure was pressed into service as the headquarters for the
club; later it was moved to its current location on Corona
Del Mar.

Nancy Donaldson, the dean of a Los Angeles high
school, and female friends—also educators and adminis-
trators—cooperated to buy, renovate, furnish, and finally
operate The Old Yacht Club Inn. Just a short distance from
lovely Cabrillo Beach, the OYCI has five tastefully decorated guest rooms, with an additional four in the historic
Hitchcock House located just next door.

The Castellamare room is my favorite: hardwood floors,
bedspread and drapes with a brightly colored flower print,
and a whirlpool bathtub. I also like the Portofino room,

with its queen-size canopy bed, and shades of baby blue, tan, and cream woven through its decor. All rooms are decorated with antiques, and the front rooms catch the sun and a delicious afternoon breeze. There is a small decanter at bedside for guests whose slumber is improved by a sip of sherry or two.

Guests are invited to share the living room as well as the spacious front porch. Arriving guests are offered a glass of wine or a cup of tea in the living room. There is a fireplace here, but no television. As a native of the area, Nancy Donaldson is well-equipped to steer guests to the best restaurants and nearby attractions. Bicycles are available to guests, as are beach chairs and towels. Those who arrive on Amtrak or at the airport can arrange to be picked up and transported to the inn.

The breakfast is fuller than most, usually featuring egg dishes, with fresh fruit, juice, homemade breads (zucchini and banana), and coffeecake. Nancy will also cook dinner for guests on Saturday evenings by advance request. My advice to you: Request it—she's an excellent cook!

Simpson House Inn

121 East Arrellaga Street
Santa Barbara, California 93101
(805) 963-7067 or (800) 676-1280

INNKEEPERS: *Glyn and Linda Davies; Gillean Wilson.*

ACCOMMODATIONS: *13 rooms, all with private bath; double, queen-, and king-size beds.*

RESERVATIONS: *Four to six weeks recommended.*

MINIMUM STAY: *Two nights on weekends.*

DEPOSIT: *Full amount.*

CREDIT CARDS: *AE, DC, MC, Visa.*

RATES: *Moderate to expensive.*

RESTRICTIONS: *No pets.*

Glyn and Linda Davies fought city hall to save their 117-year-old Victorian from demolition, and happily for bed and breakfast lovers, they won. The home was built in 1874 by a Scotsman, Robert Simpson, for his daughters Margaret and Mary. When it was first erected, just after the Civil War, it had neither electricity nor indoor plumbing, but it has come a long way since that era. The Davies have devoted over 10 years to the restoration of Simpson House, including tracking down original maps of the area, poring over old photographs of the home, and making trips to Europe to select just the right furniture. Today a grand inn stands as proud testimony to the Davies' devotion to their task.

Once you venture behind Simpson House Inn's sandstone walls and eugenia hedges, you'll find it hard to believe you are just blocks away from downtown Santa Barbara. The resplendent Eastlake Victorian sits on an acre of lush green lawns covered with gardens and oak and magnolia trees. You can put your bags in your room and join the croquet game that's probably just starting on the side lawn, or jump on one of the inn's bicycles and go exploring.

Keeping with the turn-of-the-century theme of the house, the guest rooms all have American and European antiques, lace curtains, and Oriental rugs. Rooms are named in honor of Robert Simpson, the original owner, and his family members. The Robert and Julia Simpson Room has a king-size brass bed and a comfortable sitting area as well as a private bath. French doors open out to the room's private deck. English lace sets the mood for the Margaret Simpson Room with its oak antiques and a brass and porcelain queen-size bed. An antique spool bed, original artwork, and a Victorian pull-chain toilet characterize the Katherine McCormick Room. The Sun Room is reminiscent of an English garden with its white wicker furniture with rose and green chintz cushions and matching fabric on the queen-size brass bed. Four luxurious suites are now contained in the property's beautifully restored 1878 barn; also available are three private newly constructed cottages.

The Simpson House living room is painted a stunning Wedgwood blue. Lace curtains accent the windows and French doors that lead out onto the veranda. Inviting overstuffed rose-colored chairs and sofa are grouped on an Oriental rug near the fireplace. The walls are lined with shelves overflowing with beautifully bound books and antique artifacts. Potted palms and fringed lamp shades help complete the Victorian feel.

Breakfast is served on the veranda from 8:30 to 9:30 a.m. Newspapers are available for perusal over a steaming hot cup of fresh-ground Viennese roast coffee. Be sure not to miss the homemade granola from the extensive selection of cereals at the help-yourself cereal bar. All fruits and vegetables served at Simpson House are organically grown, some in Glyn and Linda's own backyard. Freshly squeezed orange juice is poured prior to the first course of mixed fruit, grapefruit, or baked pear. Also on the menu are strawberry crepes dusted with powdered sugar or baked Huevos Santa Barbara (eggs, salsa, and grated Monterey and cheddar cheeses) along with English scones topped with double whipped cream and homemade lemon curd.

Late afternoon brings forth wines produced at local wineries served with baked Brie and French bread or pear chutney with cream cheese and crackers.

Inn on Summer Hill

2520 Lillie Avenue
P.O. Box 376
Summerland, California 93067; (805) 969-9998

INNKEEPERS: *Mabel Shults and Verlinda Richardson.*

ACCOMMODATIONS: *16 rooms, all with private bath; queen- and king-size beds.*

RESERVATIONS: *Four weeks recommended.*

MINIMUM STAY: *Two nights on weekends and over holiday periods.*

DEPOSIT: *Full amount.*

CREDIT CARDS: *AE, MC, Visa.*

RATES: *Expensive to very expensive.*

RESTRICTIONS: *Children discouraged. No pets.*

There are some things in life that are simply a labor of love, and the Inn on Summer Hill is one of them.

For over 20 years Mabel Shults has received acclaim for her interior design skills when it comes to decorating (or redecorating) California country inns and hotels. Some of her well-known projects have included Los Olivos Grand Hotel, the Hilton in Oxnard, the charming Blue Whale (Cambria), and San Luis Obispo's Apple Farm. But it was in the late 1980s that someone suggested she and her married daughter Verlinda (Shults) Richardson cooperate to design, build, and finally operate their own secluded seaside village resort.

The California Craftsman-style Inn on Summer Hill has 16 guest rooms that are filled with custom-made furniture. Mabel's professional trademarks are quite evident: they include an exuberant use of decorative items and fabric—up to seven different fabric patterns are interwoven through coverlets, dust ruffles, canopies, pillows, table skirts, and curtains. Each "mini-suite" also includes a stereo, television, and video cassette player hidden inside an armoire, a Jacuzzi tub for two, wood-burning fireplace, small refrigerator stocked with soft drinks, and balcony with Pacific Ocean view.

One of the few bed and breakfasts that employs a full-time professional chef, Inn on Summer Hill meals are a cut above the rest. My Saturday morning began when a copy of the *Los Angeles Times* was delivered to the door along with a hand-written card noting the day's weather report. While breakfast in the room was an option, I chose to sample from the help-yourself buffet of fresh melon, homemade bread pudding, granola and milk, blackberry muffins, and flaky croissants. Meanwhile the chef was engaged preparing the day's entrée: potato pancakes with fresh dill and sour cream sauce.

Also known for their outstanding hors d'oeuvres and dessert buffets, the inn offers amenities almost too numerous to mention: alarm clocks, coffee thermoses, fresh flowers, extra pillows, an outdoor spa.

Set in the rolling foothills of Santa Barbara, Summerland is noted for its quaint antique stores. Although Californians have long been aware of this coastal village which was founded as a spiritualist colony in the late 19th century, it was President Bill Clinton's 1992 Thanksgiving weekend visit that put Summerland on the national map. Some six miles north of Summerland, Santa Barbara's beaches, hiking trails, shopping, and historic buildings beckon. Of special interest is Mission Santa Barbara on the upper end of Laguna Street, the 60-acre botanic garden on Mission Canyon Road, and the city's art museum.

La Mer Gaestehaus

411 Poli Street
Ventura, California 93001; (805) 643-3600

INNKEEPER: *Gisela Flender Baida.*

ACCOMMODATIONS: *Five rooms, all private bath; double, queen-, and king-size beds.*

RESERVATIONS: *Four to six weeks recommended.*

MINIMUM STAY: *Two nights on weekends.*

DEPOSIT: *First night's lodging.*

CREDIT CARDS: *MC, Visa.*

RATES: *Moderate to expensive.*

RESTRICTIONS: *No children under 12. No pets.*

In the mood to do something drastic? Reserve two seats on the midnight flight to Paris and stay at that quaint country inn on the Seine. Then hop across the channel and visit that little bed and breakfast just outside London. What's that you say? Not enough time, too expensive? If it's the hospitality of a European bed and breakfast inn you seek, then look no further than Ventura. Because the hillside La Mer, overlooking the Pacific Ocean, brings a little bit of Europe to the southern coast of California.

You won't have any trouble spotting the inn once you're in the vicinity: It's the Cape Cod-style Victorian with the American, French, German, Norwegian, and Austrian flags waving a message of welcome from the front porch. At sunset, the German-born innkeeper, Gisela Baida, keeps the front windows gaily lit.

A step up into the lavender-colored parlor is a step back to 1890 when the home was first built. The French walnut clawfoot love seat with matching walnut coffee table set the tone. On chilly nights you can curl up here in front of the Pennsylvania Dutch pot-bellied stove or make your personal calls from the old-fashioned-style telephone. A beautifully carved buffet is pressed into service during morning hours to display Gisela's homemade cakes.

After filling your plate at the buffet you can dine in the rustic Bavarian breakfast room that has a panoramic view of the city of Ventura or at a secluded table for two on the deck outside the kitchen. Gisela encourages her guests to get acquainted and share their travel stories over the morning meal. The fresh-squeezed orange juice and coffee precedes the Black Forest ham and soft boiled eggs that Gisela always offers her guests. Save room for the Muesli (a cereal with raisins, almonds, granola, and coconut) and be sure to sample one (or all) of the fresh-baked breads (banana, pumpkin, and pumpernickel). Fresh fruit complements an assortment of Fontina, Jarlsburg, and Steppenkaese cheeses. The homemade German cakes (*Traenchenkuchen*, which means "tear drop," and *Bienenstich*, or "bee sting") are quite unique.

The five guest rooms (each with a private entrance) also have a distinct European flavor. Peter Paul Rubens is the representative from Germany. Then there's the English Queen Anne. Captain's Coje is the Norwegian theme room, and Wienerwald, Austrian. Elegant is the word that comes to mind when attempting to describe the powder blue Madame Pompadour room. You sleep under a ficus tree that stands behind a queen-size antique Louis XIV bed. There's a brocade love seat, an ideal spot to rest after a day of picnicking at the beach, and a cast-iron pot-bellied stove. In the evening you can relax on your private balcony and watch the sun sink into the Pacific.

La Mer is located in Ventura with its miles of "undiscovered" beaches, antique stores, the Channel Island National Park, and historic mission San Buenaventura. Ask Gisela to pack your lunch so you can spend the day playing at the ocean or exploring the hills behind the inn. An even lazier day can be spent aboard an antique horse carriage ride that ends up at the nearby Oak Creek Winery.

La Maida House

11159 La Maida Street
North Hollywood, California 91601; (818) 769-3857

INNKEEPER: *Megan Timothy.*

ACCOMMODATIONS: *Seven rooms and five suites, all with private bath; twin, double, queen-, and king-size beds.*

RESERVATIONS: *Three weeks recommended.*

MINIMUM STAY: *Two nights.*

DEPOSIT: *First night's lodging.*

CREDIT CARDS: *MC, Visa.*

RATES: *Moderate to very expensive.*

RESTRICTIONS: *No pets.*

All the great things you've been hearing about La Maida House are true. This 25-room, 7,000-square-foot Italian villa is the crème de la crème of the small inns. Its marble fireplace, spiral staircase, French doors, beveled glass mirrors, and bubbling fountains are reminiscent of the glamorous Hollywood of the '30s and '40s. The house was actually built in 1926 by one T. G. La Maida, a fruit and vegetable rancher. The largest guest room, Cipresso, overlooks the cypress trees along La Maida Street. Its canopied bed, ceiling fan, and wicker furniture remind one of warmer climes—perhaps Zimbabwe, where innkeeper Megan Timothy hails from.

Other touches I like here: AM/FM clock radios, refrigerators, and private-line telephones in the guest rooms; down comforters and wool blankets; a copy of the *Los Angeles Times* delivered to the door; bathroom scales for the weight conscious; full laundry and dry-cleaning service on request; and Megan will even prepare dinner for a tired and weary traveler with a little advance notice.

"Our guests are guests in the true sense of the word," says Megan. "In Africa when we had house guests we catered to their every little whim. That's what I'm striving to re-create here."

A woman of many talents, this Megan: a caterer by profession, a patron of the arts, a sculptor in stained glass, a photographer extraordinaire, an interior designer, and even a one-time professional folk singer.

Everything here is homemade, right down to the blended yogurt-fruit juice beverages served at breakfast and the "padkos" (an African tradition of "food for the road") Megan gives guests as a parting gift. What for many other innkeepers is the lull in their day, is for Megan the busiest part; she was baking oatmeal cookies when I arrived in the early afternoon. Megan keeps chickens for fresh eggs, grows her own fruits, vegetables, and herbs, and makes her own jams and preserves.

Writers, producers, directors, and celebrities are entered on La Maida's guest list. Part of the reason is that the inn is so close to most of the major studios (Universal, Disney, Columbia, Warner Brothers, NBC). La Maida has even seen a little moviemaking of its own. The house was featured in scenes of *Quincy* and the popular television shows *Unsolved Mysteries* and *Simon and Simon.*

Other nearby attractions include the Hollywood Bowl (Megan will provide a preconcert supper), the Huntington Library and Gardens, the Norton Simon Museum, and the Los Angeles County Museum of Art. (La Maida is a quick 10 minutes from the Burbank/Hollywood airport.)

Speaking of art, Megan's breakfast is a feast of edible art. The fare includes freshly baked breads (scones, brioches, or oatmeal muffins), an attractive carved-fruit platter with Tunisian oranges (sprinkled with rosewater and cinnamon), and a refreshing fresh fruit-yogurt drink such as peach-rosewater-honey or mint-pepper. (Bing cherries partially dipped in bittersweet chocolate were served at bedside.)

So the question is: Is it Hollywood or Zimbabwe? Perhaps it's the best of both.

Salisbury House

2273 West 20th Street
Los Angeles, California 90018
(213) 737-7817 or (800) 373-1778

INNKEEPERS: *Sue and Jay German.*

ACCOMMODATIONS: *Five rooms, three with private bath; twin, double, queen-, and king-size beds.*

RESERVATIONS: *Three to four weeks recommended.*

MINIMUM STAY: *None.*

DEPOSIT: *First night's lodging.*

CREDIT CARDS: *AE, MC, Visa.*

RATES: *Moderate.*

RESTRICTIONS: *No pets.*

"Our inn guests are our house guests," asserts Sue German, Salisbury House's dynamic hostess. "They're welcome, they're cared for, and most of all, they're cared about." Sue also says she tends to look at matters from a traveler's, rather than an innkeeper's perspective. Having herself been made to feel at home in bed and breakfasts in several foreign countries, her professional goal was to create a comparable feeling for visitors despite the enormity of Los Angeles.

Located just minutes from downtown Los Angeles and the freeway, Salisbury House is ideal for both the business and vacation traveler. Besides downtown, the mid-Wilshire, Beverly Hills, Century City, and Westside districts are readily accessible. Vacationers or getaway weekenders can use the inn as home base for museum or library visits, beach-going, theater entertainment, or theme park junkets.

The classic Craftsman-style home, built in 1909, had only three previous owners before Sue and Jay came along. The first, a physician whose office was downtown, reputedly owned one of the first automobiles in the area. This pocket of family homes on wide streets with big old trees finds friendly neighbors sitting out on the porch. It is so well maintained, in fact, that numerous movie and television production crews have filmed in the neighborhood; Salisbury House itself has even been used as a feature film location.

The living room of Salisbury House is made cozy by a grand piano and pendulum clock, wood-burning tile fireplace, deep blue floral print sofa and love seat, wood-beamed ceiling, and Oriental carpets. Original light fixtures and stained- and leaded-glass windows are found throughout the house.

Three of the guest rooms are named for their predominant color: the Rose, Green, and Blue rooms; the fourth is the Sun Suite where gay floral wallpaper combines with sunshine to give the main room and its sitting porch a bright, cheery look. The fifth room is the Americana Attic Suite occupying the home's entire third floor. This air-conditioned accommodation contains a spacious sitting area, a king-size brass bed, braided rugs, a color television, a telephone, and a private bath with antique clawfoot tub. All of the inn's beds are supplied with down comforters and feather pillows.

Sue's mouth-watering breakfasts are served in the home's inviting dining room on weekdays between 7:30 and 9:00 a.m.; weekends, between 8:00 and 9:30 a.m. Coffee and tea are brewing about a half hour earlier. The buffet includes entrees like chicken or fresh peach crepes, Belgian waffles with strawberries and cream, apple puffed pancakes, or asparagus omelettes. On weekends a fresh fruit cobbler or Sue's own bread pudding bursting with fruits and nuts may appear. And with the homemade baked goods, granola, and fresh fruit accompaniments, it's a cinch that no one will leave the table hungry.

Christmas House

9240 Archibald Avenue
Rancho Cucamonga, California 91730; (909) 980-6450

INNKEEPERS: *Jay and Janice Ilsley.*

ACCOMMODATIONS: *Six rooms, four with private bath; double and queen-size beds.*

RESERVATIONS: *Three to four weeks recommended.*

MINIMUM STAY: *None.*

DEPOSIT: *First night's lodging.*

CREDIT CARDS: *AE, DC, MC, Visa.*

RATES: *Moderate.*

RESTRICTIONS: *No pets.*

It's Christmas in July in Southern California, or just about any other month of the year as well. The Yuletide spirit is imaginable because Christmas House was named for the gala gatherings held here each December by the Cousins and Whitson families, both former owners of the three-story Queen Anne-style Victorian home. And to think what a sight the stately manor must have been in its heyday when it was surrounded by some 80 acres of vineyards and citrus groves. Even now it is visible for nearly a block around, distinguished by more than a dozen tall palms.

Built in 1904, Christmas House was discovered by present-day owners Jay and Janice Ilsley in 1983. On the auction block and in a disreputable state at the time, the dwelling still showed its potential elegance in stained-glass windows, intricate woodwork, and wood and tile-faced fireplaces (a total of seven altogether in the home). Two years of extensive renovation later, greater Ontario's first and only bed and breakfast inn was born.

Located in the foothills of the San Gabriel Mountains, 37 miles east of downtown Los Angeles, Christmas House is within an hour's drive of most Southern California cultural and recreational attractions. Christmas House also appeals to business travelers due to its close proximity to the Ontario airport, just five minutes south.

Guests enjoy the parlor, library, formal dining room, and wide veranda during their stay at Christmas House. Period antiques help to capture the home's original grandeur. The reception room and parlor, for instance, are furnished with

1860s Eastlake-style parlor sets. Both rooms have fireplaces and Oriental carpets as well as original brass light fixtures and shades that are also common to the library.

The only downstairs guest room holds a queen-size white iron bed fashioned in the Victorian style. Known as the Garden Suite, this cheery sunlit room's white wood shutters and French doors open to a brick courtyard garden area with private spa covered by a gazebo. Upstairs, I sojourned in the Celebration Suite with its mahogany canopy bed draped in lace, bay windowed alcove, and two fireplaces, one in the bedroom and one in the sitting room. In the restored carriage house are Elizabeth's Room (named in honor of Elizabeth Whitson, the last grandame of the estate) and The Carriage Room (queen-size sleigh bed, parlor stove, and private spa). The Carriage Room's armoire hides a television and VCR as well as a library of classic films (including *It's A Wonderful Life*), a popcorn maker, and popcorn.

Silver service and antique china and linen set the mood for the 7:00 to 9:00 a.m. breakfast Monday through Friday and 8:00 to 9:30 seatings Saturday and Sunday. Watermelon granité garnished with fresh mint from the garden or chilled pear soup are sometimes the starters. Faces glow when Janice appears with her custard-filled strawberry crepes made with triple cream sherry. Ice water, fresh-squeezed grapefruit juice, and coffee are also available on the fresh-flower-graced rectangular dining table.

The inn's generous midweek stay discounts and corporate rates are worth a mention. But its biggest drawing card is special event weekends. Murder mysteries, called "Dead and Breakfast," give overnighters the opportunity to play out their fantasies as detectives, murderers, or victims as buried clues are unearthed to shed light on whodunit. The murder mystery package includes a wine tasting and champagne reception, gourmet dinner, sleeping arrangements, and to-die-for breakfast.

The *Los Angeles Times* named Christmas House one of the most romantic destinations in the Inland Empire. I adore it most in spring or fall, but if you feel you just must visit in December, plan to attend the inn's annual Christmas Eve day production of Dickens' *A Christmas Carol* when Ebenezer Scrooge receives guests and ghosts between the hours of 1:00 and 6:00 p.m.

Channel Road Inn

219 West Channel Road
Santa Monica, California 90402; (310) 459-1920

INNKEEPERS: *Susan Zolla and Kathy Jensen.*

ACCOMMODATIONS: *14 rooms, all with private bath; double, queen-, and king-size beds.*

RESERVATIONS: *Three to four weeks recommended.*

MINIMUM STAY: *None.*

DEPOSIT: *First night's lodging.*

CREDIT CARDS: *AE, MC, Visa.*

RATES: *Moderate to expensive.*

RESTRICTIONS: *No pets.*

Featured in many architectural guidebooks and touted by prestigious publications such as *Travel & Leisure* and the *New York Times*, the Channel Road Inn offers history, romance, and an outstanding location—one block from the beach in Santa Monica Canyon and 20 minutes from LAX.

Designed by architect Frank Kegley, the home is a rare West Coast example of the Shingle Clad Colonial Revival style. It was built in 1910 for Thomas McCall, a Scotsman who emigrated to Texas in the 1880s and managed to amass a fortune from oil and cattle.

The home's inviting living room is filled with furnishings evocative of a 1920s California beachfront property. Silk upholstered sofas and chairs in pastel colors complement a lavender Chinese rug. The library, brimming with volumes ranging from romantic novels to Southern California travel, is furnished in white wicker highlighted by green chintz. Framed photographs of the Thomas McCall family have been lovingly placed throughout the house by living McCall descendants.

Fourteen individually decorated guest rooms and suites scattered throughout the three-story residence are each equipped with telephone and television. Some have antique four-posters, others wicker bedroom sets; one room, the Patio Room, is handicapped accessible. Among the many little indulgences seen to by Channel Road Inn hostesses are bubble bath, bathrobes, goose-down pillows, fresh fruit and flowers, and breakfast in bed.

Assorted pastries and muffins are served as part of a full complimentary breakfast which also includes hot and cold cereals, apple-filled French toast, a California fruit platter, and tea, coffee, and freshly squeezed orange juice. Afternoons bring wine, cheese, tea, and other refreshments. The chocolate chip cookie jar is always full.

Life-long residents of Santa Monica, innkeepers Kathy Jensen and Susan Zolla are pros when it comes to recommending sightseeing spots and upscale restaurants. For starters they suggest shopping the boutiques along chic Montana Avenue or visiting the Getty Museum or Will Rogers Park. The inn provides bicycles for the short jaunt to Santa Monica Pier or a ride along the 30-mile oceanside bike path that runs from Santa Monica to Venice Beach, Marina Del Rey, and beyond. Aching leg muscles rejuvenate themselves in Channel Road Inn's hillside hot tub.

The Seal Beach Inn

212 Fifth Street
Seal Beach, California 90740; (310) 493-2416

INNKEEPER: *Marjorie Bettenhausen.*

ACCOMMODATIONS: *23 rooms, all with private bath; twin, double, queen-, and king-size beds.*

RESERVATIONS: *Two to three weeks recommended.*

MINIMUM STAY: *Two nights on weekends.*

DEPOSIT: *First night's lodging.*

CREDIT CARDS: *AE, DC, MC, Visa.*

RATES: *Moderate to expensive.*

RESTRICTIONS: *Children discouraged. No pets.*

The Spanish called it Rancho Los Alamitos; the German burghers who followed knew it as Anaheim Landing. Bay City was the rather slick monicker cooked up by developers in the 1920s. Today this sleepy coastal village is known as Seal Beach (after the many seals that once flocked to the beaches here), but it is in many ways just as quiet now as it was in former days—which for those of us who wish to get away from it all is a big plus. Yet the nearby convergence of four major freeways makes Los Angeles and destinations in Orange County easy to get to when it's time to return to the real world.

The style of The Seal Beach Inn is French Mediterranean, a perfect choice for this part of the state. When one first hears of its 23 rooms, one imagines that this might be a motel that serves breakfast. Not a bit of it! The rooms are equipped with antiques and warm, quality furnishings, carefully designed to impart a Continental country inn flavor. (All rooms have private baths, and kitchen bars are available in most.) Prints, objets d'art, collectibles, and books abound in most rooms. There is a pool, as one might expect in Southern California, and there is also an attractive garden with roses, geraniums, hibiscus, and begonias, among scores of other flowers.

Seal Beach Inn saw its inception in the 1920s, when Seal Beach was a wide-open gambling and resort area, which makes the European feeling of this place all the more remarkable. ("The closest thing to Europe since I left there," reads one guest-register encomium.) Hardwood floors and wood paneling are everywhere. Antique lamp-posts and a brick courtyard, blue awnings and white-painted fence, and an antique British telephone booth all add to the ambience.

Proprietor Marjorie Bettenhausen goes out of her way to provide those little extras that make a bed and breakfast different from any other kind of accommodation. Current magazines and the *Los Angeles Times* are available in the library; there is even an ironing board and iron available for guest use. Just one block from the ocean, the inn is also close to the Old Town section of Seal Beach (the high per-centage of artists and craftspeople living in the area is ob-vious in the boutiques and shops), the Long Beach marina, and a total of four shopping areas on various waterfronts. And the inn is just 15 to 20 minutes by car from Disneyland and Knott's Berry Farm.

Breakfast in the dining room begins at 7:30 a.m. and lasts until 10:00. The croissants and freshly baked breads, homemade granola, Belgian waffles, fresh fruits and juices, cheeses, egg casserole or quiche, freshly ground coffee, and selection of imported teas make this a wonderful morning meal.

Marjorie enjoys what she does, as becomes obvious when one talks to her about her work. "Every day it's some-thing different," Marjorie told me. One interesting moment came when two attractive French girls admitted sadly that they had run out of money. What to do? Before a call could be placed to the French Embassy, two French pilots checked in, and *voilà*! The next day the two young women were flown—free of charge—back to Paris. A charming story, and one that might have an interesting follow-up.

Lord Mayor's Inn

435 Cedar Avenue
Long Beach, California 90802; (310) 436-0324

INNKEEPERS: *Reuben and Laura Brasser.*

ACCOMMODATIONS: *Five rooms, all with private bath; twin, double, and queen-size beds.*

RESERVATIONS: *Six weeks recommended.*

MINIMUM STAY: *None.*

DEPOSIT: *First night's lodging.*

CREDIT CARDS: *AE, MC, Visa.*

RATES: *Moderate.*

RESTRICTIONS: *Not appropriate for children. No pets.*

For better or worse, Lord Mayor's Inn is located in the heart of downtown Long Beach. Yet, it is truly a blessing to its surrounding neighbors, business travelers who frequent nearby government offices or the new World Trade Center, and Southern California vacationers heading for Catalina Island or the Queen Mary. Lord Mayor's can also be praised for extending overnight rates that are quite agreeable—under $100 (with breakfast and afternoon refreshments) for two people. Laura and Reuben Brasser's home has even earned AAA's three-star rating.

Formerly the residence of the city's first mayor, Charles H. Windham, this spacious 1904 Edwardian underwent a three-phase, four-year renovation before it turned bed and breakfast. In 1992 it received the prestigious Great American Home Award from the Washington, DC-based National Trust for Historic Preservation.

As you approach the house from the front lawn, notice the five different shades of gray used in exterior decoration, the granite porch pillars that traveled to Long Beach around Cape Horn, and the rounded dentil that is repeated again inside on the living room fireplace. The entry, like all of the downstairs, glistens with golden oak woodwork. Living and dining rooms sport 10-foot ceilings, hardwood floors, and original brass hardware. Opposite the living room is Reuben's office, which is furnished with a matching antique clawfoot desk and sideboard, and a library open for guest perusal.

The dining room's cherrywood oval table is dressed for breakfast according to guests' needs up until 9:00 a.m. Homemade elderberry jam enlivens Laura's special popovers. Fresh strawberries are topped with lemon curd, and fluffy scrambled eggs are laced with herbs from the backyard garden. Reuben offers a prayer for the well-being of his guests along with fresh-squeezed orange juice and coffee.

Five guest bedrooms access second-floor sun decks. The Eastlake Room takes its name from its furnishings, the most unique of which is an 1870 Eastlake folding chair. Beppe's Room showcases a four-poster bed and a collection of Laura's grandmother's hats. The original bedroom of Mayor Windham's daughter, called Margarita's Room, has twin 18th-century Austrian beds, a marble-top dressing table, and a framed and dated 1686 sampler handed down through Laura's family. A Hawaiian wedding bed from the early 1900s distinguishes the Hawaiian Room; it is draped with a popcorn stitch coverlet. The Fireplace Room, the original master bedroom, has the only photo of Mayor Windham in the house on its fireplace mantel. The room is also furnished with a four-poster bed.

Lord Mayor's Inn renders a wide variety of services to the community besides its unique overnight accommodations. These include Victorian teas, murder mystery weekends, luncheons, formal dinner parties, weddings, group tours, and arts and crafts demonstrations. "Long Beach has given so much to us through the years," say Laura and Reuben. "Now we feel like we're giving something back."

The Inn on Mt. Ada

398 Wrigley Road
Avalon, Santa Catalina Island, California 90704
(310) 510-2030

INNKEEPER: *Susie Griffin.*

ACCOMMODATIONS: *Six rooms, all with private bath; double and queen-size beds.*

RESERVATIONS: *Two to four months for weekdays; eight months to one year for weekends.*

MINIMUM STAY: *Two nights on weekends and over holiday periods.*

DEPOSIT: *First night's lodging.*

CREDIT CARDS: *MC, Visa.*

RATES: *Very expensive.*

RESTRICTIONS: *Children discouraged. No pets.*

There are several bed and breakfast inns on Santa Catalina Island, but the crème de la crème of the consortium is undoubtedly the Wrigley Mansion. Also known as The Inn on Mt. Ada, the 10,000-square-foot home, with its 22 rooms, six working fireplaces, 11-room servants' quarters, carriage house, and five-and-a-half acres planted in hibiscus, eucalyptus, palm trees, and succulents, was once the summer home of William Wrigley, Jr., chewing gum magnate, and his wife, Ada.

Built in 1921, the Georgian Colonial is listed on the National Register of Historic Places and is also a California State Historical Landmark. Spectacular views of Avalon Harbor with its multitude of sailboats, quaint village shops, and famed landmark casino are beheld from the hilltop home's splendidly manicured grounds.

In the cozy den, once Wrigley's billiard parlor, a brick and wood mantel fireplace enhances an English drawing room feel. The palatial-sized living room's walls are lined with built-in bookshelves. Overstuffed wingback chairs mix comfortably with white, green, and coral upholstered sofas. A baby grand piano sits near French doors that lead to the terrace. The sunroom is furnished in wicker with mint green and blue floral upholstered cushions. Its rows of glass-paned windows also overlook Avalon Harbor. A telescope, allowing an even closer view, is provided on the veranda just off the sunroom where white wicker rockers are interspersed among green and white striped umbrella tables and chairs.

During the inn's convivial wine hour, a spread of hot and cold appetizers is laid out. Among the offerings are an artichoke chili cheese spread with crackers, ham and asparagus roll-ups, or possibly a Mexican fiesta platter. Bowls full of mixed nuts sit alongside wine decanters and soft drinks, as well as bottles of Calistoga water.

Breakfasts are individually served at cozy tables for two between the hours of 8:30 and 10:00 a.m. The first course is always a fruit dish, such as baked apples or fresh blueberries bathed in cream. French toast is served with a side of bacon; mushroom and cheese omelettes are accompanied by bagels. There is always plenty of coffee, tea, cocoa, milk, and freshly squeezed orange juice. A light deli-style lunch and a full dinner are also complimentary to overnight guests.

Each guest room comes complete with its own golf cart. (How's that for unique?) Color televisions are supplied on request. Of the six bedrooms, the Grand Suite (formerly the Wrigley's upstairs living room and Mr. Wrigley's bedroom and bath) has the most tailored look. Its canopied bed faces a marble fireplace. The adjoining Small Suite (Mrs. Wrigley's former bedroom), has an ecru lace canopied and draped bed, a vanity table, small fireplace, and its own library with sitting room and chaise longue. A corner bedroom with a queen-size four-poster and moss green tiled fireplace once hosted the Prince of Wales (who later became King Edward VIII of England), and former presidents Calvin Coolidge and Woodrow Wilson. (During his term of office, Warren Harding used the entire property as his western White House.)

Passage to Santa Catalina Island can be obtained by ferry boat, helicopter, or plane from the mainland. Catalina Cruises and the Catalina Express depart out of Long Beach and San Pedro. Island Express helicopter service is also available from these two cities. Boat service from San Diego is provided by Sea Jet and Catalina Pacifica. The Catalina Flyer (Catalina Passenger Service) runs on a limited schedule but does transport passengers from Newport Beach to Catalina Island on weekends year-round.

The Carriage House

1322 Catalina
Laguna Beach, California 92651; (714) 494-8945

INNKEEPERS: *Vernon, Dee, and Tom Taylor.*

ACCOMMODATIONS: *Six suites, all with private bath; twin, double, queen-, and king-size beds.*

RESERVATIONS: *Three to four weeks recommended.*

MINIMUM STAY: *Two nights on weekends.*

DEPOSIT: *First night's lodging.*

CREDIT CARDS: *Not accepted.*

RATES: *Moderate to expensive.*

RESTRICTIONS: *None.*

Southern California has its own unique style when it comes to bed and breakfast—especially when contrasted with the inns of the North Coast. Perhaps the climate evokes a more casual atmosphere; perhaps it has something to do with the architectural styles of the area as well. Take The Carriage House as a case in point. Here you have six suites surrounding a central brick courtyard in a horseshoe-shaped fashion. (This arrangement is similar to Eiler's Inn, the other Laguna Beach bed and breakfast.)

Each suite features its own parlor, separate bedroom, and fully equipped kitchen. Room decors play on themes like Green Palms (forest green walls and carpet, white woodwork, white wicker furniture, a ceiling fan, and, as one would expect, potted palms), Lilac Time (cranberry and lilac tones, French doors that open to the courtyard), Primrose Lane, Mockingbird Hill, Mandalay, and Home Sweet Home (calico and gingham).

The focal point of the inn is Grandma Bean's dining room, where guests enjoy a buffet-style breakfast from 8:30 to 10:00 a.m. of hot and cold cereals, coffeecake and English muffins, fresh fruit, two different juices (orange is one), coffee, and tea. This is a family-owned and -operated affair (Dee Taylor and husband Vernon are the resident innkeepers while son Tom is co-owner) located on a quiet residential street just two blocks from the beach and a few more from the heart of the village.

Laguna is a town *with* and *in* which people fall in love. Hand holding is as popular here as jogging and cycling, and stealing a kiss as common as stealing the show—in this case the show is the annual Festival of Arts and Pageant of the Masters held each year throughout July and August.

Blue Lantern Inn

34343 Street of the Blue Lantern
Dana Point, California 92629; (714) 661-1304

INNKEEPERS: *Roger and Sally Post; Tom Taylor.*

ACCOMMODATIONS: *29 rooms, all with private bath; twin, double, queen-, and king-size beds.*

RESERVATIONS: *Four to six weeks recommended.*

MINIMUM STAY: *None.*

DEPOSIT: *First night's lodging.*

CREDIT CARDS: *AE, MC, Visa.*

RATES: *Expensive to very expensive.*

RESTRICTIONS: *No pets.*

Roger and Sally Post have come the closest to opening what may be considered the country's first chain of bed and breakfasts. It all started on California's central coast, when, nearly 20 years ago, they acquired the Green Gables Inn in Pacific Grove. This was soon followed by the opening of their Gosby House in 1976, also in Pacific Grove. Next came The Cobblestone Inn of Carmel. And finally, Petite Auberge and the White Swan Inn, both located in downtown San Francisco. Just when we thought we had heard the last of it, the Posts emerged from a four-year hiatus to open yet another inn—only this time in *Southern* California.

Their Blue Lantern Inn is situated high on a bluff above Dana Point yacht harbor. Panoramic views of the Pacific Ocean and guest rooms filled with New England furniture, Jacuzzi tubs, and fireplaces are touches characteristic of the Cape Cod-like atmosphere. French doors welcome guests to the entry of the sand-colored, wood-frame building trimmed in white with its first-floor reception area, sitting room, dining room, and cozy library.

The decor throughout the inn is resplendent in hues indicative of the southern coast where Dana Point is located: seafoam green, lavender, periwinkle, and sand tones. Original art print wallpapers, soft quilts, and patterned carpets set the stage for traditional bedroom furnishings. Additionally, each guest room is supplied with oversized beach towels, fluffy terry cloth robes, a refrigerator, color television set, and a ministereo. Typical of my champagne taste, I opted for the Tower Room, which has a vaulted ceiling, king-size bed, and 180-degree view of the coast and the yacht harbor.

A bounteous buffet breakfast is served in the sunny dining room, but may also be taken back to your private terrace. The ever-changing menu could include a vegetarian quiche, egg-based casserole, or hot-off-the-griddle pancakes. There's always homemade granola, a fresh fruit platter, and a selection of homemade breads and muffins. Beverages (coffee, tea, milk, and three kinds of juice) are also included. Wine and hors d'oeurves are prepared each afternoon and set out in the library; evening time brings fresh-baked cookies along with turn-down service. (Good thing the inn also has an exercise room!)

Dana Point is perched along the southern coast just a block west of Highway One. Laguna Beach is a mere five miles farther to the north. On sunny days the area is a paradise of outdoor activities on white sand beaches: Sailing, windsurfing, deep sea fishing, and parasailing facilities are all available. Shops and art galleries abound in both Laguna and Dana Point, and several excellent restaurants are within walking distance of the Blue Lantern, the sixth inn of the Posts' collection.

The Bed & Breakfast Inn at La Jolla

7753 Draper Avenue
La Jolla, California 92037; (619) 456-2066

INNKEEPER: *Pierrette Timmerman.*

ACCOMMODATIONS: *16 rooms, 15 with private bath; twin, queen-, and king-size beds.*

RESERVATIONS: *Three to four weeks for weekends.*

MINIMUM STAY: *Two nights over weekends and holiday periods.*

DEPOSIT: *First night's lodging.*

CREDIT CARDS: *MC, Visa.*

RATES: *Moderate to expensive.*

RESTRICTIONS: *No pets.*

The only bed and breakfast inn in La Jolla, this lovely dwelling was built in 1913 by architect Irving Gill, who for many years had worked side by side with his better-known contemporary, Frank Lloyd Wright. Gill was a pioneer of modernism—his work known for its machinelike quality and precision detail. It has been said that this stucco box-like structure with its prominent arches best exemplifies his Cubist style.

Sitting pretty in the heart of La Jolla's cultural complex (surrounded by the Museum of Contemporary Art, a school, church, public recreation center, and the Women's Club), the inn harbors 16 guest accommodations: 11 in the original structure, five in the addition (a matching new building dovetailed to the old). Rooms are charmingly appointed, and all but one come with private bath. My evening was spent in The Shores, a twin-bedded room just off the upstairs guest parlor and sun deck. There was a decanter of sherry in the room and a basket filled with apples and oranges. Other niceties included floral print comforters with matching pillow shams and dust ruffles on the beds, a pedestal-base breakfast table with two chairs, a supply of current magazines of interest, a digital alarm clock, fluffy towels, and European lotions and soaps in the bath. A television set, VCR, and ice maker were located in the combination parlor/library. Umbrella tables and chairs as well as a chaise longue were found on the deck.

Pacific View is another room that commanded my attention with its fireplace, antique mantel clock, corner bookshelves, double French doors, pineapple post bed, blue upholstered love seat, and fine writing desk. The premier attraction, however, is the Holiday Suite with its canopied (king) four-poster, eight-foot armoire, tile and brick fireplace, tailored white chintz sofa and wingback chair, Oriental carpet, view of the Pacific, and abundance of healthy plants.

Breakfast spots are many and varied: the dining room, the garden, the sun deck, or your bedroom. If you choose the latter, a delightful tray holding freshly squeezed orange juice, coffee and tea, granola, and a basket filled with croissants and quick breads accompanied by sweet butter and jam is delivered to the door of your room. Breakfast hours span 7:30 to 9:30 a.m. The inn stocks an ample supply of sightseeing literature and restaurant information; there is a pay telephone for guest use in the downstairs hall.

A picnic of sandwiches, fresh fruit, chocolates, and champagne or sparkling cider can be prepared for your day out with a little advance notice. The possibilities in and around this seaside community include a visit to the nearby Scripps Aquarium or the University of California at San Diego campus. Main street shops and restaurants are within easy walking distance, and the beach is just one block away. Wine hour is scheduled back at the inn at 4:00 p.m.

Heritage Park Bed & Breakfast Inn

2470 Heritage Park Row
San Diego, California 92110
(619) 299-6832 or (800) 995-2470

INNKEEPERS: *Nancy and Charles Helsper.*

ACCOMMODATIONS: *10 rooms, seven with private bath; double, queen-, and king-size beds.*

RESERVATIONS: *Three to four weeks for weekends and holidays.*

MINIMUM STAY: *Two nights on weekends.*

DEPOSIT: *Half of full amount.*

CREDIT CARDS: *MC, Visa.*

RATES: *Moderate.*

RESTRICTIONS: *No pets.*

Two blocks from Old Town San Diego—the first permanent Spanish settlement on the California coast, now filled with museums, art galleries, and restaurants—sits Heritage Park Bed & Breakfast Inn. Just imagine the setting: a quiet seven-acre park formed solely for the preservation of endangered Victorian homes. Among the cobblestone walkways and gardens stand seven classic Victorian structures from the 1800s. Built in 1889 for Harfield and Myrtle Christian, this particular Queen Anne is characterized by a variety of chimneys, shingles, a two-story corner tower, and an encircling veranda. Featured in *The Golden Era* magazine in 1890, it was called "an outstandingly beautiful home of Southern California." Recently, a panel of judges for San Diego's "People in Preservation" awards declared the remodeling job that took the house back to its original floor plan "one of the most enchanting projects we've seen and a major contribution not only to the park, but to the city as well."

This 10-room inn is completely decorated with antiques and collectibles of the 1800s. The formal front parlor contains period settees, Eastlake parlor tables, and a mahogany Eastlake-style fireplace with moss green tiles against a backdrop of William Morris wallpaper. Carpet reproductions from the 1800s blend with Oriental rugs designed to match Tiffany glass patterns.

Breakfast, served between 8:30 and 9:30 a.m., is packed to go for business people or travelers who need to get on the road early—another considerate touch. Heritage Park specialties include a chili cheese bake, French toast with apple cider syrup, homemade granola, broiled grapefruit and poached pears, and warm orange-flavored rolls or fresh-baked scones served with clotted cream and lemon curd.

Guest chambers follow themes in both name and decor. The Garden Room boasts a Floral Basket wall covering from the American Folk Art Collection, a sunflower-motif burled walnut Eastlake bed, and an 1880 triple-style mirrored vanity with built-in corner curios. The Victorian Rose Room has a white and brass iron bed and a pink rose motif. The Turret encompasses the home's turret tower with its 180-degree view. Country Heart is the least expensive room with stenciled-heart walls and towel racks, heart-shaped pillows, and a brass and iron bed. The largest room, Queen Anne, contains a four-poster with a hand-crocheted, tassled canopy, an Eastlake settee, and a walnut armoire. Other rooms are Coral Tree Lookout, Nosegay, Morning Glory Room, Forget Me Not (mahogany sleigh bed), and the Manor Suite.

A film from the inn's collection of old classics is shown in the parlor each night around 7:00 p.m. *Magnificent Doll* starring Ginger Rogers and David Niven was playing the day I visited, but *It's A Wonderful Life* with Jimmy Stewart and Donna Reed is said to be the most popular with the guests.

Special occasions come often at this inn. Nancy puts together packages of champagne, chocolates, roses, and bubble bath for honeymoon or anniversary couples. Her coup, however, is a very romantic five-course candlelight dinner served in the inn's private dining room. Also offered is a Victorian Hat Box Supper with lighter fare of salad, fruit, cheese, bread, and dessert which guests can enjoy on the veranda.

The inn celebrates Christmas with an annual Victorian candlelight tour that runs the entire month of December. The house has trees laden with candles, bows, and heirloom ornaments. Antiques and gift items are offered for sale. Hot wassail completes the time-honored scene. During the rest of the year, the ornaments that decorate the house are the congenial friends who frequent it. Heritage Park Bed & Breakfast Inn—what a hit!

Brookside Farm

1373 Marron Valley Road
Dulzura, California 92017; (619) 468-3043

INNKEEPERS: *Edd and Sally Guishard.*

ACCOMMODATIONS: *11 rooms, nine with private bath;
queen-size beds.*

RESERVATIONS: *Two to three weeks recommended.*

MINIMUM STAY: *Two nights on weekends, three over
some holiday periods.*

DEPOSIT: *First night's lodging.*

CREDIT CARDS: *MC, Visa.*

RATES: *Inexpensive to moderate.*

RESTRICTIONS: *No pets.*

I whizzed along Star Route 94 through downtown Dulzura
without even realizing it: the town consisted of one small
cafe and a post office. Several miles later, my car turned
around and headed back in the other direction, I spotted
Marron Valley Road and the country farmhouse surrounded by shady oak trees known as Brookside Farm.

Needless to say, this is a rural setting where time slows
to a crawl. Somewhere between the gravel parking lot and
the barrel-roof barn, I, too, lost some momentum. The four
acres of grounds and gardens, gently flowing stream, lazy
hammock, whirlpool spa, and menagerie of peacocks,
goats, chickens, pigs, pheasants, and kittens settled any
thoughts of looking for the nearest shopping mall.

The refurbished 1928 residence of Edd and Sally
Guishard is located 30 miles east of San Diego and 10
miles north of Tecate, a Mexican border town. Its sunny sitting room, stocked with games, books, magazines, and
puzzles, also cradles a cozy wood-burning parlor stove. The
dining room with upright piano, wind-up Victrola, and
tables covered in cream-colored lace is adjacent to a
homey kitchen where Edd prepares guest meals. His lifetime in the restaurant business makes for delicious daily
breakfasts (and optional four-course weekend dinners) that
incorporate vegetables and fruits picked fresh from the
property's gardens and orchards.

Each of the Farm's 11 bedrooms radiates a personality of its own through the use of period furnishings and hand-woven rugs on hardwood floors. Queen-size beds are the rule; most are covered with handmade quilts. I spent a peaceful night in the atypical Victorian-style Captain Small's Room which sheltered an 1880 vintage mahogany bed. Most quarters express a rustic sense of whimsy with names and themes like Hunter's Cabin, The Carpenter's Shop, and The Wash House.

The Guishards can be especially credited for their special event weekends, some of which include Honeymoon in June, a Fourth of July picnic, Labor Day square dance and barbecue, and semiannual wine tasting dinners. Swell as these are, something you'll always be sure to remember about Brookside Farm is its motto: One day in the country is worth one month in town.

Loma Vista Bed & Breakfast

33350 La Serena Way
Temecula, California 92591; (909) 676-7047

INNKEEPERS: *Dick and Betty Ryan.*

ACCOMMODATIONS: *Six rooms, all with private bath; queen- and king-size beds.*

RESERVATIONS: *Three to four weeks recommended.*

MINIMUM STAY: *Two nights through holiday periods.*

DEPOSIT: *First night's lodging.*

CREDIT CARDS: *DC, MC, Visa.*

RATES: *Moderate.*

RESTRICTIONS: *No pets.*

Just 60 miles north of San Diego and 90 miles southeast of Los Angeles are two of Southern California's best kept secrets—the Temecula Valley wine country and Loma Vista Bed & Breakfast. If it's jobs, kids, or simply boredom you're looking to escape from, this 5,400-square-foot California Mission-style home overlooking acres and acres of rolling hills covered with vineyards just might do the trick.

The first and only bed and breakfast in Temecula, Loma Vista was built and opened in 1988 by Dick and Betty Ryan, both in their late 50s and retired from banking and teaching respectively. The couple took to the trade with a flair for entertaining: "We love people," Betty notes, "even though we realize they don't come here *just* to visit us."

It is the Ryans' nightly happy hour and daily gourmet breakfast that encourages the spirit of camaraderie between guests and hosts. Locally produced wines, cheese, and pâté are served on the patio between 6:00 and 7:00 p.m. A 9:00 a.m. breakfast runs to cranberry and walnut muffins, fresh fruits and juice, eggs with refried beans and avocado, waffles, or chicken mushroom crepes, coffee, tea, and champagne. It is served family-style in the dining room.

Loma Vista guest quarters are individually decorated and fittingly named: Fume Blanc (furnished with white wicker), Zinfandel (Queen Anne traditional-style with a balcony that looks to the Palomar Observatory), Sauvignon Blanc (Southwestern decor), Chardonnay (country oak furnishings and a bath with old-fashioned pull-chain toilet),

Merlot (cherrywood queen bedroom suite; faces the San Jacinto Mountains), and Champagne (black lacquer furnishings, Art Deco decor). The rooms offer either queen- or king-size beds; all are air conditioned and have private baths with tub/showers.

Temecula is an official California State Historial Site due to its intact historic buildings and roots in the settling of the Old West. Twelve wineries in the area take advantage of the valley's unique microclimate and well-drained decomposed granite soils to produce and offer tastings of award-winning wines to the public. Annual wine-related events are the Barrel Tasting (first weekend in February), Hot Air Balloon and Wine Festival (May), and the Nouveau Wine and Food Tasting (third weekend of November).

Bed and Breakfast Reservation and Referral Services

Following is a list of agencies that book reservations and refer travelers to bed and breakfast inns as well as to accommodations in private homes. These services have gained tremendous popularity, and the rooms in private homes include breakfast along with overnight lodging at rates that are very affordable (starting at $35 per night).

Operations vary. Some services charge the traveler an annual membership fee, while others take their commissions from the host. In some cases the agencies provide lists or directories of the homes they contract with and leave the booking arrangements up to you.

American Family Inn/Bed & Breakfast San Francisco
P.O. Box 420009
San Francisco, CA 94142
(415) 479-1913; (415) 921-BBSF (fax)
A reservation service with homes and inns in San Francisco, Marin County, Monterey/Carmel, the Wine Country, and the Gold Country. Rates range from $45 to $150 per night; no membership fee.

Bed & Breakfast International
P.O. Box 282910
San Francisco, CA 94128-2910
(415) 696-1690; (415) 696-1699 (fax)
A reservation service representing homes and inns in San Francisco and the greater Bay Area, the Wine Country, Tahoe, the Monterey Peninsula, Yosemite, Los Angeles, San Diego, and other areas of travel interest in California. Rates from $50 to $125, double occupancy; no membership fee. Send a self-addressed, legal-size stamped envelope, or call for a free brochure.

Rent-A-Room International
11531 Varna Street
Garden Grove, CA 92640
(714) 638-1406
Represents homes in Southern California; rates from $35/single, $45/double per night.

Northwest Bed and Breakfast
610 S.W. Broadway, Suite 606
Portland, OR 97205
(503) 243-7616
A reservation service for California homes as well as
homes throughout the western United States and British
Columbia. Room rates from $45/single, $55/double. Directory available for $7.95.

Accommodations Referral
P.O. Box 59
St. Helena, CA 94574
(707) 963-8466 or (800) 499-8466 (in California)
A referral service for nearly 150 properties in Napa Valley
including small inns, bed and breakfasts, hotels, country
clubs, and (monthly) private estate rentals. Room rates
start at $45 per night. No fee to client.

Bed & Breakfast Homestay
P.O. Box 326
Cambria, CA 93428
(805) 927-4613
A reservation service for bed and breakfast lodging in
private homes. Geographic coverage: Hearst Castle country and the central California coast. Room rates $50 to
$90.

Megan's Friends
1776 Royal Way
San Luis Obispo, CA 93405
(805) 544-4406
A membership organization that provides a reservation
service; $10 one-time membership fee. Listings include
private homes and guest cabins on the central coast
(primarily in San Luis Obispo and Santa Barbara counties). Lodgings in Solvang and Cambria (near Hearst
Castle) are also covered. Room rates starting at $60.

Eye Openers Bed & Breakfast Reservations
P.O. Box 694
Altadena, CA 91003
(213) 684-4428; (818) 798-3640 (fax)
A reservation service for bed and breakfast homes and
inns throughout California. Rates from $40 per night;
one-time membership fee of $10. Send $1 and a self-
addressed, stamped envelope for brochure.

Bed & Breakfast of Los Angeles
3924 East 14th Street
Long Beach, CA 90804
(310) 498-0552 or (800) 383-3513
A reservation service for California homestays, guest
homes, small inns, and bed and breakfasts. Over 300
listings throughout the state. Room rates start at $45/
single, $50/double. Directory available.

Napa Valley Tourist Bureau Reservations
P.O. Box 3240
6488 Washington Street
Yountville, CA 94599
(707) 944-1558
A reservation service for bed and breakfast inns, homes,
hotels, and country clubs in the Napa and Sonoma valley
areas. Rates from $55 to $225; no fee.

Tahoe North Visitors and Convention Bureau
P.O. Box 5578
Tahoe City, CA 96145
(916) 583-3494 or (800) 824-6348 (nationwide)
A reservation service for the north Lake Tahoe-Truckee
area representing over 100 lodging properties, eight of
which are bed and breakfast inns. Room rates start at $60.

Wine Country Bed & Breakfast
P.O. Box 3211
Santa Rosa, CA 95402
(707) 578-1661
Reservation service for homes within a 35-mile radius of
Santa Rosa: Healdsburg, Kenwood, Sebastopol, Santa
Rosa, and vicinity. Rates in the $80 to $100 range. No
membership fee.

Co-Host, America's Bed & Breakfast
P.O. Box 9302
Whittier, CA 90608
(310) 699-8427
A reservation service with homes throughout California.
Rates from $40 to $85; no membership fee. Specializing
in considerations for the disabled, senior citizens, and
families with children.

Wine Country Reservations
Box 5059
Napa, CA 94581
(707) 944-1222
Reservation service for the entire Napa Valley. Room
rates from $65 up; no fee to client. Brochures available for
$2 to cover postage and handling.

Carmel Tourist Information and Roomfinder Service
Box 7430
Mission Street between 5th and 6th
Carmel, CA 93921
(408) 624-1711
Handles accommodations in bed and breakfasts, hotels,
motels, and cottages in Northern California. Specializes in
the Monterey/Carmel area. Free service; room rates from
$60 up.

Napa Valley Reservations Unlimited
1819 Tanen Street
Napa, CA 94559
(707) 252-1985 or (800) 251-NAPA (in California)
Reservation and referral service for Napa Valley accommodations (bed and breakfasts, hotels, resorts). No booking or membership fee. Average bed and breakfast rate is
$75 to $125 for two.

Napa Valley's Finest Lodging
1557 Madrid Court
Napa, CA 94559
(707) 224-4667
Information and reservation service for all of Napa Valley.
Rooms in homes, inns, hotels, and motels. Rates from $90
per night. Brochures sent on request; no fee to client.

Seashore Bed & Breakfasts of Marin County
Old Creamery Building
P.O. Box 1239
Point Reyes Station, CA 94956
(415) 663-9373
Referral service for homes and guest cottages located
along the Marin County seashore. Rates from $45 to $135.
No fee; free brochure available.

Kids Welcome
3924 East 14th Street
Long Beach, CA 90804
(310) 498-0552 or (800) 383-3513
A reservation service specifically designed to meet the
need of people traveling with children. Representing over
150 homestays, guest homes, small inns, and bed and
breakfasts throughout California. Room rates average $50
to $75. Directory available.

Bed and Breakfast Associations

Regional associations assist the traveler with information on bed and breakfast accommodations in their geographic area by providing group brochures and central telephone referral services. The associations listed below welcome your call or letter.

Bed & Breakfast Innkeepers of Santa Cruz County
P.O. Box 464
Santa Cruz, CA 95061
(408) 425-8212
An association referral service. Phone or send for free brochure with self-addressed, stamped envelope.

The Inns of Point Reyes
P.O. Box 145
Inverness, CA 94937
(415) 485-2649
An information and referral service. Free brochure available.

Seashore Bed & Breakfasts of Marin
Old Creamery Building
P.O. Box 1239
Point Reyes Station, CA 94956
(415) 663-9373
Call or write for free brochure.

Bed & Breakfast Inns of Sonoma Valley
P.O. Box 125
Sonoma, CA 95476
(707) 996-INNS or (800) 284-6675
Telephone referral service for five member inns. Phone or write for free brochure.

Wine Country Bed & Breakfast Inns of Sonoma County
P.O. Box 51
Geyserville, CA 95441
(707) 433-INNS or (800) 354-4743
Telephone referral service for 14 inns. Booklet and wine road map available for $1.

Bed & Breakfast Association of Napa Valley
P.O. Box 5059
Napa, CA 94581-0059
(707) 944-1222
Central reservation service for 30 inns. Send $2 for brochures to cover postage and handling.

Mendocino Coast Innkeepers Association
P.O. Box 1141-LB
Mendocino, CA 95460
(707) 964-0640
Phone or write for handy guide depicting eight Mendocino Coast inns. Comes with location map of the 80-mile Mendocino Coast.

Amador County Bed and Breakfast Inns
P.O. Box 322
Ione, CA 95640
(209) 274-4468
Send for free brochure with self-addressed, stamped envelope.

Gold Country Inns of Tuolumne County
P.O. Box 462
Sonora, CA 95370
(209) 533-1845
Information service for room availability. Send for free brochure including descriptions of 11 inns.

Inns of Grass Valley and Nevada City Association
P.O. Box 2060
Grass Valley, CA 95959
(916) 477-6634
Telephone referral service for 12 member inns; offers information on room availability. Send for free brochure.

Bed & Breakfast Inns of the Auburn Area
601 Lincoln Way
Auburn, CA 95603
(916) 885-5616
Phone or write for free brochure.

Sacramento Innkeepers' Association
2120 G Street
Sacramento, CA 95816
(916) 441-5007
Call or write for free brochure.

Yosemite Bed & Breakfast of Mariposa County
2669 Triangle Road
Mariposa, CA 95338
(209) 966-2456
Send for free brochure.

Santa Barbara Bed & Breakfast Innkeepers Guild
P.O. Box 90734
Santa Barbara, CA 93190
(800) 776-9176
Free brochure available.

Bed & Breakfast Innkeepers of Southern California
P.O. Box 15425
Los Angeles, CA 90015-0385
Send legal size, self-addressed, stamped envelope for free
brochure.

California Association of Bed & Breakfast Inns
2715 Porter Street
Soquel, CA 95073
(408) 462-9191 (Office) or (800) 284-INNS (Traveling
Tour)
This statewide organization of professionally run inns
offers a free computer-generated list of its members
(sorted by geographical region) as well as the "Traveling
Tour" phone service which provides a direct transfer to
the inn of your choice for reservations.

Professional Association of Innkeepers
International (PAII)
P.O. Box 90710
Santa Barbara, CA 93190
(805) 569-1853
Want to be an innkeeper? Find all the information you
need to get off to a great start from this trade association
for the bed and breakfast and country inn industry. Work-
shops, publications, take-to-the-bank research, product
information and discounts, and a member hot line. Phone
or write for membership details.

Bed and Breakfast Publications

Guidebooks to bed and breakfast inns, homestays, and reservation services. Most are available, or can be ordered, through your local bookstore.

Country Inns of California
$11.95
by Jacqueline Killeen
101 Productions/The Cole Group, Inc.
4415 Sonoma Highway
Santa Rosa, CA 95409
Reviews of country inns and bed and breakfast inns.

The Complete Guide to Bed & Breakfasts,
Inns & Guesthouses
$16.95
by Pamela Lanier
Ten Speed Press
P.O. Box 7123
Berkeley, CA 94707
Covers the United States and Canada.

Bed & Breakfast in California
$11.95
by Kathy Strong
The Globe Pequot Press
P.O. Box 833
Old Saybrook, CT 06475

Country Inns and Back Roads—California
$10.00
by Jerry Levitin
HarperCollins Publishers, Inc.
10 East 53rd Street
New York, NY 10022

Bed & Breakfast Homes Directory—West Coast
$12.95
by Diane Knight
Knighttime Publications
890 Calabasas Road
Watsonville, CA 95076
Lists bed and breakfast accommodations in small,
owner-occupied inns and private homes in California,
Oregon, Washington, and British Columbia.

Bed and Breakfast U.S.A.
$14.00
by Betty Rundback and Peggy Ackerman
Penguin Books USA, Inc.
375 Hudson Street
New York, NY 10014

Bed & Breakfast North America
$15.95
by Norma Buzan
Betsy Ross Publications
127 West Spruce
Missoula, MT 59802
A directory of bed and breakfast reservation services,
small inns, and individual guest houses in the U.S.,
Mexico, and Canada.

*The Bed & Breakfast Guide for the U.S., Canada,
and the Caribbean*
$16.95
by Phyllis Featherston and Barbara F. Ostler
The National Bed & Breakfast Association
P.O. Box 332
Norwalk, CT 06852
Lists over 1,600 individual bed and breakfast homes and
family-run inns and provides access to 8,000 more
through a Reservation Service section. Add $2 for postage
and handling when ordering by mail.

Inspected, Rated & Approved B&Bs and Country Inns
$14.95
The American Bed & Breakfast Association
10800 Midlothian Turnpike, Suite 254
Richmond, VA 23235
Includes 600 bed and breakfasts and country inns across
the United States. Add $3 for shipping to order by mail.

California Bed & Breakfast Inns
Free
California State Office of Tourism
Department B&B, 801 K Street, Suite 1600
Sacramento, CA 95814
A statewide directory of more than 250 bed and breakfast
inns. Write for a free copy.

*The National Trust Guide to Historic Bed & Breakfasts,
Inns and Small Hotels*
$13.95
by Suzanne G. Dane
The Preservation Press
1785 Massachusetts Avenue, NW
Washington, DC 20036
Lists more than 500 historic lodgings across the United
States.

Frommer's Bed & Breakfast North America
$14.95
by Hal Gieseking
Prentice Hall Press
Division of Simon & Schuster, Inc.
15 Columbus Circle
New York, NY 10023
A directory of bed and breakfast reservation services that
book stays in private homes; some individual inns.

Bed & Breakfast Directory for San Diego
$3.95
by Carol Emerick
B&B Resources
P.O. Box 3292
San Diego, CA 92163
Includes information about bed and breakfast homes and inns located throughout San Diego County. Order by mail; postage included.

Bed and Breakfast Directory
Free (to members)
AAA-California State Automobile Association
ATTN: Touring Department
150 Van Ness Avenue, P.O. Box 1860
San Francisco, CA 94101-1860
Directory of bed and breakfast inns for Central and Northern California as well as Nevada. Free to members of the American Automobile Association. For a copy, drop in to your nearest AAA district office and show your membership card, or write or phone with your membership number.

Bed & Breakfast Southern California
$3.00/members
$6.95/non-members
AAA-Automobile Club of Southern California
Travel Publications Department
2601 South Figueroa Street
Los Angeles, CA 90007
Directory of bed and breakfast inns for Southern California, available to members of the American Automobile Association for $3. For a copy, drop in to your nearest AAA district office and show your membership card, or write to the above address with your membership number. The guide is also available to the general public for $6.95.

Fodor's Bed & Breakfasts and Country Inns—California
$15.00
Edie Jarolin, Editor
Fodor's Travel Publications
201 East 50th Street
New York, NY 10022

California Country Inns & Itineraries
$14.95
by Karen Brown
Karen Brown's Guides
P.O. Box 70
San Mateo, CA 94401
Add $3.50 for shipping and handling when ordering
by mail.

Best Places To Stay In California
$14.95
by Marilyn McFarlane
Houghton Mifflin Company
2 Park Street
Boston, MA 02108
Descriptions of 250 accommodations throughout California. Add $2.50 for shipping if ordering by mail.

America's Wonderful Little Hotels and Inns
$19.95
by Sandra W. Soule
St. Martin's Press
175 Fifth Avenue
New York, NY 10010

Recommended Country Inns West Coast
$12.95
by Julianne Belote
The Globe Pequot Press
P.O. Box 833
Old Saybrook, CT 06475

Bed & Breakfast and Country Inns
$17.95
by Tim and Deborah Sakach
The Association of American Historic Inns
P.O. Box 336
Dana Point, CA 92629
Lists 1,200 inns across the country. For mail orders,
phone toll free 1-800-397-INNS nationwide.

The Non-Smoker's Guide to Bed & Breakfasts
$9.95
Robyn Martins, Editor
Rutledge Hill Press
513 Third Avenue South
Nashville, TN 37210
Covers more than 1,150 bed and breakfasts in the United States, Canada, and Puerto Rico.

The Annual Directory of American Bed & Breakfasts
$18.95
Julia Pitkin, Editor
Rutledge Hill Press
513 Third Avenue South
Nashville, TN 37210
Complete descriptions of more than 6,000 bed and breakfasts in the United States, Puerto Rico, the Virgin Islands, and Canada. Add $2 for postage when ordering by mail.

Bed & Breakfast Guide—California
$15.00
by Courtia Worth, Terry Berger, Naomi Black, and Lucy Poshek
Prentice Hall, Division of Simon & Schuster
15 Columbus Circle
New York, NY 10023

Bed & Breakfast Guide—Pacific Northwest
$15.00
Prentice Hall, Division of Simon & Schuster
15 Columbus Circle
New York, NY 10023
Covers Oregon and Washington.

The Inn Guide
$12.75
Toby Smith, Publisher
P.O. Box 3383
Santa Rosa, CA 95402
Annual directory of nearly 700 California bed and breakfast inns, small restored hotels, and period lodges and resorts. Order by mail; price includes shipping and California sales tax.

Newsletters

Yellow Brick Road
Bobbi Zane, Publisher
2445 Northcreek Lane
Fullerton, CA 92631
Reviews of bed and breakfast inns along with news of areas and events of travel interest. Published monthly; $39/year. Sample copies: $4.

Publications on How to Open and Operate a Bed and Breakfast Inn

So, You Want To Be an Innkeeper
$12.95
by Davies, Hardy, Bell, and Brown
Chronicle Books
275 Fifth Street
San Francisco, CA 94103
Contains a wealth of information for the novice or veteran—everything from balancing the budget to balancing the teacup—plus how-tos, anecdotes, and case histories based on the authors' own experiences.

How To Open and Operate a Bed & Breakfast Home
$10.95
by Jan Stankus
The Globe Pequot Press
P.O. Box 833
Old Saybrook, CT 06475
A step-by-step look at the challenges and rewards of setting up and operating a bed and breakfast home.

Open Your Own Bed & Breakfast
$14.95
by Barbara Notarius and Gail Sforza Brewer
John Wiley & Sons, Inc.
Professional Reference and Trade Division
605 Third Avenue
New York, NY 10158-0012

Inn Marketing Newsletter
Norman Strasma, Publisher
P.O. Box 1789-L
Kankakee, IL 60901
News of people, places, and events of the inn business throughout the United States. The emphasis is on marketing and promotions of bed and breakfasts and inns. Published 10 times a year. $47/year; sample copy $3.

innkeeping
JoAnn M. Bell, Publisher
P.O. Box 90710
Santa Barbara, CA 93190
A newsletter for owners/operators of bed and breakfast and country inns. Subject matter ranges from inn promotion to policies and procedures. Issued monthly; $65/year.

Cookbooks from Bed and Breakfasts

Cinnamon Mornings
$17.95
by Pamela Lanier
Running Press Book Publishers
125 South 22nd Street
Philadelphia, PA 19103
A collection of breakfast, brunch, and teatime recipes from America's foremost bed and breakfast inns.

Bread & Breakfast: Best Recipes from North America's Bed & Breakfast Inns
$9.95
by Linda Kay Bristow
101 Productions/The Cole Group, Inc.
4415 Sonoma Highway
Santa Rosa, CA 95409
Regional specialties and treasured family favorites including dishes like Fresh Peach Soup, My Great Aunt Fanny's Date Cake, Minnesota Wild Rice Waffles, and Virginia Ham and Apple Pie.

Cooking & Traveling Inn Style
$12.95
Bed and Breakfast Innkeepers of Northern California
A combined bed and breakfast inn guide to Northern California and breakfast recipe cookbook. For Visa or MasterCard purchase, phone 1-800-284-INNS.

Grant Corner Inn Breakfast & Brunch Cookbook
$12.95
by Louise Stewart
Grant Corner Inn
122 Grant Avenue
Santa Fe, NM 87501
Features Southwest regional specialties for breakfast and brunch; tried and true recipes. Order by mail; add $3 for postage and handling.

*The American Country Inn and Bed & Breakfast Cookbook,
Volume I*
$14.95 Paperback
$22.95 Hardcover
by Kitty and Lucian Maynard
Rutledge Hill Press
513 Third Avenue South
Nashville, TN 37210
Over 1,700 recipes from 500 inns. Add $2 for postage
when ordering by mail.

*The American Country Inn and Bed & Breakfast Cookbook,
Volume II*
$16.95 Paperback
$24.95 Hardcover
by Kitty and Lucian Maynard
Rutledge Hill Press
513 Third Avenue South
Nashville, TN 37210
A 600-page book packed with recipes from inns in the
United States and Canada; more recipes from California
than any other state. Add $2.50 for postage when ordering
by mail.

Index

Abigail's **174**
American River Inn **184**
Arbor Guest House **78**
Archbishops Mansion **8**

The Babbling Brook Inn **30**
The Ballard Inn **242**
Bartels Ranch **96**
Bath Street Inn **244**
Beazley House **80**
The Bed and Breakfast
    Inn **10**
The Bed & Breakfast Inn at
    La Jolla **274**
Belle de Jour **62**
Blackthorne Inn **48**
Blue Lantern Inn **272**
Blue Quail Inn **246**
Boulder Creek Bed and
    Breakfast **162**
Brookside Farm **278**
Brookside Vineyard **82**

Campbell Ranch Inn **68**
The Carriage House **270**
Carter House Inn **152**
Casa del Mar **42**
Chaney House **210**
Channel Road Inn **262**
Chateau des Fleurs **28**
The Chichester-McKee
    House **188**
Christmas House **260**
Cliff Crest Bed & Breakfast
    Inn **32**
The Cobblestone Inn **224**
The Coloma Country
    Inn **186**
Country Garden Inn **84**
Country House Inn **234**
Country Inn **142**
Court Street Inn **194**
Cross Roads Inn **86**

Dunbar House, 1880 **200**

An Elegant Victorian
    Mansion **154**
Elk Cove Inn **124**

Foothill House **108**
The Foxes **192**

The Gables Bed &
    Breakfast Inn **58**
Gaige House **56**
Garden Street Inn **236**
Garratt Mansion **2**
The George Alexander
    House **64**
The Gingerbread
    Mansion **150**
Glendeven Inn **130**
The Gosby House Inn **16**
Gramma's Rose
    Garden Inn **4**
Grandmere's Inn **176**
Grape Leaf Inn **66**
Green Apple Inn **74**
Green Gables **218**
The Grey Whale Inn **144**

Headlands Inn **134**
The Heirloom **198**
Heritage Park Bed &
    Breakfast Inn **276**
Hilltop House **98**
Holly Tree Inn **46**
The Hope-Merrill
    House **70**

Indian Creek Bed &
    Breakfast **190**
The Ink House **100**
The Inn at Depot Hill **34**
The Inn on Mt. Ada **268**
Inn on Summer Hill **252**

The J. Patrick House   **230**

John Dougherty House   **136**

Joshua Grindle Inn   **138**

Karen's Bed &
  Breakfast Inn   **170**

The Kendall House   **178**

La Belle Epoque   **88**

La Maida House   **256**

La Mer Gaestehaus   **260**

La Residence Country
  Inn   **90**

Llamahall Guest
  Ranch   **202**

Loma Vista Bed &
  Breakfast   **280**

Lord Mayor's Inn   **266**

The Lost Whale Inn   **156**

Magnolia Hotel   **92**

The Mansion at Lakewood   **6**

The Mansions Hotel   **12**

Mayfield House   **212**

Meadow Creek Ranch   **164**

Mill Rose Inn   **26**

Mountain Home Inn   **38**

Murphy's Inn   **182**

Oak Hill Ranch   **206**

Oak Meadows, Too   **166**

Olallieberry Inn   **232**

Old Milano Hotel   **118**

Old Monterey Inn   **222**

The Old Yacht Club
  Inn   **248**

Oliver House   **102**

The Pelican Inn   **40**

Pudding Creek Inn   **146**

Pygmalion House   **60**

Quail Mountain Bed &
  Breakfast   **110**

Rachel's Inn   **128**

Red Castle Inn   **180**

The Red Victorian   **14**

Rockwood Lodge   **208**

Roundstone Farm   **44**

The Ryan House, 1855   **204**

St. Orres   **122**

Salisbury House   **258**

Sandpiper House Inn   **126**

Schlageter House   **168**

Scott Courtyard   **112**

Sea View Inn   **226**

The Seal Beach Inn   **264**

Seal Cove Inn   **24**

Seven Gables Inn   **220**

Shady Oaks Country
  Inn   **104**

Silver Rose Inn   **114**

Simpson House Inn   **250**

The Spencer House   **16**

Sunset House   **228**

Sybron House   **94**

Ten Inverness Way   **50**

Thistle Dew Inn   **54**

Trinidad Bed &
  Breakfast   **158**

Union Hotel   **240**

Union Street Inn   **18**

Victorian Farmhouse   **132**

Victorian on Lytton   **22**

Whale Watch Inn   **122**

Washington Square Inn   **20**

The Wedgewood Inn   **196**

Whitegate Inn   **140**

Ye Olde' Shelford House   **72**

Zinfandel Inn   **106**